STAY ALERT
STAY ALIVE!

A Guide to Counterterrorism for Everyday Life

CIA DISCLOSURE

All statements of fact, opinion or analysis expressed are those of the author and do not reflect the official position or views of the Central Intelligence Agency (CIA) or any other U.S. Government agency. Nothing in the contents should be construed as asserting or implying U.S. Government authentication of information or CIA endorsement of the author's views. The CIA has reviewed this material in order to prevent the disclosure of classified information.

Copyright © 2011 by Empire Books, LLC.

All rights reserved. No part of this publication may be reproduced or utilized in any form or by any means, electronic or mechanical, including photocopying, recording, or by any information storage and retrieval system, without prior written permission from *Empire Books, LLC*.

EMPIRE BOOKS
P.O. Box 491788
Los Angeles, CA 90049

First edition
05 04 03 02 01 00 99 98 97 1 3 5 7 9 10 8 6 4 2
Printed in the United States of America

Library of Congress: XXXXXXXXXXXXX
ISBN-10: XXXXXXXXXXX
ISBN-13: XXXXXXXXXXXXXXXX

Library of Congress Cataloging-in-Publication Data

STAY ALERT
STAY ALIVE!

A Guide to Counterterrorism for Everyday Life

- *Spot*
- *Respond*
- *Survive*

Jim C. Blount

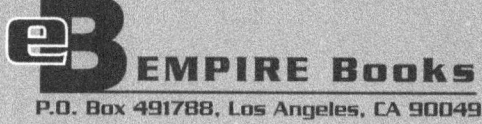

EMPIRE Books
P.O. Box 491788, Los Angeles, CA 90049

About the Author

Jim Blount is a retired 28-year veteran of the Central Intelligence Agency. His assignments at CIA included tours of duty in the Counterterrorist Center, where he served as a training supervisor, and the Office of Security. Throughout his career he received numerous awards, including the Director's Award from the Director of Central Intelligence and also from the Director of the FBI.

Prior to joining the CIA, Mr. Blount served in the US Navy and was employed for eight years as a local police officer in Virginia. He holds a B.S. Degree in Criminal Justice and M.S. in Public Administration. He is currently the owner and CEO of International Threat Assessment, LLC, a company providing high-risk training and consulting services to public and private clients worldwide.

His chief hobby is running and he enjoys participating in road races throughout Virginia and the United States. He is the father of five grown children and resides with his wife, Nancy, in Williamsburg, Virginia.

Acknowledgments

Gratitude and thanks go to my numerous former instructors, colleagues, coworkers and mentors, many of whom are still fighting the good fight on active duty with the CIA and therefore cannot be named individually. You all know who you are.

I owe a deep debt of gratitude to Jose M. Fraguas, Director of Empire Books for taking a big chance on a first-time author. Thanks, Jose, for all your help and guidance.

And last, but certainly not least, to my wife, Nancy, I owe my appreciation for being my editor, typist, advisor and my encourager. You helped make the dream come true.

TABLE OF CONTENTS

	INTRODUCTION vi	
	PROLOGUE viii	
1	TERRORISM - *What Is It?* 1	
2	THE TERRORIST METHODOLOGY: *Thinking Like A Terrorist* 9	
3	INTRODUCTION TO THE COMBAT TRIAD 19	
4	SURVIVAL SKILL ONE: *Awarness* 21	
5	SURVIVAL SKILL TWO: *Action* 35	
6	SURVIVAL SKILL THREE: *Mindset* 41	
7	THE TERRORIST AMBUSH 45	
8	RESPONDING TO THE THREAT: *Anticipation, Recognition and Action* ... 55	
9	ARE YOU A TARGET? 59	
10	YOUR VEHICLE: *How Safe Is It Really?* 63	
11	THE ATTEMPTED ABDUCTION: *Submit or Resist?* 67	
12	IDENTIFYING AND UTILIZING YOUR WEAPONS 75	
13	PROTECTING YOURSELF ON THE ROAD 81	
14	STAYING SAFE AT HOME: *Threats to Your Home's Security* 85	
15	STAYING SAFE WHILE YOU TRAVEL: *Part 1 - Your Hotel* 105	
16	STAYING SAFE WHILE YOU TRAVEL: *Part 2 - In The Air* 111	
17	SAFETY IN THE PUBLIC DOMAIN 121	
18	HOSTAGE SURVIVAL 127	
19	MAKING YOURSELF A "HARD" TARGET 141	
20	MANAGING FEAR AND STRESS 151	
21	SHOULD YOU CARRY A FIREARM? 157	
22	THE CBRN ATTACK: *Chemical, Biological, Radiological and Nuclear* ... 167	
	CONCLUSION 171	

Introduction

In 28 years of employment with the Central Intelligence Agency, I have spent much of my time training Agency employees who were being assigned to high-threat areas overseas. I have often been asked why I haven't written a book on the means of avoiding a terrorist incident or surviving an attack. CIA employees serve in some of the most dangerous places on earth. It was my job to see that they were given the tools to detect, defeat and disrupt terrorist operations directed against them. Although there is no way to ensure one-hundred-percent success in any endeavor, it remains a fact that many Agency employees have successfully survived terrorist threats and incidents in recent years.

Contained in this book is not "the" way, but simply "a" way to detect, defeat and disrupt a terrorist attack against yourself and your family. There is no magic bullet that will protect you in any and all circumstances. There are no guarantees that following this book to the letter will prevent your becoming the target of a terrorist group. There is no doubt in my mind, however, that by following these time-honored and tested principles you will be safer and better prepared than most citizens.

The tactics and techniques in this book have been practiced by U.S. Government employees who live, work and serve in dangerous environments. We have a phrase that we use in my business – "written in blood", and these techniques have truly been "written in blood". Simply stated, we learn through the failures and experiences of others. In the world of counter terrorism it is often through the shed blood and sacrifice of innocent lives that we learn our most valuable lessons.

This book is intended for use by anyone who is or will be living, working or traveling overseas. There is no doubt that the world has changed in the last few years and we must be prepared for the worst, even as we hope for the best. Whether you travel for business or pleasure; whether you are a civil servant living overseas or a tourist traveling overseas for only a few days; a diplomat, journalist or a wife and mother, the information contained in this book should be considered an essential guide in your quest for personal safety.

Today's terrorist makes no distinction between soldier and businessman, man or woman, child or adult, student or missionary. Terrorists are, by and large, cowards. Like the schoolyard bully, they pick on the weak and unprepared. To the terrorist we are all targets of opportunity – we are fair game. When they are faced, however, with an adversary who is well trained and versed in the terrorists' own tactics, and most importantly is willing to fight,

most of these "bullies" will retreat and seek out an easier target. The techniques provided in the following chapters are the "tools" that will help you to:

◆ **Spot a terrorist incident before it occurs**

◆ **Respond quickly to a terrorist incident**

◆ **Survive an attack**

As a society, we must become better prepared to detect and defeat terrorism, wherever and whenever it rears its ugly head. My goal is to help you, the reader, to stay alert and stay alive through the diligent practice and incorporation of those techniques in your daily life. ❖

"The confrontation that Islam calls for with these godless and apostate regimes does not know Socratic debates, Platonic ideals or Aristotelian diplomacy. But it knows the dialog of bullets, the ideals of assassination, bombing, and destruction and the diplomacy of the canon and machine-gun."

--- Al-Qaeda Training Manual

PROLOGUE

Imagine you are sitting in your car at a stoplight on your way to work. It's a routine day, sunny and a little chilly. As you are listening to traffic reports on the radio and thinking about your day ahead, you suddenly hear a popping sound, much like a car backfiring. Then you hear it again and again. You look up to see a man walking between the two rows of cars stopped at the light. He has an automatic weapon in his hand and as he passes by each car, he randomly puts the barrel of the gun in the window and fires. The expression on his face evokes terror among the trapped commuters as he continues working his way down the line of vehicles -- and he is approaching you. What do you do?

You may be thinking this couldn't happen in the United States, but it did. It happened right in front of one of the most secure facilities on this planet, and on a major highway just outside our nation's capital. On January 25, 1993, I was on a domestic assignment for my employer, the Central Intelligence Agency, when I heard the news. An apparent terrorist attack at the CIA Headquarters Main Gate had left two employees dead and three wounded. I knew the area well as I had traversed that same intersection hundreds of times myself. The main gate at CIA was located approximately 300 yards from Virginia Route 123, a busy commuter access road into Washington, D. C. Each morning hundreds of CIA employees sit at the Route 123 light waiting to turn into Headquarters and begin another day of work at the world's premier intelligence agency. Listening to the sketchy reports on the radio as I sat in my non-descript black government vehicle, I wondered how this could possibly have happened. In my mind's eye I imagined myself in that place, as I had waited at that very light numerous mornings, on days just like this one, sitting, thinking of the day ahead and all the projects waiting for me in that cavernous CIA building known as the George Bush Center for Intelligence. Although I had spent my career as a CIA Security and Counter Terrorist Officer, I could not imagine a terrorist attack at that particular location. Overseas, yes, but not at the front door to CIA Headquarters. After all, this area is well patrolled by the Fairfax County Police, as well as by CIA Security Protection Service Officers. These officers, known as "SPOs" in CIA vernacular, are highly trained, federally certified officers and are well armed and trained to respond to in-extremis incidents. I felt certain that if any of those officers had been present during the crisis, the attack and the attacker would have been short lived. Unfortunately, due to jurisdictional and bureaucratic rules, they weren't there.

Because I was approximately five hundred miles away from headquarters at the time of the attack, I had to rely on news reports and television coverage for most of my information about the attack. Investigation subsequently revealed that Mir Aimal Kansi, a Pakistani native, had apparently acted alone in the attack. According to the reports, Kansi, just as the morning rush hour approached, hid in the shrubbery near the traffic light leading to the CIA main gate. At an opportune moment he approached several cars stopped at the red light and began firing his AK-47 assault rifle, the standard issue weapon of terrorists everywhere. He randomly and indiscriminately fired into several vehicles parked at the light, ultimately killing two CIA officers and wounding three others.

I immediately thought of the victims, people much like myself, with families and with hopes and dreams for the future. I wondered if I could have, somehow, made a difference if I had been there. Perhaps I would have been one of the victims -- but then again, maybe not. Having spent my entire adult life in the military, civilian law enforcement and in the CIA and having experience in martial arts and weapons, maybe in those first critical minutes I could have saved not only myself, but others as well. Just maybe I could have presented Mir Kansi with his worst nightmare -- facing a trained, armed individual who was ready, willing and capable of taking his life as quickly and efficiently as he had taken the lives of those innocent Agency employees.

Thanks to a joint CIA and FBI effort, Kansi was subsequently captured in his native Pakistan and extradited to the United States to stand trial. He met his just reward in the death chamber of the Virginia State Penitentiary on 14 November 2002. As I read the news of his execution, I couldn't help but wonder just how many other Mir Aimal Kansis were out there, trained and eagerly waiting for their opportunity to take more innocent lives. ❖

CHAPTER 1

"Terrorism has become the systematic weapon of a war that knows no borders or seldom has a face."

~ Jacques Chirac

TERRORISM

WHAT IS IT?

The American Heritage Dictionary defines terrorism as "the unlawful use or threatened use of force or violence by a person or an organized group against people or property with the intention of intimidating or coercing societies or governments, often for ideological or political reasons". Merriam-Webster's Dictionary of Law adds that terrorism is "a violent and intimidating gang activity". The United States Federal Criminal Code (Chapter 113B or Part I of Title 18, United States Code) defines terrorism as "activities that involve violent or life threatening acts that appear to be intended (i) to intimidate or coerce a civilian population; (ii) to influence the policy of a government by intimidation or coercion; or (iii) to affect the conduct of government by mass destruction, assassination, or kidnapping". The United Nations described terrorism as any act "intended to cause death or serious bodily harm to civilians or non-combatants with the purpose of intimidating a population". Pay particular attention to the key words, "intimidation", fear", "and violence". The goal of terrorists is to instill a paralyzing fear in people by threats, intimidation and violence. It is the fear and intimidation that distinguishes terrorism from conventional or guerilla warfare.

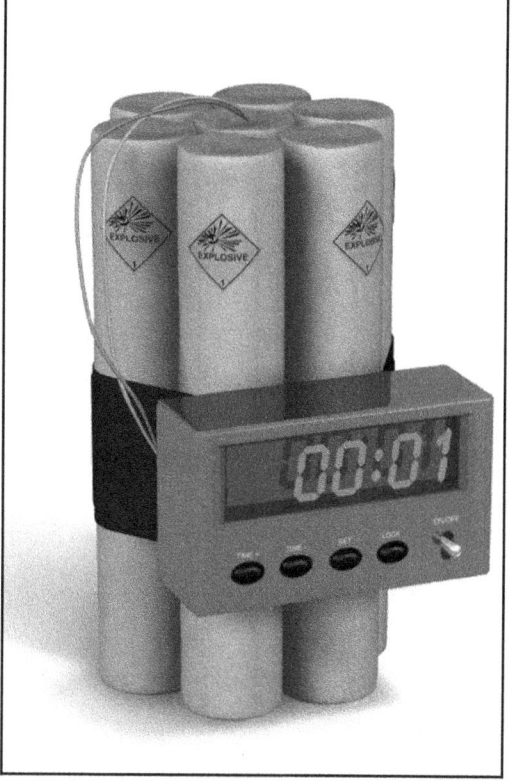

On their website, the FBI defines two types of terrorism in the United States; these are domestic and international. Domestic terrorism involves "groups or individuals whose terrorist activities are directed at elements of our government or population without foreign direction." International terrorism is perpetrated by "groups or individuals whose terrorist activities are foreign based and/or directed by countries or groups outside the U.S. or whose activities transcend national boundaries".

Terrorism is a worldwide epidemic. Until recently there were only a few areas in the world that were plagued by terrorism. The United States was the target of very few terrorist incidents prior to the 1980s and most Americans felt secure in their own country. That is not the case in today's world. As we know only too well, terrorists can and do operate in almost every country of the world. No person is immune from a terrorist attack and no country is exempt from the plague of terrorism.

Terrorism: Alive and Well

Terrorism, in one form or another, has been around for centuries and there is no indication it will go away anytime soon. In fact, the opposite is happening. Since the 1980's the world has witnessed a dramatic increase in the number and complexity of terrorist events. Following is a partial list of some of the key terrorist events that have occurred in the past three decades.

1976   **Beirut, Lebanon:** US Ambassador Francis Meloy, Economic Officer Robert Waring and their Lebanese driver were kidnapped and murdered while on their way to a meeting in Beirut.

1979   **Tehran, Iran:** Iranian radicals seized the US Embassy in Tehran, taking 66 hostages. Of the 66 hostages taken, 52 of them were held for a total of 444 days.

1981   **San Salvador, El Salvador:** Three American nuns and a missionary were murdered on December 4.

1983   **Beirut, Lebanon:** The terrorist organization, Islamic Jihad, drove a truck bomb into the US Embassy in Beirut, killing 63 people and wounding 120.

Beirut, Lebanon: A coordinated truck bomb attacked US and French forces in Beirut, killing 242 Americans and 58 French military personnel.

Athens, Greece: A US Naval officer was shot and killed while stopped at a stop light in Athens. The terrorist group, November 17, claimed responsibility for the attack.

1984   **Beirut, Lebanon:** Malcolm Kerr, President of American University in Beirut, was slain by two gunmen as he stepped off an elevator near his office. Islamic Jihad took responsibility.

Beirut, Lebanon: Twenty-two people were killed, including two Americans, and seventy were wounded when a van exploded in front of the US Embassy annex.

Beirut, Lebanon: CIA Station Chief William Buckley was kidnapped and murdered by the Islamic Jihad on March 16.

1985   **Cruise ship, Achille Lauro:** During the hijacking of this cruise liner, a wheel chair-bound US citizen was killed and pushed overboard by Palestinian terrorists. Over 700 people were held hostage during the ordeal.

Rome and Vienna, Italy: Gunmen from the Abu Nidal terrorist organization killed 16 people and wounded 105 others in coordinated attacks directed at the Rome and Vienna airports.

1986 **Berlin, Germany:** Two US servicemen were killed and 79 others injured in the bombing of a Berlin discotheque. Libyan terrorists were responsible for the attack.

1987 **Athens, Greece:** Sixteen US military personnel were injured during an attack on a bus; the terrorist group, November 17, conducted the attack.

Barcelona, Spain: Terrorists bombed a bar frequented by US servicemen, killing one American.

1988 **Naples Italy:** Five people were killed and fifteen wounded in an attack on a USO Club; the attack was carried out by the terrorist organization known as the Japanese Red Army.

Lockerbie, Scotland: Pan Am Flight 103 exploded over Lockerbie, Scotland, killing 258 people on board the plane and another 11 people on the ground. Libyan terrorists were behind this attack.

Athens, Greece: The US Defense Attaché was killed when a car bomb exploded outside his residence.

Beirut, Lebanon: US Marine Corps Lieutenant Colonel Higgins was kidnapped and murdered by elements of the terrorist organization, Hezbollah.

1989 **Manila, The Philippines:** The terrorist group, The New People's Army (NPA), assassinated US Army Colonel James Rowe. The NPA also murdered two US government contractors in September of that year.

Frankfurt, Germany: Deutsche Bank chairman, Alfred Herrhausen, was assassinated by the German terrorist organization, The Red Army Faction.

1990 **The Philippines:** A terrorist group known as the New Peoples Army murdered two US Air Force personnel on May 13.

1992 **Colombia, South America:** Terrorists kidnapped two American businessmen.

Manila, The Philippines: The Philippine terrorist organization known as Red Scorpion Group kidnapped a senior business official in Manila.

1993 **New York City:** The first World Trade Center bombing in New York City resulted in 6 people being killed and 1000 injured. Extremist Islamic terrorists committed the attack.

CIA Headquarters, Langley, Virginia: A terrorist attack by a lone gunman at the entrance to CIA Headquarters left two Agency employees dead and three wounded. Mir Amal Kansi, a Pakistani national, was subsequently charged and executed for the attack.

Colombia, South America: The Revolutionary Armed Forces of Colombia (FARC) kidnapped three American missionaries.

Colombia, South America: FARC terrorists kidnapped American, Thomas Hargrove, on September 23.

1995 **Karachi, Pakistan:** Two gunmen opened fire on a US Consulate van, killing two US diplomats and wounding a third. Islamic militants were suspected of this attack.

Tokyo, Japan: Terrorists released a nerve gas, known as Sarin, in the Tokyo subway system, killing 12 people and injuring 5700 other people.

Oklahoma City, Oklahoma: Domestic terrorists used a truck bomb to destroy the Murrah Federal Building in Oklahoma City on April 19, killing 166 people and injuring additional hundreds.

Kashmir, India: A Kashmiri terrorist group abducted six foreigners, including two US citizens. One hostage was later beheaded.

1996 **Saudi Arabia:** The bombing of the Khobar Towers killed 19 US servicemen and wounded 515 other people.

Columbia, South America: FARC rebels kidnapped a US citizen. He was later released after the terrorists demanded a one-million-dollar ransom.

Colombia, South America: Another US citizen was kidnapped and held for nine months before he was released.

Colombia, South America: The FARC kidnapped an American geologist working in Colombia on December 11. He was later found murdered.

Lima, Peru: Terrorists from the Tupac Amaru Revolutionary Movement (MRTA) burst into a party at the Japanese ambassador's residence, taking several people hostage. The terrorists held 81 of the hostages for several months.

1997 **New York City:** A terrorist opened fire at an observation deck atop the Empire State Building in New York City, killing one person and wounding several others.

Karachi, Pakistan: Two gunmen murdered four American employees and one Pakistani employee of the Union Texas Petroleum Company as they left the Sheraton Hotel in Karachi. The attacks occurred following a Virginia jury verdict finding Mir Amal Kansi guilty of murdering two CIA employees.

Luxor, Egypt: Gunmen opened fire, killing 58 tourists and four Egyptians. Twenty-six others were wounded in the attack.

Colombia, South America: Terrorists kidnapped several US citizens on February 14, February 24, and March 7, eventually releasing most of them.

Republic of Yemen: Yemeni terrorists kidnapped a US businessman on October 30, releasing him on November 27.

1998 **Kenya and Tanzania:** US Embassy bombings in Kenya and Tanzania resulted in killing 224 people and injuring scores of others. Al-Qaeda claimed responsibility.

Bogotá, Colombia: FARC terrorists kidnapped 28 people, including five US citizens, at a roadblock near Bogotá. The terrorists also killed three people and wounded 14 in the same incident.

Cundinamarca, Colombia: Colombian terrorists followed a US businessman and his family to their home in Cundinamarca and kidnapped his 11-year-old son. They held the boy from November 15 to January 21, before finally releasing him, demanding a one-million-dollar ransom.

1999 **Colombia, South America:** FARC terrorists kidnapped and murdered three US citizens who were working in Colombia. (In 1999 alone, terrorists kidnapped a total of 165 persons, including eleven US citizens.)

Nigeria: Armed terrorists stormed an oil platform in Nigeria and kidnapped three workers, including an American and an Australian citizen. Several other oil platform seizures were conducted shortly thereafter.

2000 **Republic of Yemen:** The American naval vessel USS Cole was attacked on October 12. Seventeen American sailors were killed and 39 wounded in the Al-Qaeda-led attack.

Ecuador: Also on October 12, terrorists in Ecuador kidnapped ten employees of a Spanish energy consortium, including five Americans. One American was later murdered and after the oil companies paid a ransom of 13 million dollars, the others were released.

Kyrgyzstan, Uzbekistan: Terrorists representing the Islamic Movement of Uzbekistan kidnapped four American tourist mountain climbers. The hostages were subsequently able to escape after spending several days in captivity.

Athens, Greece: The Greek terrorist organization, 17 November, assassinated a British Defense Attaché in an ambush-type attack.

2001 **New York City and Washington, D.C.:** On September 11, in the worst terrorist attack on American soil, hijackers flew two passenger airliners into the World Trade Center in New York City, and another one into the Pentagon in the nation's capital. One airliner crashed in a field in Pennsylvania. In all, 2,973 people perished in the coordinated attacks orchestrated by Osama Bin Laden and the Islamic Fundamentalist terrorist group, Al-Qaeda.

United States: A number of anthrax attacks were conducted in various locations in the United States during the period of October and November. The attacks were directed at the American news media and members of Congress.

The Philippines: Terrorists from the Abu Sayyaf organization kidnapped thirteen tourists, including three Americans, and three staff members from a resort area in the Philippines. During a series of rescue attempts by the Philippine military, two hostages were killed and nine escaped. The two remaining hostages were held in captivity until June 2002.

2002 **Pakistan:** The Wall Street Journal reported that Daniel Pearl, on assignment in Pakistan, was kidnapped. He was later tortured and murdered by Islamic militants.

Colombia, South America: Armed terrorists on motorcycles shot and killed two US citizens. The victims were in Colombia trying to negotiate the release of their father, who was

being held hostage by the FARC.

Karachi, Pakistan: Terrorists attacked a Christian Church, killing five people, including two US citizens, and wounding 46 others. The church was one that was frequented by personnel from the US Embassy.

Pakistan: Armed terrorists attacked a Christian school attended by the children of missionaries. Six people were killed and one injured in the attack.

Bali, Indonesia: A car bomb exploded outside of a nightclub in Bali, killing 202 people and injuring 300 more. Among the dead were 88 Australian and seven American tourists. Al-Qaeda claimed responsibility for the attacks.

Moscow, Russia: Chechen terrorists seized a theater in Moscow, Russia, taking more than 800 people as hostages. A rescue attempt was conducted; however, 100 hostages lost their lives during the ordeal, including one American citizen.

Kenya: A suicide car-bomb attack on a hotel in Kenya killed fifteen people and wounded forty.

2003 **Morocco:** Twelve suicide bombers attacked several targets in Morocco, killing 43 people and wounding 100. Targeted were a Spanish restaurant, a Jewish enclave, a hotel, and the Belgian Consulate.

Jakarta, Indonesia: A car bomb exploded outside of a Marriott Hotel in Jakarta. Ten people were killed and one hundred-fifty were wounded, including two Americans.

Bogotá, Colombia: FARC terrorists attacked two bars frequented by Americans, killing one person and injuring 72 others.

2004 **Beslan, Russia:** Muslim terrorists stormed and took over a school in Beslan. Russian police and military units assaulted the school in a rescue attempt three days later. A total of 355 hostages, about half of them children, were killed and 500 were wounded. Al-Qaeda was believed to be responsible for this attack.

Saudi Arabia: Paul Johnson, an American engineer working for Lockheed-Martin, was kidnapped in Saudi Arabia. His Al-Qaeda captors beheaded him five days later.

Riyadh, Saudi Arabia: Terrorists shot and killed Robert Jacob, an American working for a US defense contractor.

Riyadh, Saudi Arabia: Gunmen shot a BBC correspondent and his cameraman, critically wounding the correspondent and killing the cameraman.

Kobar, Saudi Arabia: Twenty-two people, mostly foreigners, were killed and twenty-five injured during a shooting spree and hostage standoff in Kobar. Al-Qaeda claimed responsibility.

Iraq: A militant Islamic website shows an American, identified as Nick Berg, being beheaded in Iraq. Civilian workers Jack Hensley and Eugene Armstong were also kidnapped and beheaded.

Yabu, Saudi Arabia: In an attack on a Western Oil Company office in Yabu, terrorists killed six people. Their bodies were subsequently dragged through the streets.

Fallujah, Iraq: Militants in Fallujah killed four US civilian contractors in an ambush. At least two of the bodies were dragged through the streets and hung from a bridge over the Euphrates River.

Madrid, Spain: One hundred ninety-one people were killed and more than eighteen hundred injured after a series of coordinated terrorist bombings against the Madrid, Spain train system. This was the deadliest terrorist attack against Europe since the Lockerbie aircraft bombing in 1988.

2005 **London, England:** Terrorist bombings in London killed fifty-two people and injured hundreds more in a coordinated attack on London's transportation system.

According to the National Counter Terrorist Center (NCTC), approximately 11,000 terrorist attacks occurred in 2005 alone, resulting in over 14,500 deaths. Non-combatants that were victims of terrorist attacks (wounded or killed) included over 6500 police officers, 1000 children, 300 government officials, 170 members of the clergy or other religious figures, 140 teachers and 100 journalists. Fifty-six Americans were killed by terrorist incidents in 2005 alone. Armed attacks and bombings accounted for the vast majority of fatalities in 2005, according to the NCTC. Suicide bombers accounted for about twenty percent of all deaths.

By far, these incidents are not the only terrorist attacks to occur within the past couple of decades. They are, however, a representative example of the world in which we live today. Every American owes it to himself or herself to be vigilant in these perilous times. All of these incidents are different in many respects, but all have one common denominator: None of the victims expected it would happen to them. Terrorism can happen anytime, anywhere in the world. The U.S. State Department currently lists 31 countries on their website where Americans should not travel. Some of these are Colombia, Sri Lanka, Pakistan, Nepal, The Philippines, Saudi Arabia, Haiti, Kenya, Nigeria, the West Bank and Gaza Strip of Israel, Algeria, Lebanon, Syria and Uzbekistan. Yet Americans travel, live and work in most, if not all of these countries. And as we learned only too well in 2001, the United States is not immune to acts of terrorism. The National Counter-Terrorism Center stated that the "homegrown" variety of terrorist attacks -- that is, attacks by terrorists residing in the host country, are a particularly noteworthy phenomenon. You owe it to yourself and to your loved ones to be prepared. Preparation is the key to successfully thwarting a terrorist attack. Being fearful and intimidated does nothing to help you prepare for the possibility of dealing with a terrorist incident. Being in denial will not equip you to face a violent encounter with a terrorist and live through it.

Knowledge, awareness and preparation can go a long way toward helping you dissipate the fear of the unknown and gain an understanding of the terrorist mindset. It is human nature to fear what we do not understand. The key to defeating fear is to gain knowledge and understanding of the terrorist methodology. Chapter Two will deal with the terrorist mindset and methodology in planning and preparing for an attack.

Are you at Risk?

The Western world has declared an international war on terrorism. No longer are acts of terrorism confined to Third World countries. Every country in the world is subject to the scourge of terrorism and no country is immune from a violent outbreak of terrorism occurring at any given moment. No longer are the wealthy industrialists and political leaders the only ones who have to worry about a terrorist attack. Certainly, wealthy industrialists and political leaders are prime terrorist targets, but now just about anyone can be the target of a terrorist incident. In the past several years we have seen military personnel, government officials and employees, Christian missionaries, Jewish businessmen, tourists, nurses, students, teachers, truck drivers and a host of people in other occupations suffering at the hands of terrorists throughout the world.

Do not make the assumption that because you are a tourist in a relatively friendly country, you won't be the victim of a terrorist incident. Terrorism can strike anyone, anytime, anywhere, and you need to be ready. ❖

"The key battleground in the war on terrorism is in the minds of the American public."

~ *Patrick J. Kennedy*

THE TERRORIST METHODOLOGY

Thinking Like A Terrorist

Ten Steps of the Terrorist Cycle of Operation

There is a common misconception that terrorist attacks simply occur with little or no prior planning. While it is true that some terrorists do take advantage of random opportunities to conduct "target of opportunity" attacks, the vast majority of terrorist acts are well planned and rehearsed. Knowledge of how terrorists go about selecting a victim, conducting surveillance and planning the attack can be very useful in detecting when something is amiss and will help you to plan accordingly. The ideal time to defeat a terrorist attack is before it starts. In most cases there is ample indication that something is happening. Once the attack is underway, you are already "behind the power curve", so to speak. The time to act is well before the attack even begins. If you know what you are looking for, you can spot clues that an attack is about to take place. The well-trained mind can pick up on these subtle clues and begin to take evasive action. Obviously, the earlier in the cycle of operation you can detect a problem, the better chance you have of defeating it. This requires practicing what I call "anticipation mindset"-- that is, living in an attitude of "relaxed awareness" being alert to subtle changes in your environment. No one wants to live in a fearful, paranoid state all the time; however, being aware of your surroundings is only common sense.

We will discuss more on that later, but first you must be aware of what signs and indicators to watch for. Once the attack begins it may be too late. The following is what is commonly referred to as the "terrorist cycle of operation". Not all terrorists strictly adhere to this formula for conducting an attack, but most of them do use several of these techniques. Knowing what to look for and acting accordingly is the key to your survival!

Step one: The Target Study

The target study is the first phase of the terrorist operation. During the target study phase terrorists discuss, in general, the viability of conducting an operation in a particular country or at a particular site. A list of potential targets is discussed among the leadership of the terrorist group planning the attack. This list usually contains multiple potential victims that would satisfy the group or individual's goals. Generating this list does not require exposure of personnel or plans and is usually done in a secret location, thus detection during the target study phase of the operation is extremely remote. It is in the target study phase that a list of possible victims is drawn up and the decision is made to go forward with the plan to conduct an attack on a generalized target. Who are these victims?

Categories of Victims

Generally, there are three categories of terrorist victims. These catagories apply to the victims of criminals as well -- victim by selection, victim by location, and victim by association. It might be worthwhile to briefly discuss each one of these.

Victim by selection

In this category, the terrorist or criminal element will go through an extensive process to determine the viability of attacking a particular victim or target. The "victim by selection" is not a random target of opportunity, but a well thought out and discussed selection. It is based on several factors, such as accessibility, predictability and symbolic value. In the case of victim by selection, the overall perceived security profile and actions of the intended target could very well determine whether the terrorist group (or criminal) continues with the operation or aborts and moves on to an easier target. Even single assailants have used a process that involves narrowing a group of potential victims down to one who is capable of being attacked. Proactive countermeasures are generally successful in keeping a potential target from being selected. Steps that you can take to limit your chances at being selected as a victim will be discussed in later chapters.

Victim by location

Victim by location can best be described as being in the "wrong place at the wrong time". The victims of the 9-11 hijackings could be described as victims by location. Innocent bystanders during a bombing are "victims of location". In the case of victim by location, a specific individual is not selected, but becomes a victim because they happen to be at a particular location when a terrorist or criminal event occurs (wrong place at the wrong time). The CIA employees murdered in January 1993 while waiting to enter the Headquarters compound could be considered examples of victims by location.

Victim by association

This scenario can resemble both "victim by location" and "victim by selection", but has some very significant differences. In victim by association, an individual becomes a victim because of his association or proximity to a person or place during an attack. A person may become a victim simply because he is a member of a particular political, religious ethnic group or nationality, or because he works for a particular company or government organization.

Don't assume that, just because you are not a high-ranking government official or high-profile private citizen you are not subject to a terrorist attack. Being an American tourist, businessman, government employee or armed services member automatically qualifies you as a suitable target. The fact that most high profile people have some type of security presence around them actually makes them a much harder target than the average citizen. History is replete with examples of tourists and low or mid-level government officials and military personnel who are victims of terrorist attacks. In fact, the numbers prove that many more "average" citizens are victims of terrorist incidents than are "high profile" individuals.

Step Two: Surveillance of the prospective target

During the initial surveillance phase of the operation, terrorists will deploy individually, in pairs or in groups to conduct surveillance on the selected targets. Terrorists may "disguise" themselves as tourists in order to take photographs of a potential attack site. A good surveillant will try and blend in with the local environment and be as unobtrusive and "invisible" as possible. He will take photographs and/or videos, not only of the potential attack site, but also of other areas of interest such as monuments, statues and various tourist attractions. That way, if he is stopped and his film is checked, he has a good cover story. He can say that he is simply a tourist taking pictures of typical tourist sites or places of interest. Interspersed with those pictures, however, will be photographs and/or videos of the prospective target site.

During this phase the terrorists will be trying to determine if a particular site or individual is a viable target. They will look for things like security, (both physical and personnel security employed at the site), ease of ingress and egress to the target site, and the possibility of inflicting maximum damage on the target while expending minimum effort.

It is important to note that a final decision on the target selection will probably not have been made yet, and this phase of the operation is considered to be part of the selection process. The Initial Surveillance phase is the first opportunity you, as a potential victim, will have to detect that something unusual is going on. Pay particular attention to anyone taking pictures of you, your home, your vehicles, your workplace, your children, your children's school or play areas, or any other place frequented by you or your family on a regular basis. We can't stop people from taking pictures, unless they are in a restricted area such as a classified government or military installation, but we can take note of anything that arouses our suspicion. Does it look unusual or out of place to you? Do the people taking the pictures look out of place (i.e. not fit in with the environment)? Do they look uncomfortable and unsure of themselves? Are they taking more pictures than most people would or showing an inordinate amount of interest in a particular place? Are they taking notes? Are they trying a little too hard to be unobtrusive? Are they being furtive or secretive when police or security officers are in the area? Do they ask too many questions? Are they asking personal questions of you, your family, employees, etc.?

It is important to note that the surveillance or information-gathering stages of the operation are vulnerabilities that can be exploited to your advantage. If something does not look right to you, this may be your "sixth sense" telling you that something is wrong. You may not be able to pinpoint what it is exactly, but it is important to make a mental note of the participants and their actions as you observe them. You may very well see them again during another phase of the operation. This is where a notebook or a small digital camera can come in handy. If you see one or more suspicious people or a suspicious vehicle, simply jot down a license plate number and a description of the occupants. Better yet, take a picture. If they can take a picture of you, why can't you take a picture of them? If it turns out to be nothing, there's no harm done. But if it turns out to be something, then you may well have thwarted a terrorist attack before it has even begun. The fact that you are paying attention to them sends an unmistakable message to the terrorists that you are alert, you are paying attention to them, and you are not likely to be taken by surprise. That may be all it takes to make them give up on you and direct their attention to another target. Most likely they will choose someone not as alert or as knowledgeable as you are. They will probably pick someone who is not paying attention to his surroundings and, therefore, is an easier target.

Technology and the Internet have made information collection far more sophisticated than in the past. The ability to obtain personal information, maps, and even satellite imagery has made the terrorist's job that much easier. Most terrorist and criminal groups, however, use, nearly exclusively, the old-fashioned surveillance techniques to gather their information and plan their attack.

Step Three: Target Selection

After the initial target surveillance, the terrorists will come together again to finalize their selection of a target. "Target selection" is the process by which a group of potential victims is narrowed down to the one they deem vulnerable enough to successfully attack. The terrorist surveillance teams will make reports, review photographs and videos, share notes and diagrams and have discussions for the purpose of identifying and selecting the most logical and vulnerable target. This meeting will most likely be conducted in a private, secure facility; however, it is entirely possible that it could be conducted in a public site such as a restaurant, café, coffee shop, or other similar location. Like the "target study phase" of the operation, detecting anything out of the ordinary during the "target selection phase" is extremely difficult, if not impossible.

During the target selection phase of the operation, the terrorists will select and identify a target based on several criteria, to include:

- Importance of the target. If the target is an individual, what is the position or job the target holds? Is he or she important enough to garner attention from the press? Can a ransom be demanded? In the event the target is a building or other significant landmark, what is the importance of the target? In the case of the World Trade Center and the Pentagon, Al Qaeda wanted to strike at the financial and military symbols of the United States. Terrorists want to extract the maximum "terror value" from an attack. The higher profile the target, the more "terror value" they get.

- Political value: Is the target a person or a location of political value? Will attacking this person or location give the terrorist organization political leverage? Will the attack make a political "statement" in itself? Will attacking this target gain sympathy and/or support from other terrorists groups, individuals or countries or will it incur the wrath of like-minded organizations and therefore be counter productive?

- Vulnerability of the target: Is the target a "soft" or a "hard" target? In other words, does the target have adequate security measures in place; or in the case of an individual, does he or she practice sound security procedures? Is the prospective target alert and aware of his surroundings? In the case of buildings and other physical locations, how effective is the physical security? Are the security officers alert and prepared? Are the people going into and out of the buildings reasonably well protected? Can vehicles get close to the building? Can individuals gain access to the facility with minimum risk? How likely is it that the operation will be a success?

- Risk to the terrorists: What is the likelihood of escape? Is this a suicide mission or is it important that all of the terrorists get out alive? What will happen to them if they are captured? (While these are legitimate questions the terrorist may ask himself, it is important to note that "risk to the terrorist" is, in reality, the least important criteria in target selection).

While you probably can't do anything about your assumed importance or your political status, you certainly can do something to make yourself less vulnerable as a target and place the terrorist at greater risk. A committed terrorist does not mind, and even may look forward to giving his life for his "mission". He absolutely does not, however, want to fail. The big risk to the terrorist is not the risk of his life -- it is in the risk of failure. Making yourself into a "hard" target increases the chance that the terrorist will fail in his mission. This, in turn, decreases your vulnerability to an attack. Selected victims tend to be predictable, accessible, and of some symbolic value. We will discuss how you can transform yourself into a "hard" target in subsequent chapters.

Step Four: Target Surveillance

Once target selection is finalized, an additional surveillance is usually conducted on the appointed target. Because the terrorists have now limited their choices to only one or two targets, instead of the original multiple selections, they are able to devote more resources to the selected target. This phase of the operation may take the form of foot surveillance, vehicular surveillance, or a combination of the two. At this point in the cycle of operation, the terrorist needs more up-to-date and better intelligence about the target. The terrorist surveillants will again resort to taking pictures and videos, drawing diagrams and taking notes. This time, however, they will do so in far more detail than during the initial surveillance. This phase of the operation is critical, both for the terrorist, and for the selected target. One goal the terrorists hope to accomplish during this particular target surveillance operation is to collect information to determine exactly where and when the intended victim is most vulnerable to an attack. The terrorists will want to note things such as daily traffic routes, times of departure and arrival, security measures employed (both physical and personnel security), and anything else that may be useful in planning the attack. The terrorist surveillants will want answers to the following questions: What route does the target take to and from work and home every day? Does he or she employ any type of security services such as security guards or police officers? Is his or her vehicle armored? Does the intended victim leave home, work, or school at the same time every day? Is he "time and place predictable"? Is he alert and aware of his environment or is he, like most people, "off in his own world"? Is he armed? If so, what are his weapons? If there are security guards or police officers employed for protection, how well armed are they? Are the officers professional security/police officers or are they "Rent-a-Cops"?

The terrorist may use "cover for status" to obtain intelligence information about you. In other words, he may pose as a worker performing maintenance on the road near your home or office or

some other such ruse to gain information about you, your family or your employees. Be alert to anything out of the ordinary near your residence or place of employment. The ingress and egress areas leading to your home and office are commonly known as "chokepoints". A chokepoint is an area through which you must pass on your route to and from work, home, school, church, or any place that you or your family frequent on a regular basis. Typically, chokepoints are areas where the victim's movement is stopped or slowed considerably. Good examples would be at stoplights, stop signs, narrow roadways with parked vehicles or other obstacles, and other areas in which your forward progress is impeded. These are danger areas that you simply cannot avoid during your daily travels, and they are prime areas for terrorist attacks. Pay particular attention to anything out of the ordinary whenever you approach a chokepoint along your route.

Step Five: Attack Planning

The terrorists may conduct planning meetings for the attack in a public area, such as a café or restaurant, but most likely will conduct them in a private, secure facility, such as the home of one of the terrorist conspirators. It will be very difficult, if not impossible, for you to detect anything unusual during the planning stage of the operation. According to the Al Qaeda training manual, "After intelligence has been gathered and surveillance is conducted, the final attack plan will be created, modified and agreed upon". The development of the attack plan is a critical step in the cycle. Usually, the operational planning stage and surveillance of the prospective target will be simultaneous. The terrorist leadership will continually receive current reports concerning the activities of the target. Once again photographs, videos, maps, diagrams and notes will be reviewed and utilized in developing the final plan of attack. Escape from the target is not a consideration for those terrorists who are willing to die while executing their plan. As stated before, terrorists are much more concerned about failing in their operation than they are about escaping or surviving. Make no mistake -- the terrorist of today has no qualms at all about dying for his cause -- and taking you with him.

Step Six: Final surveillance of the target

At this stage of the cycle, the terrorists will conduct a final surveillance of the target. They do this to essentially verify that nothing has changed in terms of the target's security posture. They will want answers to the following questions: Has the target changed anything about his route, timing, manner of transportation, etc.? Has security around the target been increased? Is security more vigilant and better armed? Is it possible the terrorists have been detected?

This is one of your final chances to detect and deter the attack before it begins. To the trained eye and alert individual, the terrorists have presented several opportunities for discovery by now. By its nature, surveillance is a manpower- and time-intensive activity. It is at this point that the terrorist is most vulnerable to detection. Pay attention to what is going on around you.

Step Seven: Practice and rehearsal of the attack

Practice and rehearsal of the impending attack will begin, based on all the information gathered during the surveillance portions of the Terrorist Cycle of Operation. The "practice attack" will take into consideration what they believe to be the "target's" utilization of security measures or "security posture". Since most practice, rehearsal and training is done covertly, the chance of your detecting anything during this stage is remote. Although not common, there have been situations where terrorist groups "practiced" at the actual site on which they planned to conduct the attack.

The group that will actually carry out the attack will most likely not be the same group that did the surveillance. The individuals who actually execute the attack are considered "specialists", and may consist of suicide bombers, assassins and other trained personnel. According to the Al-Qaeda training manual, "concurrently Commander has begun tuning up the Special Operations Group members--shooting, physical and mental preparation, etc. The Special Operations group is given the target and the attack plan".

The Dry Run

There is a directive in the Al-Qaeda training manual that states, "the Special Operations Group goes through at least one dry run before the attack". Terrorists use dry runs during the final stages of operational planning to simulate the actual attack. Unlike surveillance, which can occur weeks or even months before an attack, dry runs are usually conducted just prior to the attack and can be an indication that an attack is imminent. Dry runs can expose strengths and weaknesses in the attack plan and can also allow the terrorist group to adapt or alter their plan as necessary. Terrorists will use dry runs to test your alertness and security procedures, and to verify that you are a "soft" (easy) target. Psychological preparation is another benefit of conducting dry runs, in that they allow the terrorist to become comfortable with the attack plan and help to allay any fears they might have prior to conducting the operation.

Every dry run conducted by the terrorist group provides you with an opportunity to detect them during their operational planning phase. Generally, the first few practice runs will be conducted in a semi-secure environment, thereby making them difficult to detect. However, most terrorist groups conduct at least one dry run in "public" prior to the actual operation. Be aware of any suspicious activity in the vicinity of your home, workplace or frequent travel routes. Look for people and/or vehicles approaching you and then turning away abruptly. The terrorists could be conducting a "probe" to further determine your weaknesses.

Terrorist groups have used dry runs frequently in the past to include the 9/11 attacks, the 2005 London bombings, and the August 2006 plot to blow up airliners while in route over the Pacific Ocean using liquid explosives. They may carry out only one dry run prior to the attack or they may conduct multiple dry runs. Detecting dry runs is one of the very last chances you will have to protect yourself prior to the actual attack.

Some of the things you will want to be aware of that may indicate a dry run is taking place are:

- Individuals exhibiting unusual behavior, such as approaching you or your vehicle and then turning away abruptly.
- Individuals who appear nervous or who display anxious behavior.
- A vehicle following you closely, while another vehicle pulls up alongside or darts in front of you quickly.
- Individuals obviously attempting to gain a position close to you in a public location.
- Two or more individuals who appear to be signaling or communicating with each other in a non-verbal manner.
- Individuals with an unusual interest in your security procedures.
- Individuals who approach security personnel and engage in small talk.
- Individuals wearing disguises.
- Individuals who approach you to make small talk, ask the time, etc., or persons who appear to be staring at you and then abruptly look away when you turn in their direction.
- Anyone who appears to be intently focused on you or who is staring at you for no apparent reason.

If you suspect that someone is engaged in a dry run, you must notify the authorities immediately. Go to a secure location and stay there until the situation is resolved. Immediately change your routine and your route. Remember -- a dry run generally occurs immediately prior to an attack. Act now. You may not get a second chance!

Step Eight: Deployment of the attack plan

In this step, terrorist "hit teams" begin to deploy to the attack sight. They may deploy individually, in pairs, or in teams. They may be on foot, in vehicles, on public transportation, or a combination thereof. This is one of the final opportunities you have to detect the attack prior to its initiation. Counter-surveillance is a useful tool for detecting terrorists during their deployment to the attack site and will be discussed in subsequent chapters. If you suspect that an attack is about to take place, it is critical that you get to a safe place immediately.

Step Nine: Target identification

Once the "hit" team has deployed to the attack site, which will usually occur at a chokepoint, they must communicate with each other in order to correctly identify the target. They may use radios, cell phones, hand signals, or simply give a quick glance or nod at their co-conspirators. If explosives are to be used, the terrorists probably won't use radios or cell phones for fear that the explosives will detonate prematurely. (Some radio and cell phone signals will detonate explosives).

The target identification step is the last surveillance an intended victim has a chance to see. This is your absolute last chance to detect an attack before it starts. Once again, you should remain alert,

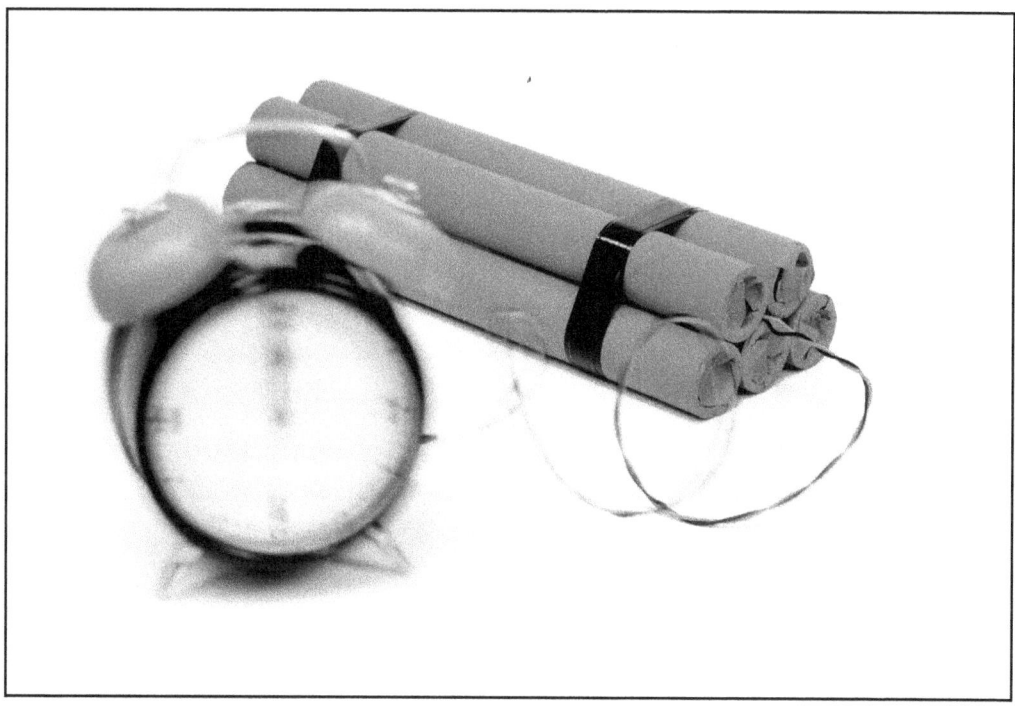

particularly at chokepoints, and pay attention to any strange or unusual behavior. It is not too late to avoid the attack, but the amount of time you have to react is now measured in seconds.

Step Ten: The attack

Upon receiving a pre-determined signal that the target is on the "X", (the point at which the attack takes place, commonly referred to in my business as "the X", also known as the "kill zone"), the attack will commence. By now it is too late to detect, preempt or defeat the attack before its onset. Your goal at this point is to get off the "X" as quickly as possible and to get out of the area. We will discuss this in later chapters. If, however, the cycle of operation gets to the attack phase, you have probably committed some serious errors. The goal is to detect the operation at some point in the terrorist cycle and to prevent it from ever getting to the attack stage.

Types of Terrorist Attacks

The types of terrorist attacks vary widely according to the terrorist groups' resources and capabilities. The three types of attacks we will discuss in this book include:

- Kidnappings
- Assassinations
- Explosive attacks

Kidnapping

Imagine this scenario: You leave for work at the same time you do every other day and you take the same familiar route you have taken for years. It is dark, traffic is light, and your mind is on the dozens of things you have to accomplish that day. As you pull to a stoplight you sip your coffee and notice an SUV in the lane next to you. You think nothing of it and turn your attention to the radio weatherman. You don't know it, but the people in the SUV are watching you, as they have been for weeks. Before the light turns green, three masked men jump out of the vehicle, jerk the doors open, and pull you out of your car. They throw you in the back of their SUV and take you to a pre-determined safe house. There they blindfold you, take a video of you in captivity with a gun held to your head, and make demands for your release. When their demands are not met within the specified time frame, they may videotape your execution and dump your body alongside a highway.

This type of scenario has occurred far too many times in the Middle East and elsewhere in the world, and could be coming to America soon. Kidnapping has been a favorite tool of terrorist groups for many years and shows no sign of abating any time soon.

Webster's New World Dictionary defines kidnapping as "to seize and hold or carry off a person against that person's will, by force or fraud, often for ransom". Kidnapping is extremely complex, involving access to the intended victim, transportation, and control of the victim over an extended period of time. Aircraft hijackings, such as what occurred on 9/11, are an extreme example of kidnapping. Terrorists may kidnap an individual for monetary purposes or for other reasons, such as making a political statement or the demand for release of other terrorists held in confinement.

Assassination

Although we tend to associate assassination with high-profile political figures, that is not always the case. The simple fact that you are an American traveling overseas can mark you for assassination. There are numerous examples of ordinary American citizens becoming victims of assassination by terrorist or criminal elements while living or traveling abroad. Webster defines assassination as "to murder by surprise attack, usually for payment or for zealous belief".

Assassinations in the form of sniper attacks have occurred in the United States as well as abroad. Pakistani terrorist Mir Amal Kansi shot five people using an AK-47 assault rifle, killing two employees at CIA Headquarters in Langley, Virginia in 1993. Two random snipers terrorized the Washington, D. C. metropolitan area in October of 2002. In late 2003 and early 2004, sniper shootings on Ohio interstates resulted in one death. Anyone can be the victim of an assassin's bullet.

Explosion

An explosive attack, such as a bomb placed on your route to work, involves technical knowledge, resource acquisition, and time on target for emplacement and detonation. Often the use of a bomb will require that the terrorist use two sites -- a bomb site (the location where the bomb actually explodes) and an observation/triggering site. Most terrorist groups today are well versed in the art of bomb making, and law enforcement has seen a dramatic increase in the use of explosives by terrorist and criminal elements over the past decade. The use of explosives as an instrument of terror has been around since the invention of the first explosive device and shows no sign of abatement. Improvised explosive devices (IEDs) are becoming more sophisticated as the technology in electronics and in ordnance becomes more advanced. Explosives have been used extensively by terrorists in both the United States and overseas as an effective terror tool.

Chapter Three will deal with what I call, "the combat triad". These are skills you should adopt in order to detect, disrupt or defeat a terrorist attack, should you find yourself in that unfortunate position. ❖

CHAPTER 3

"The credit belongs to the man who is actually in the arena; whose face is marred by dust and sweat and blood; who strives valiantly; who errs and comes up short again and again; who knows the great enthusiasms, the great devotions, and spends himself in a worthy cause; who, at the best, knows in the end the triumph of high achievement; and who, at the worst, if he fails, at least fails while daring greatly, so that his place shall never be with those cold and timid souls who know neither victory nor defeat."

~ Theodore Roosevelt

INTRODUCTION TO THE COMBAT TRIAD

We are at war. Like it or not, Americans are in a global confrontation unlikely to end anytime soon. Unlike most wars, the war on terrorism affects combatants and non-combatants alike. There is no "front line" and, as we in the United States learned the hard way, civilians aren't immune from attack. On the contrary, terrorists prefer to attack civilian targets. Civilians are less likely to be armed, well trained or have the ability to deal with a terrorist attack. As I said earlier, terrorists are, by and large, cowards and make the weak and unprepared among us their victims. I completely agree with Lieutenant Colonel Dave Grossman, who authored the book, *On Combat*. In his book he compares the majority of people in our society to sheep and refers to them as "kind, gentle, productive creatures that only hurt one another by accident". I think this is an apt description. Most people in our country have fortunately not been exposed to violence, murder and mayhem on a regular basis. Until June 15, 1974, I included myself in this category. That day was the day I raised my right hand and took the oath of office as a police officer. That was the beginning of a radical transformation in my perception of the "dark side" of human nature. I was astonished at the violence I encountered on a daily basis while working as a street cop. Before becoming a police officer I had no real concept of rampant crime; and facing the reality that anyone could become a victim at any moment was a harsh truth.

The lesson in reality hit me hard and it didn't take me long to realize the importance of never leaving home unarmed. It wasn't that I'd become paranoid or scared, but I had become a realist. I saw firsthand the criminal acts that the underbelly of society was capable of perpetrating against the "sheep" and I was determined not to become one of those sheep. Until I became a street cop I had no idea how vulnerable most people were. Like most civilians, I thought "it" would never happen to me. My eight years as a street cop changed that perspective dramatically. I quickly learned that the police cannot possibly protect everyone and the ultimate responsibility for my safety and security was mine.

Based on this newfound revelation, I was motivated to begin working on the skills necessary to protect myself. I practiced my shooting skills daily as if my life depended on it (it did). I studied martial arts and obtained a black belt in karate, as well as lesser belts in other disciplines. I began running for fitness, lifting weights and studying everything I could get my hands on concerning street combat. I read and re-read books like *No Second Place Winner*, by legendary Border Patrol Agent Bill Jordan; *Fast and Fancy Revolver Shooting* by old time pistelero Ed McGivern; *Kill or Be Killed* by Colonel Rex Applegate; and *Get Tough!* by British Commando Major W. E. Fairbairn. Although somewhat outdated in terms of tactics, these books are still considered classics and contain very valuable information, especially concerning the "combat mindset". I was determined not to become some bad guy's "prey". Instead, I became a predator of the criminal predators. I went hunting for those elements in our society that preyed on the "sheep".

Colonel Grossman, in his book, *On Combat*, described the terrorists and criminals of the world as "wolves" that prey on the innocent and unsuspecting "sheep". He stated, "there are evil men in this world and they are capable of evil deeds. The moment you forget that or pretend it is not so, you become a sheep. There is no safety in denial". I couldn't agree more. The next time you find yourself denying the fact there are evil men out there who want to harm you or your family, and if that denial leads you into a state of complacency and unwillingness to prepare, just look in the mirror and say "baaa".

The "Combat Triad" and Your Safety

There are basic skills necessary to decrease your chances of becoming a victim of a terrorist incident. What I refer to as the Combat Triad consists of three critical components:

- Awareness
- Action
- Mindset

They are the foundational skills with which you should arm yourself and in the next three chapters we will look at how honing the skills of Awareness, Action, and Mindset are essential keys to survival in this dangerous world of terrorism. ❖

CHAPTER 4

"Let us never forget that terrorism at its heart, at its evil heart, is a psychological war. It endeavors to break the spirit and resolve of those it attacks by creating a lose situation."

~ *Norm Coleman*

SURVIVAL SKILL ONE:

AWARENESS

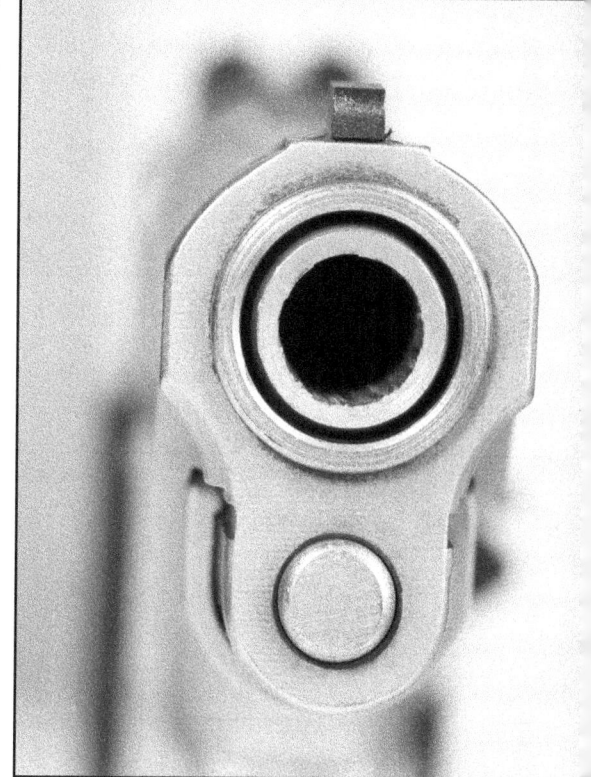

Once a terrorist attack has begun, it is very difficult, if not impossible, to remove oneself from the scene without being harmed. The ideal situation is to detect a terrorist attack before it begins. This is where threat awareness plays a critical role in counter terrorism. Your survival depends on your ability to detect a potential terrorist incident before it has begun. A great military commander once said that losing a battle is forgivable, but being surprised is not. The best weapon you have in your personal war against becoming a terrorist victim is awareness of your surroundings and the ability to maintain an alert, vigilant demeanor at all times.

Cooper's Colors

Any discussion of threat awareness would be incomplete without mentioning "Cooper's Colors". Colonel Jeff Cooper was a former Marine Corps officer who developed an expertise in firearms and survival techniques. Founder of the famous Gunsite Institute in Arizona, Colonel Cooper set the standard for modern pistol techniques, combined with combat awareness. As a result, he developed what is widely known in law enforcement and military circles as "Cooper's Colors". In his excellent book, *Principles of Personal Defense*, Colonel Cooper adapted a Marine Corps system of readiness into four color-coded states of awareness:

White: Unaware and unprepared. If attacked in Condition White, the only thing that may save you is the inadequacy or ineptitude of your attacker. When confronted by something nasty, your reaction will probably be, "Oh my God, this can't be happening!"

Yellow: Relaxed Alert. No specific threat information. Your mindset is that, "today could be the day I may have to defend myself". You are simply aware that the world you are in is an unfriendly place and that you are prepared to do something, if necessary. You should always be in Condition Yellow whenever you are in unfamiliar surroundings or among people you don't know. You should be able to remain in Condition Yellow for long periods of time, as long as you are alert to all that is going on around you. In Yellow, you are taking in surrounding information in a relaxed but alert manner, as in a 360-degree radar sweep.

Orange: Specific Alert. Something is not quite right and has your attention. Your radar has picked up a specific alert. You shift your primary focus to determine if there is a threat, but are still aware of your surroundings. In Condition Orange you set a mental trigger: "If that person does "X", I will need to stop him". Staying in Orange can be a bit of a mental strain, but you can stay in it for as long as you need to. If the threat proves to be nothing, shift back to Condition Yellow.

Red: Fight. Your mental trigger has been "tripped" (established in Condition Orange). Take appropriate action.

The Marine Corps had one additional condition, to be avoided at all cost:

Black: Condition Black is the inability to think or respond in a reasonable manner, due to severe stress. In the training I have conducted for the CIA and numerous other agencies, I characterize Condition Black as being totally overcome with fear. In a stressful situation you become paralyzed with fear. You are unable to think, act or respond in a cohesive manner. Of the three responses available to you, Fight, Flight or Freeze, you freeze, much like a deer caught in the headlights. This is not where you want to be. If this happens you will most likely die. You can stay out of Condition Black by practicing what I refer to as "Anticipation Mindset".

Anticipation Mindset

If you are a good, defensive driver you already possess "anticipation mindset". As an example, while driving a car you might anticipate that the car in the next lane will suddenly swerve in front of you. You might anticipate that other drivers will run red lights, so you maintain caution when the light changes, careful not to bolt out into the intersection.

In the realm of personal protection, anticipation mindset is even more important. Webster's Dictionary defines anticipation as "something expected; foreknowledge; presentment". None of us should remain in a paranoid or obsessive state all the time, but it does pay to be aware of our surroundings. Particularly in unfamiliar surroundings we should always be operating in "Condition Yellow". I don't know how many times, as a police officer investigating a crime, I've heard the victim say, "I can't believe this happened to me". I always wanted to ask, "Why can't you believe it? Don't you read the paper or watch the news?" If you read the newspaper you know that bad things happen to people every day, several times a day. If you have the expectation something bad may happen, you won't be surprised and find yourself in "Condition Black" when it does. Expect the unexpected. If it doesn't happen, there's no harm done. But if it does, you are that much ahead of the reactionary curve and better able to initiate your plan of action.

Anticipation Mindset is a component of Combat Mindset. Anticipation Mindset is essentially "problem solving" before facing the problem. Much like in a chess match, you should think three steps ahead of what is currently happening. Practicing visualization helps in Anticipation Mindset. If you can imagine the scenario in your mind and think about how you should react, you are way ahead of the game. In practicing visualization you have already faced the violent encounter a hundred times in your imagination and you know how you are going to react. When the real thing happens, you don't have to think about it -- you respond as your "trained" mind tells you.

People who are attuned to their security environment constantly play the "When/Then" game. They are thinking, "When (not if) this happens, then this is what I will do". The "When/Then" game is critical to your development as a warrior in the art of survival. You are mentally preparing yourself for action. Physical preparation is extremely important, but as any good football coach will tell you, mental preparation is just as important. If you say to yourself, "I am a victim, and if something happens I will be at the mercy of my attackers", then you have no hope of ever surviving a violent confrontation. On the other hand, if you say to yourself, "When something happens, then I will react aggressively, violently and without hesitation. I will survive, regardless of what I have to do, and the terrorists will be at my mercy", you are well on your way to developing the right combat and survival mindset.

A critical objective that terrorists need to achieve during an attack is the element of surprise. Don't allow them to achieve this goal. Total surprise generally produces an unavoidable and devastating physical response. A massive amount of adrenaline is released into the blood stream, causing a loss of the fine motor skills. The unprepared mind goes into a state of shock, resulting in temporary paralysis (Condition Black). In other words, you have allowed the terrorist to "terrorize" you, which is exactly his intention. Terrorists are well aware that most people go into "Condition Black" during a violent encounter and depend on it to achieve their objectives. In the ideal terrorist ambush, the victim just sits there totally in shock (Condition Black) and the terrorists are able to "have their way with them". It is the initial shock and surprise of the attack that the terrorists use to their advantage. You must deny them this important asset. To do this, you must be in the appropriate state of awareness and have a full understanding of what is going on around you. If you are aware, you can react. If you are not aware of what is going on around you, your reaction time will be far too slow, greatly increasing your chance of becoming a victim.

Anticipation Mindset or "counter-surprise training" can prepare you to overcome this reaction so that you are able to function and effectively execute your plan to survive and escape the attack. Awareness and Anticipation Mindset consist of two critical components, planning and observation. Planning is a key element in awareness and Anticipation Mindset.

Planning

There is an old saying, "Failure to plan is planning to fail". A well thought out plan, vigorously executed, is the key to surviving a terrorist incident. Most people panic in an emergency situation (Condition Black), because they are:

- Not expecting bad things to happen (not practicing anticipation mindset) and
- Not trained on what to do in a violent encounter (no prior planning).

Once the attack has been initiated, your mind will be too overwhelmed at that point to plan an effective response. Develop a plan of action beforehand; know what you are going to do in an attack (play the "When/Then" game) and continually practice "Anticipation Mindset".

Here are some things to keep in mind when developing a plan of action:

- Keep it Simple. You will not remember a complicated plan in a stressful situation, such as a terrorist attack.
- Mentally rehearse your plan often, so that if and when an incident occurs your response will be immediate. I can't stress enough the importance of mental preparation. Mental preparation prepares your mind to react instantly in an emergency. Play the "When/Then" game, ("When "X" happens, then I will do "Y") to get your mind prepared for the worst.
- Physically rehearse the plan if possible. This will enable you to work out the "kinks" in your plan and hard wire your mental plan to your physical response. I believe that it is very important to physically rehearse your plan; however, it is *imperative* that you mentally rehearse your plan if you have any hope at all of being successful.
- Share your plan with your family. If they are with you, discuss what you are going to do if "X" happens. Get them mentally prepared, as well as physically ready to respond to an incident.
- Be flexible. Have more than one plan in mind. In addition to your primary plan, develop secondary and tertiary plans. In case "plan A" doesn't work, go to plan "B", and if that fails, have a plan "C". Above all, be prepared and expect the unexpected. Once again, keep all of your plans simple enough that you will easily remember them in an emergency, and be able to react immediately.
- Constantly re-evaluate your plans and be willing to modify your options as your personal situation develops. Live in Condition Yellow, practicing "Anticipation Mindset".
- Have your plan(s) reviewed by a trusted friend or a security professional, listen to what they tell you and be willing to take their advice.

Observation

Being alert and aware of your surroundings at all times is a critical element in detecting and defeating a potential terrorist attack. I make a habit of watching people go about their daily activities and I have generally noticed that most people are totally oblivious to what is going on around them. Many career criminals report choosing their victims based on whether or not they "looked like a victim". In other words, were they alert and aware of their environment? Were they paying attention to what was going on around them? If they were alert, aware and paying attention to their surroundings, the criminals would usually look for someone else to victimize.

Terrorists use the same criteria in evaluating whether a person is a potential target. Someone who gives the appearance of walking around "in a fog" is, more than likely totally oblivious to what is going on around him. In this condition he is not likely to pick up on any surveillance being conducted on him by terrorists and will become an easy target. Surveillance is a crucial element in the success of any terrorist operation. Many terrorist organizations are very good at conducting surveillance and their record of operational successes proves this. Surveillance by an experienced operator can be very difficult to detect, even under the best of circumstances.

You can, however, learn to detect surveillance if you develop and use good observation skills. "Counter-surveillance" is just another way of developing an awareness of what is going on around you. Prior to residing or traveling overseas, CIA employees receive extensive training in counter-surveillance. This valuable skill has, I'm certain, saved many lives. We will never know for sure, since terrorists don't tend to advertise their failures. I firmly believe that simply giving the impression that you are alert and aware is sometimes enough to thwart a terrorist or criminal attack. If the terrorists, during surveillance of you, suspect you have discovered them, they will most likely (but not always) abort their operation and choose a "softer" target. Remember, the biggest fear a terrorist has is not the fear of death, but the fear of failure. If he thinks he has been discovered and the operation has been compromised, he may very well give up rather than risk failure.

Terrorists and criminals depend heavily on the element of surprise to achieve their goals. Several studies conducted on criminals serving time in jail indicate that this is true. The criminals in the study were in prison because they committed crimes against people, i.e., murder, rape and armed robbery. They were interviewed and asked the question, "What is it that you look for in choosing a victim?" The vast majority of these convicted felons reported that the main criteria they considered in choosing their victims was the apparent lack of awareness the victims had of their surroundings. You need to deprive the terrorist of this important tactic by being alert and aware, both in unfamiliar surroundings and during your daily routine. Continually work on developing good observation skills.

Observation skills consist of the following elements:

- Awareness of your environment (neighborhood, travel routes, office building, school, etc.)
- Awareness of other individuals in your vicinity
- Awareness of your immediate surroundings
- Awareness of any suspicious groups of people in your vicinity
- Awareness of your intuition and "gut feelings" (your "sixth sense")

Before we can understand the methods that we can use to help us detect surveillance, we must first understand what surveillance is.

Surveillance Techniques

Surveillance is described in Webster's Dictionary as "a close watch over someone; constant observation of a place or process". The purpose of surveillance is to gather as much information about the intended victim as possible. Information gleaned by surveillance will reveal patterns in the victim's daily activities. This information will then be used to plan the attack, with the goal of hitting the victim just at the time and place he is most vulnerable. There are three basic traditional forms of surveillance techniques used by terrorists.

Static Surveillance

Static surveillance is done from a fixed position such as a building, business or other public or semi-public facility. When conducting static surveillance, terrorists may establish themselves in a public location over a period of time, sometimes using disguises, such as under the pretense of performing some type of work in the area. In the 1989 assassination of Deutsch Bank chairman, Alfred Herrhausen, the terrorists disguised themselves as highway workers conducting repairs on a road that was traveled daily by the victim. Incredibly, no one, including Herrhausen's security detail, noticed anything amiss -- until it was too late.

Static surveillance is often referred to as "ambush surveillance". The surveillant sits in a predetermined location and waits for the intended victim to pass by. He then notes the time at which the victim passes, as well as other particulars, i.e. the make, model and color of the victim's vehicle, number of occupants in the car, any visible security presence, and any other information that might be useful in planning the attack. Static surveillants may be sitting in a car, truck or other vehicle, they may be on foot, seated in a restaurant, on a park bench, or at any other public location. They may have a radio or cell phone in their possession or be in a phone booth in order to phone in an immediate report to their leader or communicate with other surveillants. Surveillants may operate alone or be in pairs. The ideal situation for a surveillant is a man and woman combination, to deter undue suspicion. Most people look for male surveillants operating alone or in pairs. Rarely do they consider that females or male/female couples may be used to conduct surveillance. Although most Islamic extremist terrorist groups seem to have used men exclusively in the past, recent trends indicate that they are becoming more dependent on women to conduct surveillance. You should be particularly aware of any individuals, male or female, who seem to be at the same place, at the same time, day after day, particularly if they are often on a cell phone as you pass by.

Static surveillance can also take the form of terrorists pretending to be repairmen or other types of work crews. These "workers" may not appear to be getting much work done (although this trait may, in fact, be typical of real work crews in many parts of the world). They might give the impression they are working on a particular section of road, building, etc., when actually they are conducting static surveillance on you. If you notice that suddenly a "work crew" has shown up along your route, watch them carefully. If they seem to be paying more attention to you than to their job, you might want to consider changing your route and varying your travel times.

Another form of static surveillance is "telephonic surveillance". Be particularly aware of strange or unusual telephone calls to your residence or office at different times of the day. The caller may hang up, ask an innocuous question, or claim that he has the wrong number. In actuality, the caller may be trying to establish a pattern of when you are at a particular location. If you receive a "hang up" or "wrong number" phone call every night at the same time, this could be a clue that something is amiss. Report any suspicious or strange phone calls to the police or security immediately. Keep a log noting the date and time of the call, as well as other information, such as the sex of the caller, and any particular phrases he or she used.

Door-to-door salesmen, survey questioners, and other uninvited "guests" who knock on your door can be a common ploy used by terrorist groups to facilitate surveillance on a target. This is considered a "static surveillance" technique and is commonly used by criminal groups, as well as terrorist organizations. By knocking on your door and getting a response, they can determine when you are home, who answers the door, what kind of security you have, and other information that can be very useful to a terrorist.

In order to be successful in detecting static surveillance, you need to be aware of the following possible indicators:

- Persons observed in the same locations on multiple occasions
- Persons sitting in the same location, such as a park bench or parked car, for extended periods of time for no apparent reason
- Individuals who take a particular interest in your movements
- People who don't seem to fit in to the surrounding environment. Are they wearing inappropri-

ate clothing for that particular environment? Are they taking photographs in a non-tourist area? Are they in vehicles not common to that area?

- Individuals exhibiting unusual behavior, such as staring or quickly averting their eyes when you pass by

Vehicle Surveillance

Vehicle surveillance is considerably more complicated than either static or foot surveillance, primarily because several vehicles are required to conduct vehicle surveillance and require additional manpower. Small or unsophisticated terrorist groups may use only one vehicle, often a motorcycle, to conduct surveillance. One vehicle is far easier to spot then several; however, many terrorist groups have been successful using only one vehicle manned by one or two surveillants.

Terrorists will generally have more than one individual in a vehicle when conducting surveillance. One will do the driving while the other keeps an eye on the target, or what is referred to as the "rabbit" in surveillance terminology. The observer will usually have a radio or cell phone and will be in constant communication with other members of the surveillance team. Good surveillance teams will have one vehicle following the "rabbit", usually several cars behind the target, so as not to be easily identified. Good surveillance teams will change vehicles and/or license plates frequently and will rotate the individuals in the vehicles, or at least alter their appearance.

Other vehicles may be stationed at intersections as static surveillance and take over the "eyeball" when the rabbit passes by. (The "eyeball" is surveillance terminology for the person who has actual eyes on the target"). Simultaneously, other vehicles may be driving parallel to the target vehicle on side streets. As you can imagine, this takes a number of vehicles, manpower, and constant communication between the surveillants. Any vehicle following you for an extended period with two or more persons, especially if one seems to be always on a radio or cell phone, should be a big warning sign. Other warning signs to look for are:

- Vehicles that start and stop when your vehicle does
- Cars that signal a turn and then fail to execute the turn
- As your vehicle turns a corner at an intersection, any vehicle that proceeds slowly through the intersection while eyeballing you and talking on a radio or cell phone
- Anyone in a vehicle who seems to be paying too much attention to you and following your every move
- Vehicles driving too fast or too slow for existing conditions
- Vehicles driving the wrong way down a one-way street
- Flashing of lights between vehicles
- Any vehicle that maintains the same distance from your car at varying speeds, such as a car speeding up when you speed up, and slowing down when you slow down for an extended period of time.
- Vehicles that speed up to run through red lights
- Vehicles moving on parallel streets at approximately the same speed as you
- Vehicles that slow down and "hide" behind other cars when you slow or stop
- Any vehicle seen two or more times during the running of a route or vehicles seen in the same location on multiple occasions

- Any vehicle pausing in traffic to observe which way your vehicle is going
- Any vehicle that seems to be hesitant to pull directly behind you at a stoplight or stop sign. Surveillants are afraid of getting too close to the target vehicle for fear their cover will be blown.

The above examples occurring by themselves may not be reason for alarm; however, what you are looking for is a pattern of two or more of these events occurring consistently. You are looking for clusters of behavior. Any one of these acts alone is not reason for concern, as we observe this type of behavior every day while on the road. However, if you see two or more of these acts occurring on a routine basis, or in clusters, you need to pay attention. It may be nothing, but then again, you could be under vehicle surveillance.

Foot Surveillance

In addition to vehicle or static surveillance, terrorist groups may conduct foot surveillance on you. Depending on the size and sophistication of the terrorist group, one or more individuals may be involved as "foot" surveillants. Again, what you are looking for are patterns or clusters of behavior, not necessarily single acts.

Foot surveillance shares many of the same characteristics as vehicle and static surveillance and requires good communication among the surveillants. Foot surveillance utilizes parallel walking routes much the same as in vehicle surveillance, and will employ a surveilant as the "eyeball", whose job is to keep a close eye on the intended target. Foot surveillance can be categorized as either "tight" surveillance in which the surveillants follow their intended victim closely, or "loose" surveillance, in which they follow from a distance. Terrorist groups may use a combination of "tight" and "loose" surveillance with the goal of keeping you off guard.

Surveillants have two basic fears -- the fear of losing the target and the fear of being detected. The type of surveillance conducted by the terrorist group depends on which one of the two fears is dominant at the time. If they fear losing the "rabbit" (the person they are following) more than being detected, they will conduct a 'tight" surveillance. If, however, their predominant fear is of being detected, they will most likely conduct a "loose" surveillance and follow at a distance. Obviously, a loose surveillance is more difficult for a potential target to detect than a tight surveillance, but not impossible. Some things to be aware of when watching for foot surveillance are:

- A person turning his head away or abruptly turning around when the target looks at or approaches him.
- Anyone showing hesitation when entering a building the target has just entered.
- Someone suddenly crossing the street when the target doubles back in the direction from which he just came. (Doubling back is a counter-surveillance technique in which the target simply turns around and begins walking in the opposite direction. If anyone is following you, this tactic may fluster him to the point of becoming obvious).
- Anyone whose dress is out of place, such as wearing a coat in warm weather. He may be concealing a weapon, radio, or other communication equipment.
- Individuals walking or running quickly who seem to be trying to catch up with you. Also beware of people walking or running parallel to you, particularly if they seem out of place in the enviroment.
- People entering or leaving a store, restaurant or similar public place immediately ahead of or behind the target. Also anyone entering by a service entrance who appears to be out of place.

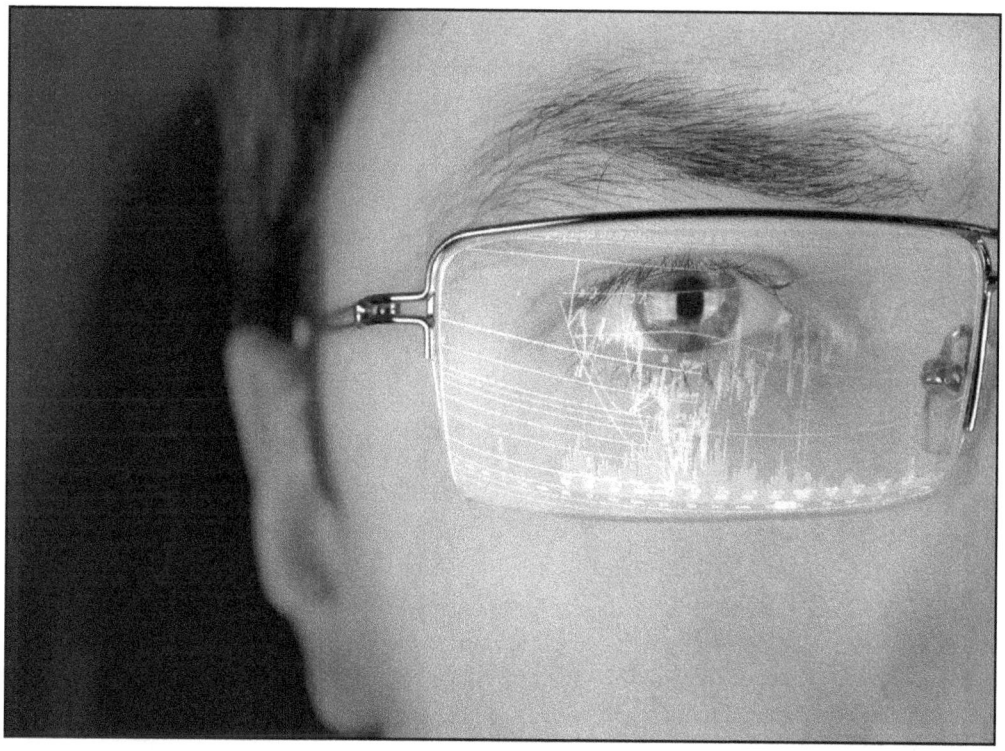

- An individual making an obvious attempt to sit near you in a restaurant, bar, cafe or other public establishment.

- Anyone "intently studying" store windows as you pass by. Surveillants often use the reflection from store windows to surreptitiously watch their targets. You can do the same, watching for anyone who might be following you, but be careful not to be obvious. (Good surveillants will spot this technique in a second).

- Any person who begins to move when the target does and stops when the target stops.

- Anyone obviously getting out of a car when the target does, particularly if he is focused on the target to the exclusion of others around him.

- Anyone close to the target using a cell phone, a radio, or on a public telephone, although in this day and time it is such a common sight that it would be almost impossible to discern.

Remember, you are looking for clusters of unusual behavior, or combinations of these events in patterns, not one or two isolated acts. In law enforcement these clusters of unusual behavior are called clues! Pay attention to them.

In foot, vehicle, or fixed surveillance, the terrorist groups may use what is known as progressive surveillance. Progressive surveillance is a technique whereby the terrorist will watch or follow the prospective target for a short period of time and then break off the surveillance for days or even weeks. He will then resume the surveillance at the point at which he left off and continue this routine until he has established the victim's pattern of movement. This type of surveillance is much more difficult to detect and is indicative of a higher level of sophistication among the terrorist group. Progressive surveillance also requires much more time to accomplish, but is a very effective tool in the terrorist arsenal.

Evidence from past terrorist attacks indicates that few attacks are executed without pre-operational surveillance of the target. Surveillance can be, and usually is, conducted at any point along your route of travel. There is one location in which the terrorist will be certain to conduct extensive surveillance, and that is what is known as the "chokepoint". Chokepoints are those locations in which the target's presence is predictable, due to the unavailability of alternative routes. The terrorist group will conduct additional surveillance here because it is usually at a chokepoint where the actual attack will occur. It is absolutely critical that you identify all of the potential chokepoints along your route and that you pay particular attention when approaching a chokepoint and traveling through one.

Chokepoints

Chokepoints are unavoidable locations you pass through on a regular basis, getting from Point A to Point B. Typical examples of chokepoints are bridges, tunnels, narrow roads, blind spots along your route, highway intersections, and arrival and departure locations, such as between your home and your office. Consider chokepoints carefully when planning your routes for your daily commute.

We have seen recently how Iraqi insurgents have used chokepoints to plant improvised explosive devices and other such ordnance along routes routinely traversed by coalition forces. These insurgents know that because of the massive numbers of locations capable of use as "chokepoints", it is impossible to protect them 24 hours a day, seven days a week. Similarly, your best possible defense is to change your routes frequently, as well as to change the times in which you normally travel those routes. If you must travel through a chokepoint during your daily routine, and most of us do, there are some steps you can take to minimize your vulnerability.

The first step is to analyze the chokepoint in terms of how you might be ambushed. Conduct an analysis on the location and ask yourself, if you were a terrorist, would you use this location as a chokepoint to attack a target. If so, how would you go about setting up the attack? Other questions to consider are, how could the bad guys set up and successfully accomplish an ambush without attracting undue attention? What physical or natural features of the terrain could they use to their advantage? What is the normal daily activity occurring at this chokepoint? Is there a police or security presence nearby? Are there ingress and egress routes that will facilitate an escape?

You must be familiar with all normal activity occurring at the chokepoint, as well as the physical features. Be aware of any unusual activity at and around the chokepoint or any activity that is thought to be out of the ordinary. Notice any changes to the physical features of the chokepoint as well. If something looks out of place or suspicious to you, change your route. If changing your route is not possible, at least consider changing the times at which you pass through the chokepoint. Above all, don't be time and place predictable.

You are particularly vulnerable to an attack at your points of arrival and departure. History has indicated that most terrorist attacks directed against their targets have occurred at one of two locations -- their home or their place of business. Knowing this information should give you an indication of where you need to be the most observant.

Think about your own residence, neighborhood and place of employment. There may be several routes you can take to and from work, but there may be only one way into your neighborhood, street, driveway or entrance to your business or office. These areas are places of predictable behavior and unavoidable presence. There are areas you have to pass through in order to get home or to work. These are perfect examples of a classic chokepoint. You may be unable to avoid these areas, but you can vary the times at which you travel through them, and you can certainly be alert and aware whenever you approach them. If past terrorist behavior is indicative of future behavior, then in all probability, when you have been targeted for an attack, it will take place at a chokepoint. Never let your guard down when approaching and traveling through these areas. Be particularly vigilant and be ready to react immediately, should you detect something amiss. Chokepoints are definite danger areas. Identify them, exercise caution around them and pay attention to anything out of the ordinary.

Vulnerabilities of Surveillants

There are two major fears that surveillants have: Fear of losing the target and fear of being detected. Surveillants must do several things in order to be successful. They must:

- Keep their eyes on the target at all times.
- Signal or communicate to other members of the surveillance team.
- Follow the target.
- Keep up with the target.
- Be ready to stop when the target stops and go when the target goes.
- Maintain their "cover for status". In other words they have to look like they belong in the area, and have a good "cover story" should the police stop and question them. They will need to be able to verbalize a reason for being in that particular place at that particular time, and their story must be plausible. They must fit in the environment and look like they belong.

Surveillants may unintentionally do some irrational things and overreact to keep from losing the target or from being detected. During vehicle surveillance they may speed up and run through red lights or recklessly weave in and out of traffic. On foot surveillance, as mentioned earlier, they may break into a run in an effort to catch up to you, abruptly stopping in the middle of the sidewalk for no apparent reason. This is so obvious that they draw attention to themselves. Static surveillants may frequent a store or restaurant that is totally out of character for them, thereby looking "out of place" for the establishment. As a trained observer, I can usually spot someone who looks like they don't belong in a particular establishment. There are certain types of individuals who frequent shops, bookstores, cafes, etc., and it is not all that difficult to spot someone who appears "out of place". Good police officers constantly utilize their observation skills to spot someone who may be about to commit a crime. A good cop can look at a suspicious individual and know instinctively that the person is up to no good. You should work on developing your "observation skills" and practice them regularly.

When terrorist surveillants do irrational acts or behave in a manner which seems "out of place", they exhibit vulnerability. Use these vulnerabilities to your advantage. If something or someone looks out of place or is acting strangely, there is probably a reason. Pay attention to these things. Make a mental note of the unusual behavior and file it away for future reference. Pay close attention to their appearance. Try to notice something unusual that makes them stand out, and make a mental note of that. Keep in mind that good surveillants will change their clothing, and possibly even their appearance, on a regular basis. There is one item, however, they hardly ever change -- their

shoes. Noticing what type of footwear a person is wearing can be a useful tool, particularly if the person is wearing unusual footwear or if he stands out in some other way. This is a trick that "counter-surveillants" employ to detect surveillance.

Surveillance Detection Techniques

We have all seen movies where the character being followed uses a variety of techniques to detect surveillance. Some of those surveillance detection "tricks" may be:

- Stopping to tie a shoe while "surreptitiously" looking about
- Abruptly changing direction and retracing steps
- Waiting until the last minute to get on or off a bus, train, etc.
- "Window shopping", using the storefront window as a mirror
- Riding short distances on public transportation and getting off suddenly when the conveyance stops
- Constantly varying the speed of walking or driving for no apparent reason
- Slowing down upon approaching a green light, waiting until it turns red and quickly running through it; or committing other flagrant traffic violations such as driving the wrong way down a one-way street, weaving through traffic or other reckless maneuvers
- Ducking into a building, down alleys or into dead end streets
- Stopping suddenly around corners or curves, then looking to see who is following

You can be certain that most of the time these "tricks" fool no one. If you try to use any of these tactics, you stand the risk of alerting them to your awareness of their presence; this could make them angry and possibly cause the situation to get ugly. If you do decide, however, that it is safe to use one of these techniques, at least try to be subtle about it. Avoid drawing attention to yourself.

A better way to handle the situation is to put surveillants to "sleep". Be the most boring and uninteresting person imaginable. Pay close attention to what is going on around you, but don't let surveillants know that you are on to them. It may incite them to act rashly, prematurely, or to change their method of surveillance. Your goal is to know what they are doing without them knowing you know. You will also want to be able to identify as many of the surveillants as possible.

It's important to have a carefully pre-planned, logical surveillance detection route that incorporates a number of "cover stops" along the route. Cover stops are those stops that are easily explained and logical in the course of your day. These cover stops should force the surveillants to change positions more often than they normally would, thereby increasing your probability of seeing the same individuals at more than one location and at disparate times.

Identifying Surveillants

Identifying anyone who may have you under surveillance is critical in establishing whether or not you are truly being watched; and it is critical for reporting the perpetrators to the authorities. Normally, you will not get close enough to identify any facial features in detail. The trick is to remember things that will help you later in confirming original sightings. Look for generalizations about the individual, for instance -- is he or she tall, short, fat, thin, or does his physical appearance stand out in some way? Does he walk with a limp? Does he have an unusual hairstyle, a beard or other distinguishing features? Also look at their clothing, especially their shoes, since they are least apt to change these. Do not be distracted by clothing such as hats, coats or jackets, since this type of clothing is easily changeable. A good surveillant will change his outer garments often during the course of an operation. Are they carrying anything? Do they wear glasses? Do they smoke or have some other readily identifiable habit?

If you can safely photograph a surveillant without his knowledge or take a picture of his vehicle, particularly the license plate number, do so. This can be extremely helpful later for identification purposes. A picture is worth a thousand words. I don't know how many times, as a police officer, I asked the victim of a crime for a physical description of the perpetrator or a description of his vehicle, only to get a generalized description that could fit the majority of the people and vehicles seen every day, several times a day. Many crime victims would simply state that "it happened so fast, I don't know what he looked like", or "I can't tell one car from another". A picture eliminates the guesswork and significantly aids in both the intelligence and investigation process.

If you can't get a clandestine picture of the surveillant or his vehicle, don't discount getting an overt one. At this point in the operation he may very well abort the operation and move on to a less astute victim. Cameras are ubiquitous today. Digital cameras are small enough to easily be carried in your pocket and many cell phones have cameras as well. If you think you are under surveillance or being stalked by someone, a camera can be an invaluable tool. After all, if he can take a picture of you, why not take a picture of him? Again, be careful when using this tactic, and do so only if you have reason to believe it is safe.

Become Predictably Unpredictable

As discussed earlier, terrorist surveillance is a tool used by the terrorists to determine patterns in your daily activity. Terrorists want to know this information for two reasons: to determine if you are, in fact, a suitable victim, and, if so, to determine the time, place and method of the attack. Predictable activity by the victim makes this determination quite easy.

There have been cases, many which have been verified, in which the victim has discouraged a terrorist attack by being unpredictable. If the terrorists can't reliably predict where the victim will be at any given point in time, they can't plan their attack as effectively. At that point, often another victim is selected. The terrorist will look for a victim who is "time and place predictable", thus an easier target.

When I first began my employment in the CIA, the Cold War was in full swing. Our main adversary was the Soviet Union and it's "Iron Curtain" allies in Eastern Europe. The infamous Soviet Intelligence Service, KGB (Komityet Gosudarstuyennoj Byezopasnosti), or Committee of State Security, literally wrote the book on surveillance. The KGB and their Eastern Bloc associates were generally regarded as the best in terms of conducting surveillance, particularly in their own countries. I had firsthand experience with this when I traveled to the former Soviet Republic and immediately noticed I was being watched everywhere I went. Sometimes the surveillance was fairly obvious, but most times it was very difficult to detect. In the old USSR, the KGB simply had to direct a shopkeeper, hotel desk clerk, restaurant waiter, traffic cop, or any other citizen to keep note of your comings and goings. The Soviets had thousands of trained surveillants and an untold number of civilians to keep watch over those they had reason to suspect. If you happened to stop in a particular kiosk to buy a newspaper, the storeowner noted the time of your arrival. If you had breakfast in a certain restaurant every day, a waiter noted the time you arrived and departed. These people were simply ordered to record your presence and report anything unusual to the KGB and, if they wanted to remain in business, they had to do it. Additionally, the Soviet Intelligence machine had thousands of well-trained people whose sole job was to conduct surveillance. When individuals have practiced all day, every day, for years and years, they become good at it. And they were the best.

Terrorist surveillance is, most certainly, not as professional or comprehensive as that conducted by the old KGB or by most other professional intelligence services. However, terrorist organizations have become quite adept in recent years in improving their surveillance capabilities, not only in their home countries, but also in free and permissive environments such as the United States. The best weapon you have to counter terrorist surveillance is to be predictably unpredictable. Never be time and place predictable. ❖

"Who Dares- - wins".

~ *British SAS Commando Motto*

SURVIVAL SKILL TWO:

ACTION

Once you become aware that you are under surveillance, and that something is amiss, you must then move to the second part of the Combat Triad, action. Before we discuss what you should do, let's first talk about what you should not do.

Don't Be Time and Place Predictable

As I just stated in the last chapter, if there is one golden rule in preventing yourself from becoming a victim of a terrorist attack it is this, -- *don't be time and place predictable*. Terrorists just love potential victims who are time and place predictable. It makes their job a lot easier. If you get nothing else from this book, I hope you will at least discipline yourself to become predictably unpredictable in your daily routine.

Humans are, by and large, creatures of habit. We all have our daily routines and most of us are annoyed when our schedules are upset. Keep a log of your daily activities and travel routes, including time of day, for a few days and you will see what I mean. We like to leave home at roughly the same time every day, walking to our cars by the same route. We like to stop at our favorite restaurant or coffee shop on the way to work, and we like to take the quickest way to work every day. The same can be said for returning

home in the evening. We generally leave work at the same time and take the quickest route home. Sometimes we like to make stops at the store, gym or other locations, and most of the time we can set our watches by the predictability of our arrival and departure times at these locations. We pass by the same places at the same time every day and give no thought to it. One fact that is extremely important for you to remember is that 80 percent of terrorist attacks occur near the target's residence. There is a reason for this. We tend to take the same routes home and arrive at approximately the same time every day. In addition, we tend to relax and let our guard down as we approach the "friendly territory" of our neighborhood. Terrorists know that there is one place we predictably return to every day, and that is our home.

In September 1977, a German terrorist group known as "Socialist Patients Kolective" (SPK), better known as the "Baader-Meinhof" terrorist group, kidnapped German Industrialist Hans Martin Schleyer in Cologne, Italy. Mr. Schleyer, who was president of the German Industrial Employers Federation and chairman of the board at Mercedes-Benz, knew he was a potential target of a terrorist attack and, as a result, employed substantial security measures. On the afternoon of 5 September 1977, five terrorists armed with sub-machine guns ambushed Schleyer's car as he was being driven home from work. Three armed bodyguards were in a second vehicle following Schleyer's car.

As Mr. Schleyer was on his usual route heading home, a car containing several members of the terrorist group forced his car off the road. At the same moment, one of the terrorists rolled a baby carriage into the road in front of Schleyer's vehicle. As his driver slammed on the brakes, a second vehicle carrying Schleyer's bodyguards ran into the back of his car. Immediately, five terrorists sitting in a van at the "chokepoint" converged on both the follow car and Schleyer's vehicle. The gunmen killed all three bodyguards and Schleyer's chauffeur, and kidnapped Schleyer. From start to finish, this entire operation took a grand total of 90 seconds to execute. Taking him to a safe haven, they offered Schleyer's life in exchange for the release of eleven imprisoned German terrorists, money, and safe transport to the country of their choice. After holding him almost five weeks in captivity without their demands being met, the terrorists murdered Hans Schleyer.

Unknown to Schleyer, his chauffeur and his "trained" bodyguards, but revealed in a subsequent investigation, Hans Schleyer's motorcade had been under surveillance for some time prior to the attack. Schleyer and his bodyguards apparently took the same route to and from his business every day and at approximately the same time. All the terrorists had to do was pick a time and wait. Armed security did no good in this instance because they allowed themselves to become complacent and easily surprised. One simple act -- changing Schleyer's route to and from work each day and possibly modifying his arrival and departure times, could have saved his life and the lives of his chauffer and bodyguards. Additionally, applying good surveillance detection techniques most certainly would have given Schleyer and his bodyguards an indication that something was amiss. Armed with this information, they may very well have been able to detect and defeat the attack before it had even begun.

Being unpredictable and making unscheduled changes in your times and routes can undoubtedly discourage a potential terrorist attack. Terrorist surveillance teams are looking for identifiable weaknesses and vulnerabilities in your daily routine. Take a serious look at your daily routine. It may be helpful if you keep a logbook of your activities indicating dates, times, and routes. Review your logbook periodically and, if you find yourself setting a predictable pattern, take measures to change your routes, times, or both.

The U.S. Department of State recommends that their diplomats traveling overseas answer the following questions relative to their security. For the sake of brevity, I have included only the ones that relate to "time and place predictability".

- What time do you normally leave for work each day?
- What are your working hours? Are they flexible?
- Do you have regularly scheduled appointments or meetings? Can the time and location of these be changed frequently?
- Do you eat lunch, breakfast, and dinner at the same time and at the same place every day?
- Do you stop for coffee, newspapers, etc. at the same location and at the same time each day?
- Do you run, bike, play golf, tennis or do other recreational activities on a regular schedule at the same location?
- Do you attend regularly scheduled social events in a predictable pattern?
- Do you have favorite stores, restaurants, bars, etc. that you frequent on a regular basis?
- If you are in school or attend academic courses, do you set a pattern in traveling to and from class?
- Do you arrive home at the same time each evening? Do you make regular stops anywhere on your way home?
- Do you have a set day for grocery shopping and other similar activities?
- Do your other family members have regularly scheduled activities that require your attendance?

SURVIVAL SKILL TWO: ACTION

- Are there any other activities you engage in on a routine, predictable basis that would make you vulnerable to a terrorist attack? For example, do you go for a walk, or walk your dog at the same time and place every day?
- Do you consciously vary your mode of travel? For instance, can you take the bus or other public transportation to work a couple of days a week instead of driving?
- Do you vary your routes to and from work, recreational events, and other routine activities
- Have you identified alternate routes to and from work, home, and other locations that you frequent on a regular basis? Are the routes and times changed frequently? Is it possible for an identifiable pattern to develop?

Actions You Can Take

We have a general rule in my business, which states, "never say 'never', and 'never say 'always'". I will, however, violate that rule and tell you that, when faced with a violent confrontation you must always, always do something. Doing nothing is not an option if you want to survive the confrontation.

In a violent emergency there are three things that you can do; fight, flight or freeze. The worst thing you can do is freeze, doing nothing at all. That leaves the other two options, fight or flight. If you are faced with several heavily-armed terrorists, fighting may not be your best option. In fact, fighting may not be much of an option at all, especially if you are faced with overwhelming numbers of terrorists with superior firepower. You might have to fight back as best as you can temporarily, but

your ultimate goal should be to leave the scene of the attack as quickly as possible. In the parlance of my profession, we call this "getting off the X".

"X" Marks the Spot – Get Out!

The exact location where the terrorists decide to initiate their attack is referred to as the "X". "X" marks the spot where the terrorists have determined the attack will probably be most successful. The attack location, or "X", is sometimes known as the "kill zone", or the "fatal funnel". Whatever you call it, this is a very bad place to be. Get off the "X" as quickly as possible. If you stay here for any length of time, you are very likely to be killed or captured. Your best hope of surviving the attack is to get out of the kill zone and keep moving until you are well away from danger.

Do the Unexpected

Generally, during an ambush type of attack, your best bet is to drive through the attack zone as quickly and aggressively as possible. If you try to retreat, withdraw, or go back the way you came, you may run into an another ambush, since this is precisely what the terrorists would expect you to do. It is always better to do what the terrorists don't expect you to do, and they clearly don't expect you to drive straight through them. What they do expect is for you to freeze, go into Condition Black and give up. Don't do it. You must resist the urge to give up. Do the unexpected -- launch a violent counterattack straight through the attack site. Think about charging aggressively straight ahead and stop for nothing or no one. Whatever you do, don't stay on the "X". If you do, you will most assuredly either die or be taken hostage. Neither is an option you should consider.

In February 1998, twelve heavily armed terrorists conducted an attack on President Edward Shevardnadze's motorcade in the former Soviet Republic of Georgia. In what was described as a "well planned and prepared military operation", the terrorists set up a roadside ambush using rocket-propelled grenades (RPGs) and automatic assault weapons. Shevardnadze's armored limousine was hit with three RPG rounds and was severely damaged while he was returning home on a well-traveled route. Fortunately, Shevardnadze's driver had the presence of mind and training to get off the "X" immediately. He drove straight ahead, through the attack, and made it to a safe location, despite the fact that the presidential limousine was barely operational. His actions that day in getting off the "X" resulted in the preservation of both his life and the life of the President of Georgia. This was the second attempt on Shevardnadze's life during his term in office. The first was a bomb attack in August 1995.

In a similar incident, President Hosni Mubarak of Egypt escaped serious bodily injury and death during a terrorist attack in Addis Ababa, Ethiopia on June 26, 1995. President Mubarak's motorcade was traveling from the airport to the downtown area when he came under heavy attack from a group of well-armed terrorists from the Egyptian fundamentalist organization known as the Islamic Group. His driver also had the training and presence of mind to get off the "X", thereby saving President Mubarak's life, although two Ethiopian Security Agents were killed during the attack.

Terrorists expect you to do what most people do when under attack -- freeze, panic and give up. This is precisely what you do not want to do. Do the unexpected. Fight to get out of the "kill zone" and off the "X". During their pre-planning and preparation, the terrorists will probably rehearse the attack and have a general idea how the attack will progress. They fully expect it to go according to their plan. They expect you to react predictably as well. When you don't react the way they think you are going to, this throws them into a tailspin, disrupting their plan of attack. Your

actions throw a "monkey wrench" into their already pre-determined outcome and this is exactly what you want to do. In their temporary state of confusion they will probably hesitate for a few seconds, or even a couple of minutes, while they are trying to figure out (a) what is happening, and (b) what to do about it. Your unexpected reaction will cause them to have to reassess the situation and adapt their plans accordingly. This lull in the action will hopefully give you time to quickly establish and act on your plan of escape.

At this point, you have the opportunity to immediately fight back using maximum aggression and violence, with the goal of stopping the attack altogether, or, failing that, at least interrupting the attack. This will, hopefully, buy you enough time to get off the "X" and out of the "kill zone" as quickly as possible. Above all, remember to do something. Something is better than nothing. If you are in your vehicle, stomp on the gas and plow straight ahead through the attack, running over anyone who gets in your way. Anything is better than becoming a sitting duck, waiting to be killed or kidnapped. Indecision leads to catastrophe. Develop a plan in your mind, mentally rehearse your plan over and over, and then execute your plan immediately and without hesitation. Do not delay and wait to see if the situation gets better. It never does. It only gets worse. Act immediately and don't allow yourself to become a victim of the "paralysis of analysis" -- over thinking your plan. Your plan of action should have been pre-determined by you, and you should know exactly what you are going to do. At that point all you have to do is execute your plan aggressively, violently and without delay. ❖

"Never give in! Never, never, never, never! Never yield in any way, great or small, except to convictions of honor and good sense. Never yield to force and the apparently overwhelming might of the enemy."

~ Winston Churchill

SURVIVAL SKILL THREE:

MINDSET

What is Combat Mindset?

Of the three components of the Combat Triad, two of them, Awareness and Action, are skills that can be taught. The one component that is internally driven and, therefore, cannot be taught is Mindset, which I will refer to as "Combat Mindset" in this chapter. Combat Mindset is the mental attitude an individual has toward survival. Combat Mindset is made up of the following components:

- Anticipation
- Competence
- Focus
- Self-Control
- Coolness under fire or stress
- Overwhelming desire to survive

When confronted with a life-threatening situation you can experience one of three reactions: Flight, fight or freeze. You can leave the scene (flight); you can stand and fight, or you can be paralyzed with fear (freeze). Of the three, flight and fight are your only options if you want to survive. The one thing you don't want to do is to freeze. Becoming paralyzed with fear will get you killed or taken hostage. There are dozens of examples of police officers who, while engaged in a gunfight, received wounds that would normally be life threatening. Instead of giving up and dying, however, they got mad, fought back, and survived. They had the right "survival mindset".

On the other hand, there are numerous examples of officers receiving non-fatal wounds during a violent confrontation, but being so traumatized and overwhelmed by circumstances and lacking the overwhelming will to live, they simply gave up and died. If you allow yourself to "freeze" during an emergency, this could very well be your fate.

An incident involving Deputy Sheriff Jennifer Fulford of the Orange County, Florida Sheriff's Department is a good example of Combat Mindset and the will to survive in action.

On May 5, 2004, Deputy Sheriff Fulford responded to a call of a residential burglary in progress. An eight-year-old boy had called the Sheriff's Office to report that some "strange men" were in his home and that he and his sister were hiding in the family van parked in the attached garage. The deputy was the first officer to arrive on the scene and immediately went into the garage to check on the children. As backup deputies arrived, two men emerged from the residence and opened fire on them. The men then entered the garage, trapping Deputy Fulford between two vehicles, and began firing on her. Despite being hit by gunfire a total of ten times, including a hit on her shooting hand, she returned fire aggressively using her "off" hand, and continued firing until both assailants were down.

The suspects were then placed into custody and the children were rescued unharmed. Deputy Sheriff Fulford could have given up and died on the scene. She certainly received a number of life-threatening wounds. Instead, she developed a "Combat Mindset" and the will to survive, adamantly determined she was not going to let a couple of thugs end her life in a stranger's garage. She refused to give up and become a victim. As a result, she continues to serve her community today as a highly-decorated law enforcement officer.

In an emergency situation you must convince yourself that you are going to survive, regardless of how dire the circumstances seem at the time. To give up is to seal your fate. You must persevere and do whatever it takes to survive the confrontation. One technique that will help you considerably is to develop what I call your "mental trigger".

Developing Your Mental Trigger

Victims of criminal activity typically make statements such as, "I can't believe it happened to me", or "I never saw it coming" when interviewed by the police after the fact. As previously stated, the one thing that you can absolutely not afford to do during a violent confrontation is to be paralyzed with fear. Decide in your mind that it can and might very well happen to you. Don't allow yourself live your life in a state of denial. Expect the unexpected and mentally prepare yourself to face a terrifying and violent situation, which is precisely what a terrorist attack is. Think about what you would do and how you would react in any given situation. Good defensive drivers constantly do this when they are behind the wheel of their vehicle. As they are driving along they are thinking about how they are going to react if the car in front of them suddenly slams on the brakes or swerves into their lane. They continually play the "when/then" game. By doing this, they have subconsciously programmed their brain to expect and then react to a reckless driver or similar emergency situation that may occur.

You can't possibly think of every emergency situation that could develop, but you can "set your mental trigger" by at least expecting something to happen. Do some "mental role playing". Play the "when/then" game -- "when "X" happens, then I will do "Y". If you decide well in advance of the incident that, should something bad happen, you are going to react immediately and you will not be surprised when an emergency situation suddenly and unexpectedly develops. By visualizing certain emergency scenarios before they happen, you are subconsciously training your mind to "expect" that scenario to occur. You are not surprised when it actually does occur. In other words, your "mental trigger" is set. When you have trained your mind in this manner, all you have to do is "pull the trigger" to go into the action mode and execute your plan. Your "mental trigger" will alert you to the fact that something significant is occurring and your mind will justify taking immediate action. That action may be to flee or it may be to fight, but it will not be to freeze because you have "trained" your mind against that. Psychologically, you will be justified in taking action to save your life. To quote Colonel Jeff Cooper:

"If you accept the fact that you may have to fight to save your life, if you train yourself to use your weapons with skill and rapidity, and if you reserve your fighting stroke for conditions in which it is justified, it is not likely that you will experience any psychological difficulties in defending yourself".

Man fights with his mind. The mind is our primary weapon. Train your mind to respond and your body will follow, doing what your "computer" (your mind) has been programmed to do. The main point, whether you decide to fight or to flee, is to do something. Doing something (fight or flight) is always better than doing nothing.

Developing an attitude that says, "it can happen to me, I expect it, and when it does, I have a plan and I will follow through aggressively and without hesitation", is the first and most important element of combat and survival mindset. You must have the mental toughness to determine that you will neither die, be taken captive nor submit in any way to terrorist demands. When a terrorist attack does occur, you won't say, "I can't believe this is happening to me and I am going to die!" Instead, you will be mentally prepared and say, "I knew this would happen, I have a plan, I am ready, and I will survive this". Get mad at your assailants, having the attitude, "how dare those bastards do this to me and my family!" Don't let them win. Instead, refuse to be surprised. Don't be a "deer in the headlights" waiting to die. Fight back aggressively, ruthlessly and with a sense of purpose. Rather than a sheep being led to the slaughter, you will be a mountain lion that is alert, aware of his surroundings and ready to defend himself at all times. You will have the mindset that, regardless of the circumstances, you will not be defeated. So which would you rather be -- a sheep or a lion? The choice is yours. ❖

"If we ever hope to rid the world of the political AIDS of our time, terrorism, one thing must be clear: One does not deal with terrorists; one does not bargain with terrorists; one kills terrorists."

~ Meir Kahane

THE TERRORIST AMBUSH

Generally speaking, there are three basic types of terrorist ambushes you should familiarize yourself with. They are:

- Mobile ambush
- Fixed ambush
- Route bombs

All ambushes have some things in common, but they differ in many ways. It is important to have a basic familiarity with each type of terrorist ambush and the knowledge necessary to counter each one.

The Mobile Ambush

The first type of ambush, the Mobile Ambush, is accomplished by terrorists on a motorcycle or in a car, truck or van. Motorcycle attacks are the preferred method of mobile attack in some of the more populated cities overseas, as they can move easily through heavy traffic in order to position themselves for the attack. Ambushes by car, truck or van usually have a driver whose sole responsibility is to drive and a passenger who acts as the gunman.

Route bombs are another favored method of assassination employed by terrorists in today's overseas environment. Both of these methods are very difficult, but not impossible, to avoid and counter.

The most effective way to counter a mobile ambush where the terrorists are using a motorcycle is to directly attack the motorcycle and its riders. A motorcycle is no match for a 3,000-pound automobile and you should not hesitate to use your own vehicle as a weapon. When you have established that you are the target of a motorcycle ambush, you should try to ram the motorcycle with your vehicle, attempting to push it off the road, into a ditch, into another vehicle or building, or, when all else fails, run over the motorcycle. Show no mercy and don't stop for anything. Keep going until you are well away from the attack site and in a location where it is safe to stop.

This ploy can also be used in the case of a mobile attack by terrorists using a car, truck or van. It will be considerably more difficult than ramming a motorcycle, and some training in how to safely and effectively ram another vehicle is recommended; it is, however, a very effective and proven method by which to counter a vehicle ambush. There are a number of schools in the United States and abroad that teach a method known as a "surgical takeout", which entails using your vehicle to spin another car out of control. Police have been using this technique for years as a method to stop fleeing drivers in a pursuit. NASCAR drivers also use this technique on a regular basis to "take out" their competition.

Another form of mobile ambush is a terrorist using a car or truck as a "blocking vehicle". This maneuver is conducted by terrorists using one blocking vehicle in front of your car; two blocking vehicles (one in front and one to the rear), or by using several vehicles to obtain a 360-degree containment of your vehicle (obviously the worst case scenario). The terrorists will then exit their vehicles and either snatch the victim from his car or assassinate him, depending on their objective.

If you find yourself victim to a "blocking" maneuver, you can still extricate yourself from the situation by driving "through the attack". Remember, the engine block is the strongest part of your vehicle. Use the engine block as a "ramming" device against the blocking vehicle. You should aim to strike the rear of the blocking vehicle, not the front. Since the engine block area is the strongest and heaviest part of any car, you need to avoid hitting that area of the blocking vehicle, if at all possible. The rear third of the vehicle, near the trunk, is generally the lightest part of the car, so aim for that area. By striking the area at the rear of the blocking vehicle, you will be able to use the force of your vehicle to help push the rear of the blocking vehicle out of the way, enabling you to drive "through" the attack and escape. Once you hit the accelerator and aim for the rear of the blocking vehicle, do not stop! Keep your foot on the accelerator until you have sufficiently pushed the blocking vehicle out of your way to get by. Keep your foot on the accelerator until you are completely off the "X" and out of the "kill zone". Keep going until you are in a safe area, regardless of what is going on with your vehicle or what is happening around you. If a terrorist gets in your way, don't stop. Run over him (and several of his buddies, if you can).

Your car is the best weapon you have. It is essentially a 3,000-pound bullet. Use it to your advantage and don't let anything or anyone stop you until you are safely out of the attack zone. Always remember to wear your seat belt. Striking the blocking vehicle will obviously cause quite an impact. The last thing you want is to be rendered unconscious or injured, becoming helpless and easy prey for the terrorists.

I have performed ramming maneuvers hundreds of times in training, and despite some damage to the front of my vehicle, I never failed to get "through the attack", off the "X" and to a safe haven.

Your vehicle may have extensive damage to the front end, the radiator may be spewing coolant and your tires may be flat, but trust me on this – your vehicle is still drivable and more than sufficient to get you out of the "kill zone". I have even successfully employed this technique while driving a small sedan against a larger blocking vehicle, such as a full-sized car or a small truck. Unless the terrorist is using a bus or a tank as a blocking vehicle, you will have an excellent chance of being successful. If you fail to make it completely through the roadblock, at the very least you may be able to distract the terrorists enough to break off their attack.

In review, if you find yourself being blocked in during an attack, aim for the rear (trunk area) of the blocking vehicle, step on the accelerator, run over anyone in your way and keep going until you are safely out of the attack zone. These things must be done in an extremely aggressive manner, so do not hesitate to use your vehicle as a "guided missile" launching a violent counterattack against the terrorists. I cannot emphasize enough the importance of not stopping, regardless of the condition of your vehicle or what is happening around you. Get well away from the attack site and to a safe location as quickly as possible!

The Fixed Ambush

A fixed ambush is an ambush that is executed from a pre-determined, stationary location. Fixed ambushes can be conducted in one of two ways—with or without a barricade. If the terrorists do not use a barricade, your best response is to drive through the attack and get off the "X" as quickly as possible. If a barricade is used, you might be able to breach the barricade and then drive through. Just as in a vehicle attack, if the barricade is breachable, take the offensive and ram through it. Run over any terrorist who gets in your way and keep going until you are well out of the kill zone.

If the barricade is not breachable, you will have to find another escape route. Sometimes the best method is to put your car in reverse and use your trunk area as a ramming device. As if you were moving straight ahead, put your foot on the accelerator and keep it there until you can safely maneuver your vehicle, enabling you to turn around and escape. Again, think of your vehicle as a 3,000-pound weapon. Don't let anything or anyone stop you from getting out of the "kill zone" as quickly as possible.

A fixed ambush will generally be one of two types—a parallel ambush or an "L" ambush.

In a parallel ambush (also known as a linear ambush), the attackers line up on the same side of the road and direct all their gunfire at the target in the same direction.

An "L" ambush is shaped like the letter "L". Some of the attackers will be in a linear fashion along one side of the road, while others will be either in front (the usual method) or to the rear, thus forming an "L" shape. In an "L" ambush, firepower is directed both laterally and longitudinally toward the target. Attackers usually will not be on directly opposing sides of the road unless they are real amateurs, as this obviously presents the risk of a "crossfire" situation in which the ambush party could end up shooting each other.

Whether you are faced with a linear attack or "L"-type ambush, your best response is to fight through the attack. The quicker you can get off the "X" and out of the kill zone, the better your chances of survival. Remember, you are in control of a 3,000-pound weapon. Use it to your advantage. There is nothing like having a car barreling toward you at high speed to mess up your concentration. Very few people have the nerve to stand there and try to take a shot when a 3,000-pound "bullet" is coming at them. As it is also extremely difficult for anyone to hit a moving target, it is important not to give your attackers a stationary target that's easy to hit. Move and keep moving.

Don't stop. What the terrorists expect you to do is to "freeze" in the kill zone (Condition Black). This is the scenario they envisioned and planned for and is the ideal situation for them. Don't do what they expect. Use the element of surprise to your advantage and do the unexpected. Put your foot on the accelerator; and get out of the kill zone, running over as many terrorists as you can in the process. Your life depends on you (A) not freezing and (B) following the correct course of action. Follow through aggressively and ruthlessly, driving at "ramming speed", not stopping until you are well out of the "kill zone".

Escaping a Fixed Ambush with "Ramming Speed"!

There is a definite art to knowing how to use a vehicle as a ramming tool. Several schools in the United States teach vehicle-ramming techniques as part of their "anti-terrorist" driving courses. Taking one of these is a worthwhile endeavor if you are going to a hostile or high-threat area. It is good to know that you can crash your car into another vehicle without causing injury to you or your passengers, and without causing so much damage to your vehicle that you will be unable to drive it off the "X" and out of the kill zone. If the bad guys start shooting at your vehicle, even hitting it numerous times, it will still function well enough to get you out of the immediate danger area. Just keep moving, don't stop for anything or anyone, and trust that your car will get you to a safe location.

When approaching an apparent roadblock or encountering a blocking maneuver (where terrorists attempting to block in your vehicle), immediately start looking for an escape route. Scan the area and try to identify a place to which you can divert quickly. This may be a side street, alley, parking lot or field, or you may have to jump the curb and drive on the sidewalk. Reversing your car is another option. Quickly glance behind you to make sure the way is clear, put your vehicle in reverse and put your foot to the floorboard. Just make sure you conduct this maneuver aggressively, being sure to stay low in your vehicle, presenting less of a target in case the terrorists start shooting at you.

If you fail to find an escape route and reversing course is not an option, you must then go through the attack. You are going to have to use your vehicle as a ramming device and ram your way through the roadblock.

Following are some techniques to use when using your car to ram another vehicle:

♦ **Buckle your seat belt!** You are going to be performing ramming techniques and high speed maneuvers and you don't want to get injured in the process. The last thing you want is to be knocked unconscious or otherwise incapacitated and unable to affect your escape; neither do you want to be sliding around on the seat, possibly causing you to lose control of your vehicle. Make sure that your windows are up and your doors are locked. You don't want a terrorist jumping in the car with you or reaching through the window to grab you or a family member. Unless you are in an armored vehicle, we all know that windows will not stop bullets. I've discovered that, for some peculiar reason, people are sometimes hesitant to shoot through a closed window. A closed window just might buy you a little extra time. Once the terrorist figures out that he can easily shoot through a glass window, you will hopefully be well on your way out of the kill zone.

Note: Even if you drive an armored vehicle, rifle caliber rounds such as the 7.62 caliber round used in the AK-47 (the terrorist weapon of choice) will eventually penetrate most armor if it is repeatedly shot in or near the same place. The bottom line: Keep moving!

- **Slow down and quickly assess the situation.** Identify where you want your vehicle to go and aim for that spot. (Generally, you will find your vehicle will go where you look, so it's important to focus on a specific area.)
- **Sit as low in your seat as possible,** once you have identified where to aim your vehicle. You want to present a low profile target in case the terrorists start shooting at you. The engine block is the best source of cover in a car. Although the doors will slow down or deflect most bullet calibers, a car door is definitely not effective cover. (Cover is anything that will stop a bullet), but it's better than nothing!
- **Slow down significantly,** but try not to stop all together. Slowing your vehicle does two things. First of all, it will put your attackers off guard and make them think you are going to comply with their demands. Secondly, you don't want to ram another vehicle if you are traveling at more than 25-35 miles per hour. Any faster than that and you stand a good chance of being injured or killed in the collision. Any less than that is likely to be ineffective in moving the other vehicle. You don't want to come to a complete stop because you take the chance of your car stalling out or spinning the wheels when you begin to accelerate.
- **Aim your vehicle.** Once you have slowed your vehicle, pick out a spot on the blocking vehicle and focus your vision on that spot. The best place to ram another vehicle is, as discussed earlier, in the trunk area, as this is where there is less weight to move. Particularly if the terrorist's vehicle is heavier than yours, you will find it much easier to move it if you hit in this general area. It is possible to move a vehicle by ramming it in the front near the engine block, but it is much more difficult. Depending on the circumstances, however, you may not have an option and you may have to ram the blocking vehicle in the engine area. Keep in mind that it may take a little longer to move the car that way, but don't give up. Eventually you will fight your way through. Your last option is to ram the blocking vehicle amidships, or broadside. When you ram the blocking vehicle broadside you are pushing the entire weight of the car, thus not using fulcrum physics to your advantage. So your best ramming option is the trunk area, followed by the engine block and, as a last resort, the middle of the car. Do not begin the ramming maneuver too far in advance of the blocking vehicle. If you do, it may alert the terrorists to what you are about to do, giving them extra time to react. There is also an increased possibility of injury to you or your passengers and excessive damage to your vehicle. Two to four car lengths away from the blocking vehicle will give you ample time to get your speed and momentum up to produce a successful ramming technique.
- **Put the accelerator all the way to the floor** and don't let up until you are well away from the kill zone. Resist the urge to let up off the accelerator when you hit the other vehicle. Keep your foot to the floor until you have accomplished your goal of pushing the blocking vehicle out of the way. Then let up only enough to safely resume driving out of the attack zone. This is totally contrary to what you would do in an accident. When we see that our car is about to hit another vehicle, our natural reaction is to slam on the brakes. You must fight the urge to hit the brakes. This is not an accident. It is a controlled crash designed to push the other vehicle out of the way enough so that you can make your escape. Keep in mind that gunmen may very well be on the side, in front, or at the rear of your vehicle trying to shoot you; so continuing to move is critical. Give them a moving target, not a stationary one! Keep moving!
- **Grip the steering wheel firmly and hold it straight.** Do not veer off at the last second, as you would do attempting to avoid an accident in normal driving conditions.

THE TERRORIST AMBUSH

- **Don't stop, don't stop, and don't stop!** Whatever you do, keep the car in motion. If you stop, you're dead. Do not stop for anything or anyone. If a terrorist gets in your way, make a speed bump out of him. It is very hard to accurately shoot at a moving target, especially when it is a 3,000-pound "bullet" coming at you at a high rate of speed. It is even harder to shoot someone when you are underneath the wheels of said vehicle while it is running over you. Keep going and don't stop until you are well away from the kill zone, regardless of what happens or who gets in your way.

The above ramming techniques will also work if two vehicles are blocking the street. Aim at a point between the two vehicles and perform the same maneuver as with a single vehicle; or if you have room to do so effectively, just ram one of the vehicles. Either way, this technique works. I have performed these ramming techniques myself many times in training and am always amazed at how well it works. Equally amazing is the fact that my car can sustain a great deal of damage, still keep moving and get me off the "X" in almost every instance.

In summary, employ the techniques of speed, surprise and extreme violence to get you through the roadblock and out of the kill zone. Put the terrorists off guard by making them think you are going to stop and comply with their demands (surprise), then quickly put the pedal to the metal (speed), and ram anyone or anything that gets in your way (extreme violence). Above all, don't stop!

Route Bombs

Last, the route bombs seem to be the preferred method of attack by the insurgents in Iraq today. Route bombs are those improvised explosive devices (IEDs) that are placed along a route and detonated at the precise moment the intended victim's car moves into the "kill zone". A route bomb can be very difficult to detect and neutralize, doing a serious amount of damage with very little risk to the terrorists. While the use of route bombs as a means of terrorist attack was somewhat sporadic in the past, the past few years have seen a much greater increase in their use. Route bombs are increasingly becoming more sophisticated and harder to detect. Route bombs were used in the attempted assassination of Venezuelan President Betancourt in the early '60s, the assassination of the President of the Spanish Government, Admiral Carrero Blanco, in 1973 and in 1988, and the attacks on US Secretary of State George Shultz during a visit to Bolivia. They were also used in the assassination of US Naval Attaché Nordeen in Greece and attacks in Colombia against the Colombian Minister of Defense and the President of Texaco-Colombia.

Route bombs are usually well concealed and, therefore, extremely difficult to detect. In each of the aforementioned cases the route bomb was placed along a route that the victim either routinely traveled or along a route that was openly published in advance. The bombs were also placed at a "chokepoint" along the intended victim's route. In the case of both President Betancourt and US Secretary of State George Shultz, the bomb was placed along a motorcade route that was well published in advance, thereby providing the terrorists with "time and place" predictability by the victim. In the Carrero Blanco case the bomb was placed in a tunnel under the street along a normally traveled route. The assassination of Naval Officer and attaché Nordeen was accomplished by a bomb that was placed in a parked car at a chokepoint near his residence. In the attempt on the life of the President of Texaco-Colombia, the bomb was concealed in a trash collector's cart at a chokepoint near the entrance to his house. During the attack on the Colombian Minster of Defense, a bomb was hidden inside a concrete block and placed at a building site located near his office at the Ministry of Defense.

In each of these cases the bombers used chokepoints along fixed or published routes to conduct the attacks. On November 30, 1989, Alfred Herrhausen, Chairman of the Duetsche Bank, was driving to work in his armored vehicle along his normal route. Approximately 500 yards from his residence Herhaussen's car was totally destroyed by a remote-controlled improvised explosive device (IED), killing Herhausen instantly. The bomb was disguised to look like a book bag or knapsack attached to a child's bicycle that was "abandoned" alongside the road.

Although route bombs can be almost impossible to detect, there are steps you can take to prevent yourself from becoming the victim of a terrorist attack that utilizes a route bomb. Probably the easiest and most efficient step you can take is to not become "time and place predictable". As previously stated, vary the routes you take during your daily routine and vary your arrival and departure times as much as possible.

Today's terrorist seems to prefer the Improvised Explosive Device, or IED, as a method of destruction. An IED is simply a homemade bomb and can be constructed by using commonly available material, such as items customarily found in any household or bought in any hardware supply store. Material obtained from other explosive devices is another way these IEDs are constructed. (Terrorists commonly use explosive material from US and coalition bombs that fail to detonate). There is ample information on the Internet, in books and in magazines on how to construct homemade bombs (IEDs), and almost anyone who obtains the materials can easily make one.

These improvised explosive devices can take the form of a car or truck bomb; a suicide bomb concealed in a backpack, belt, or clothing; shape charges used in roadside ambush attacks; pipe bombs, homemade grenades, rockets and mortars; and other similar devices. IEDS can be very difficult, if not almost impossible, to detect. Again, one of the most reliable ways to avoid an IED is to be unpredictable in your movements. It takes a great deal of planning for the bad guys to set up a route bomb and, if they can't reliably predict where you will be at any given time, they will not likely be successful.

Another way to "defeat' a route bomb is to pay attention to your surroundings. Placing a route bomb takes careful planning on the part of the terrorist group, including extensive surveillance of the proposed attack site. In setting up a route bomb, or IED, the terrorists must acquire a suitable location where they can safely and accurately detonate the bomb. They must find a suitable place to conceal the bomb from public view. And they must set the device up and conduct surveillance without attracting undue attention.

The need to conduct surveillance of the intended victim is clearly another area in the cycle of operation where the terrorist is vulnerable. Your ability to spot things that appear out of the ordinary and to assess their meaning is a key element in avoiding a terrorist IED attack. Look for things out of the ordinary, especially when living or working in a hostile environment. A child's bicycle with a backpack attached leaning up against a post may not mean anything to you. However, if it is in an area that is unusual or out of place, and if it is located near a chokepoint on your route, pay close attention. Especially if you see "workmen" in the vicinity where no apparent work had been going on before. (In the case of Carrero Blanco the terrorists pretended to be telephone repairmen working on a pole). These things are clear indications that something bad may be getting ready to happen. These "indicators" should raise a red flag in your mind, and you should adjust your security posture accordingly. Have the police or security personnel check out the vicinity and, at the very least, take an alternate route and change your times of departure and arrival. While we don't know exactly when the attack will occur, we do know that it will most likely occur at a chokepoint at or

near your residence or place of business, and it will probably occur during an arrival or departure. This is important "intelligence" information that we can, and should, use to our advantage. Don't try to justify indicators by thinking that, "it is probably nothing", or "it's just my imagination". This kind of thinking will get you killed.

If you simply "blow off" these indicators and suddenly find yourself in the "kill zone", as the bomb detonates, there is not much you can do except to get off the "X" as quickly as possible, if you are still able to do so. Sometimes terrorists use route bombs to initiate an ambush and then "finish the victim off" with small arms fire by gunmen waiting in the vicinity. Most of the time, however, the route bomb is the principle means of attack, and most IEDs are powerful enough to totally devastate the victim's vehicle. The best, and indeed the only, effective defense against a route bomb is prevention.

Success of any terrorist operation is based on the assumption that the intended victim will act in accordance with the terrorist's ambush plan. Their plan is, by necessity, a fairly rigid one. The terrorists have decided when and where to attack, and have designed their operation within certain rigid bounds of time and place predictability. Their ability to maneuver and redeploy to an alternate attack site at a different time is extremely limiting. The terrorists are counting on having the advantage of your time and place predictability in order for their plan to succeed. The terrorists have put all their "eggs into one basket", so to speak. Their only hope of success is if you act according to their expectations, based on their observations (surveillance) of your past behavior. Therefore, when you refuse to be time and place predictable, you foil their plan. The terrorists will have failed because their limited window of opportunity to attack you has passed. In most cases, they will abort their operation or move on to an easier, more predictable target.

Terrorist Ambush Planning

When they are in the mission-planning phase of an ambush operation, terrorists look for suitable locations that will meet their needs and provide for a "cover story" should they be questioned by the authorities. They generally look for fixed attack (ambush) sites that meet the following criteria:

- The attack location should be on a known route that is frequently traveled by the intended victim.
- It should preferably be located at a chokepoint (bridge, merging traffic pattern, curve in the road, stop light, gate, etc.)
- It should have terrain features that provide good cover and concealment so that the terrorists can set up the explosive device or ambush with minimal chance of being discovered.
- The attack site should have no obstacles that would hinder the terrorists movement or that would get in their way when conducting the attack.
- It should have a good observation point so that the victim can be seen prior to entering the chokepoint, the device can be armed and the attackers readied.
- It should have clear fields of fire; either in a linear or in an "L" shaped ambush design.
- The ambush site should be in a location that does not attract undue attention to the terrorists. In other words, it should be in a place that can provide them with a ready excuse for being there, or, a "cover for action". It should be somewhere they will not look out of place while conducting surveillance, assembling the bomb, or setting up the ambush.
- It should provide good avenues of approach and escape.

You, as a potential victim, should be particularly aware of any location that meets this description, and pay close attention to any unusual activity or changes you observe in that location. Use all of your senses (sight, hearing, smell) to alert you to anything out of the ordinary. In addition to your five senses, use the phenomenon known as your "sixth sense" to alert you to danger. Whether you know it or not, we all have a "sixth sense", it is just a matter of developing it and using it to our advantage.

What is The "Sixth Sense"?

When I first heard of the "sixth sense" during a lecture in my initial police academy training in 1974, I casually dismissed it as superstition or folklore. At that time I really didn't believe that humans possessed a "sixth sense"—to me it seemed a little spooky and certainly unprofessional. However, after over thirty years of operating in dangerous environments as a police officer and CIA officer, I am now a firm believer in the "sixth sense". Everyone knows their five basic senses of seeing, feeling, smelling, hearing and tasting, and you should take advantage of all of these senses to help warn you of impending danger. The "sixth sense" is not something that we normally think of as a basic sense, like the other five senses, but it is a vital part of our makeup and it can be an invaluable tool in developing "anticipation mindset and awareness". I recall many occasions when I was a police officer investigating crimes against individuals. While taking the report, the victims would tell me, "I just knew something was wrong". Although it seemed as though they had no concrete evidence, they had a "feeling" that something bad was about to happen. That was their "sixth sense" trying to warn them. It's too bad they didn't listen.

An article was published some time ago in *Psychology Today* entitled "Is There a Sixth Sense?" After conducting experiments related to the "sixth sense", the authors concluded that, "We can now demonstrate in the laboratory what at some level we have known all along: Many people literally get a gut feeling before something bad happens. Our viscera warn us of danger, even if our conscious mind doesn't always get the message".

Now that science has concluded there really is such a thing as a "sixth sense"(something that cops have always known), all we have to do now is develop it. We need to listen to it when it's trying to tell us something is wrong. I believe the sixth sense may be something more than simply an "unconscious form of perception". It may, in fact, be based on information that the brain has already received and processed from the other five senses. I base this opinion on my own experiences involving the criminal cases I mentioned earlier. When I would question these victims further, they would remember details they thought were inconsequential at the time. Maybe they had noticed something minor out of place or had observed a person who just somehow didn't seem quite right. They usually couldn't identify anything specific, but they knew something was out of the ordinary. Most of the time we discount these things and tell ourselves we're being overly sensitive or paranoid. However, I believe that these "insignificant" incidents are not really insignificant after all and are part of our "sixth sense" telling us to pay attention.

There is a reason for the uneasy feeling we get when something bad is about to happen to us. Is this reason simply based on our "unconscious perception" or has our mind cataloged pertinent information that it has gathered subconsciously, beginning the process of "connecting the dots"? A physical manifestation of this could be something like the hair standing up on the back of your neck, having chill bumps, or simply an "eerie feeling". Whatever it is, the sixth sense is a very real tool and should not be ignored. When our sixth sense is telling us that something "funny" is going on, we need to pay close attention. Then we need to quickly develop a plan and enter the decision-making process. "What are we going to do in response to this perceived threat"? The process I use for this will be discussed in the following chapter. ❖

"Terrorism, too, must be excised where it exists, which will take years, and will not happen without the total commitment of the everyday involvement of the American people."

~ *David Hackworth*

CHAPTER 8

RESPONDING TO THE THREAT

Anticipation, Recognition, Decision and Action

The "ARDA" Concept

In the 1950s, Colonel John Boyd, a United States Air Force fighter pilot, developed a concept he called the "OODA Loop" (Observation, Orientation, Decision, Action). His goal was to give fighter pilots an edge in the decision-making process that would help them make positive decisions during in-flight combat, also known as "dogfights". I have adapted his "OODA Loop" in relating to the average citizen who may find himself preparing for his own fight. I call mine ARDA – Anticipation, Recognition, Decision and Action.

Anticipation

The very nature of terrorism suggests that there may be little or no warning prior to an attack. Despite your best efforts, you may fail in noticing those pre-incident indicators of a terrorist attack we discussed the in terrorist cycle of operation. The first line of defense against a terrorist attack is to anticipate, or expect that an attack can occur. This is what I refer to as possessing an "anticipation mindset". A person who possesses an "anticipation mindset" expects that something bad might actually happen to him. If and when it does, he is not surprised. He will not be one of those victims who say, "I can't believe this is happening to me".

A person who practices "anticipation mindset" lives his life in "Condition Yellow". He or she is not surprised when something bad happens, because they are in a place, mentally, where they have accepted the fact that sometimes bad things happen to good people. The worst place any person can be is in a position of denial where he or she says, "it will happen to someone else, but it will not happen to me". This is exactly what Mr. Terrorist wants you to think. Believing that the worst can happen is the first step in the decision-making process. The second step is to recognize that an attack is actually about to occur.

Recognition

Using all of your senses, including your "sixth sense", you must quickly recognize what is going on around you. You will have only a few seconds to develop and process this information, and then decide on a course of action. To assist you in gathering this information, you must ask yourself the questions **"Who, What, When, Where, Why and How"**.

Who is conducting or about to conduct the attack? Can I identify the attackers? How many of them are there?

What exactly is happening? Am I actually under attack, or is something else going on? Are the terrorists after someone else, and I am just in the wrong place at the wrong time?

When is the attack happening? Is it imminent, or do I have a few seconds to re-direct my route? Do I have some time to conduct more analysis, or do I need to react immediately?

Where is the attack coming from? Is it from the front, rear, sides, or a combination? Is it coming from a vehicle, a building, a person on foot, or another fixed object? Where are the attackers?

Why am I under attack? At first this may seem like a ridiculous question, but consider that you may not be the object of the attack. You may simply be in the wrong place at the wrong time. This may be a random terrorist attack, or the terrorists may have targeted someone else in your vicinity. Knowing this information can determine how you react to the attack.

How is the attack being conducted? What is their method of attack? Is this an attack with small arms fire? Bombs? Rocket propelled grenades? Are they intending to kill me or kidnap me? Is this a Linear or an "L-shaped attack? Are vehicles involved or are the attackers on foot? How many attackers are there?

These are questions that need to be addressed, very quickly, before you can decide on a course of action. Once you have quickly gathered as much intelligence on the situation as possible, it is time to decide what you are going to do to extricate yourself from this situation.

Decision

After quickly evaluating and processing all of the above information, you must immediately decide on a course of action. There are only three possible ways you can react. You can fight; you can take flight; or you can freeze. As we have already discussed, what you decide to do is primarily dependent on the situation; however, freeze is never a good option. Don't be immobilized by the "paralysis of analysis". Quickly decide what to do, and then take immediate action.

Action

Once you have decided on a course of action, you must execute your plan immediately and without hesitation. Be aggressive. To paraphrase General Patton, "a poor plan vigorously executed is better that a well-thought-out plan executed half way". If you decide that fight is your best option, give it all you've got. Fight like your life depends on it, because it does. Don't stop fighting until you are off the "X" and safely out of the "kill zone". Terrorists (and most criminals) do not expect you to fight back, so do the unexpected, put them off guard and fight back. Fighting may mean ramming your vehicle into their vehicle, running over one or more of the terrorists with your car, using a firearm, or using your fists, knees, elbows (personal weapons) to affect your escape. If you do have to fight, do so with speed, surprise, and extreme violence. In other words, hit them fast, surprise them by doing what they don't expect, and do it with the utmost violence you can muster. Fight only as long as necessary to extract yourself from the situation, and then spend every amount of energy you have in getting out of the "kill zone".

Your best option, if you are able to do so, is to flee the area without fighting. Fight only if necessary to affect your escape from the "kill zone". Your objective at this point is not necessarily to kill the terrorist, but to facilitate your flight off the "X" and out of the immediate area. If you have to fight to do that, do so aggressively and show no mercy. If you don't have to fight, however, don't waste your time and energy. Instead, spend your energy in getting out of the attack zone as quickly as possible. Fight only enough to aid in your escape. It is important for you to know that the terrorists are probably better armed than you and may be better trained as well. There may be several of them and only one of you. Don't try to shoot it out if there is a clear avenue of escape available to

you. Get out of the area and keep going until you are sure you are safe. I have conducted hundreds of training evolutions with employees who are preparing to go overseas to high-threat areas. In these scenarios the instructors usually play the role of "terrorists", and the students play the role of "American businesspersons" or "government employees". In a typical scenario we attack them by utilizing a linear or "L" type ambush and use a non-lethal paintball type of ammunition. In every case where the students tried to stay and fight, they were "killed" in short order. They were out gunned and out numbered and the "terrorists" had the position of advantage over the students. We would generally refer to the lesson they so painfully learned as a "self-correcting mistake". Hopefully, in the "real world" they wouldn't do something that stupid, which was the whole point of the training.

In the cases where the students either fought back just enough to affect their escape, or immediately got off the "X" without fighting back at all, they "lived". Was the deck stacked against them? Absolutely. Was it a fair fight? Absolutely not. The instructors were better armed, better trained and always outnumbered the students. Did the students survive? The ones who got off the "X" did. And you can too. You need to know that in the "real world" the deck is going to be stacked against you in a terrorist attack. But you can live through it and survive if you utilize speed, surprise and extreme violence in affecting your escape. Above all, get off the "X" quickly. ❖

CHAPTER 9

"I am one who believes that we are engaged in a worldwide war against terrorism. We must have the serenity to accept the fact that war is not going away if we ignore it."

~ Robert Foster Bennett

ARE YOU A TARGET?

What Does the "Target" Look Like?

Any person traveling overseas on business or for pleasure should recognize the possibility that he could become the target of a terrorist organization. You do not have to be wealthy (remember, wealth is a relative term. In most of the world, even the average American is "wealthy"). You do not have to be an important government official or industrialist. The fact that you are an American (or Westerner) is enough to make you a potential target.

Foreign intelligence services have long used certain methods to successfully "spot, assess, and target" certain individuals of interest to them, and terrorist groups have successfully adapted some of these techniques for their purposes as well. In the course of traveling abroad you should be aware that there are certain indicators that may provide evidence that you are the subject of interest by a terrorist group. Remember, the first thing a terrorist group needs before developing a plan of attack is information. Just like a foreign intelligence service, their goal is to collect as much relevant information about you and your activities as possible. To obtain this information they also ask the "who, what, when, where, why and how" questions. Prior to planning an attack, the terrorists want answers to the following questions:

- **Who are you?** Are you a US Government employee? If so, are you a high level employee? Are you a businessperson? What company do you represent? If you are a tourist, are you a "high profile" or wealthy person? Are you well known in both your country and the host country? What are you doing in their country? What is your daily routine while in that country? What is the purpose of your visit? What is your itinerary? What is your mode of transportation?
- **When did you arrive?** When do you depart? If you have meetings with high level government or business officials, when are they scheduled? When do you leave and arrive at your hotel during your daily routine?
- **Where are you staying while in country?** Where is your family (if they are with you)? Where are you going while you are here? If traveling to another area of the country, where are you staying? Where is your office or where are your business meetings conducted? If you have security, where are the security personnel? Are they staying with you or somewhere else? If you are a permanent resident of that country, where do you live? Work? Go to school?
- **Why are you in their country?** Are you in their country on business or as a tourist? Are you a temporary visitor or a permanent resident?
- **How do you travel around the country?** How much money do you have? How do you make a living? How important are you? How do you travel to and from your appointments every day?

The Targeting Cycle

Intelligence officers all around the world use the "spot, assess, develop, recruit" method, also known as the "recruitment cycle", to target their "potential recruits" or to hone in on individuals who are likely to be a threat to their country. The same is true of the terrorist who is seeking a "potential victim". He uses this same basic principle that I am calling the "targeting cycle". Put yourself in the place of the terrorist and ask the question, "What would I want to know about me that would aid in carrying out an attack against me?"

"Spotting" is simply a method of locating and recognizing a target (potential recruit). The target is identified and then the information-gathering phase of the operation begins. This is where the target is officially "assessed".

"Assessing" is the intelligence officer's means of deciding whether or not this potential target is (a) worthy of recruitment, and (b) is susceptible to recruitment. This is very similar to the process by which terrorists study and select their targets. Terrorists want to know if the potential target is worth the risk involved in conducting an attack against him, and is a "soft" target.

"Developing" the target, in intelligence terminology, means that the intelligence officer attempts to get to know the target or potential recruit better. Intelligence officers will try to develop a personal relationship with the prospective target and obtain as much information about him or her as possible. Terrorists may also use this approach to develop information about their potential target.

Before terrorists can plan and conduct an attack, they need information about the victim and his habits. In an overseas environment, be especially cautious when people are attempting to get "close" to you personally. This is especially true with Third World Country nationals who are not involved in your business interests or who are not your personal friends.

Most major terrorist organizations have intelligence networks that are well organized, efficient, and very effective. Sometimes, members of terrorist groups will try and approach you themselves in an attempt to develop information about you, your family and your business. At other times they may use a "cutout" to obtain this information. A "cutout" is a person who, while not a bona fide member of the terrorist group, is sympathetic to their cause and will provide "non-lethal" services to them. Sometimes "cutouts" will work for money, but most often they do so because they are sympathetic to the terrorists' cause. There are others who are intimidated or coerced into working for a terrorist organization. They fear for their lives and the lives of their families if they don't cooperate. Still, others may cooperate with terrorist groups strictly for monetary reasons. Whatever the reason, be careful of developing relationships or providing personal information to people you don't know well.

"Recruiting" is the final piece of the targeting cycle. In intelligence work, recruitment involves enlisting an "agent" to work for an intelligence service. In essence, the intelligence officer decides that his "victim" is worthy of recruitment, and takes the necessary steps to complete the operation.

In terrorist terminology, "recruitment" would be analogous to the terrorist group finally deciding that you are a worthy target and would be a suitable victim for an attack. You have been "recruited" as a "target".

In some countries many members of the military, the police, and intelligence services are sympathetic to terrorist causes. Governments in many Third World countries are rife with terrorist sympathizers, if not actual terrorists themselves. Just because a person is a government official does not mean he can be trusted. Terrorist organizations have infiltrated many foreign governments, some at the highest levels, and while these government officials may not be "full-fledged" members of a terrorist organization, they may very well be sympathetic to them. Working closely with an employee of a host government may be unavoidable for business reasons, but be extremely cautious about allowing it develop any further than a business relationship.

Be particularly suspicious of any foreign national who you seem to "keep running into" at social or business functions, especially if this person seems to "zero" in on you at these events. He or she may very well have more than a passing interest in you and your activities, so be careful not to provide them with personal information and attempt to keep all conversations with them on a "surface" level. Be especially cautious of providing information about you and your family's routine or daily activities. If the individual seems to be prying for this sort of personal information, break off the conversation and avoid him as much as possible.

Be aware of any "accidental encounters" you have with unknown locals as well. Most foreign nationals are friendly and only want to talk to an American; however, you should never let your guard down when talking to a stranger overseas. Beware of those who approach you and want to "practice" their English. Most of these encounters are benign, but be particularly suspicious if the foreign national wants to discuss politics with you. They may also want to talk to you about your home country, your business, your family, or any number of other topics in an attempt to begin a personal relationship with you. It may very well be an innocent encounter with a friendly foreign national, but you should keep your guard up and exercise good judgment when talking to them.

In my travels I've found that, contrary to what the media would have us believe, most foreigners actually like Americans. I've actually met many more foreign nationals that I liked and trusted than ones I distrusted.

I'll relate one incident I was involved in while I was on a business trip in Cairo, Egypt. On this trip I was staying in an international hotel that catered to travelers from all over the world. It was a common occurrence to have cab drivers always hanging around. It was no problem at all for a cab driver to get good-paying fares at hotels like this one.

This was prior to 9/11, and it just so happened I had a free afternoon with nothing scheduled. There was one particular cab driver that spoke reasonably good English and always seemed to zero in on me every time I left the hotel, wanting to "show me sights of Cairo". On that day, with several hours on my hands, I took him up on his offer. I asked him to take me to the pyramids at Giza and we negotiated a fair price. Knowing that it was only about a thirty-minute drive from the hotel to the pyramids, even with the notorious Cairo traffic, I anticipated no problems. When we started out, however, I noticed we weren't headed in the direction of the pyramids. I asked the driver where he was going and he said he was taking me to his "cousin's" shop, where I could get a good deal on some Egyptian souvenirs. Since I was in the market for some souvenirs, I went along for the ride. By this time my suspicions were becoming aroused. It turned out that his "cousin" did have a shop and I made a couple of small purchases and returned to the cab.

Although I could actually see the pyramids from where we were, my driver started the cab and again headed in the wrong direction. I demanded to know where he was going; he replied that his other "cousin" owned a camel and he thought I might like to take a ride on it. By then I was getting plenty nervous and clearly didn't like the direction this situation was taking. This time, however, I got firm with him and ordered him to either take me to the pyramids at once or let me out of the cab. Believe me, had he not turned the cab around at that point, he would have had an angry customer on his hands -- and he knew it. In my mind a contingency plan was already being formed, in the event he didn't comply. I won't go into the details of that plan, although it's safe to say I would have been the proud new owner of an Egyptian cab racing through the streets of Cairo like Dale Earnhardt at the Daytona 500!

I have a colleague who actually pulled a knife on a cab driver in Pakistan and held it to his throat because the driver was headed in the opposite direction of where my friend wanted to go. Extreme? Perhaps, but my colleague is alive today to tell the story.

Remember, terrorist organizations have long tentacles reaching into all levels of society. It may sound extreme, but you cannot afford to trust anyone with whom you have not developed a close personal relationship and can attest to his or her trustworthiness. That cab driver, baggage handler, or security officer may just be trying to be friendly and helpful, and most of the time that is the case. On the other hand, they may have ulterior motives. Don't assume anything, and don't get overly friendly with someone you don't know. As polite people, we are usually fearful of offending people by refusing to indulge them and answer all their questions. After all, no one wants to be the "ugly American". It's perfectly all right to be friendly to foreign nationals, as long as you maintain certain boundaries. You must, however, fight the urge to give them personal information about yourself, your family, your friends, or your business associates. If you feel you must talk about personal issues, at least make something up. Don't give them good information that they can use against you. The chances are good you will never see them again anyway. The bottom line is you and your family's safety is at stake here. What's more important, hurting the feelings of someone you hardly know or the safety and well being of you and your family? ❖

"We need to get ready for a world where terrorism will not ever fully go away."

~ Major Owens

YOUR VEHICLE:

HOW SAFE IS IT REALLY?

The VBIED (or the Vehicle Bomb)

The vehicle bomb, or Vehicle Borne Improvised Explosive Device (VBIED), is a method of attack that has been used by terrorist and criminal organizations for decades. It is a relatively easy process for the terrorist to place and rig a bomb in your unattended vehicle so that it will detonate when you turn on the ignition or by use of a remote-controlled device. Either way, the chances of surviving a vehicle borne improvised explosive device are slim indeed.

On June 2, 1976, a bomb planted in the car of Arizona Republic newspaper reporter, Don Bolles, exploded in a parking lot in Phoenix, Arizona. Bolles lost both of his legs and one of his arms in the attack and was hospitalized for eleven days before he finally died.

In a similar attack, former Chilean Ambassador to the United States, Orlando Letelier, was killed when a bomb placed in his car was detonated in Washington, D. C. The bomb killed Letelier and his American assistant, Ronni Karpen, severely injuring her husband, Michael Moffitt.

The term "vehicle bomb", or VBIED for short, refers to an improvised explosive device that is placed in a vehicle or can describe a bomb planted in another vehicle and set to explode at a predetermined time. The term can also be ascribed to a bomb placed in a vehicle driven by a "suicide bomber", much like the ones that struck the US Embassy and the Marine Barracks in Beirut in 1983.

If you live, work, or travel overseas and have access to a personal vehicle, you should be aware of certain safety measures to detect evidence of someone tampering with your vehicle. Ideally, your vehicle should be secured at all times when not occupied by you or someone you trust. The best way to secure your vehicle is in your personal garage. If that is not an option, then a garage that has 24-hour-a-day security will work. Few people, however, have the luxury of being able to hire "round the clock" security guards to watch their car. Keep in mind that even if you can afford it, security guards have been known to wander away from their post, become distracted, fall asleep or worse yet, be "co-opted" (compromised) by a terrorist group. The same applies to a public garage with an attendant or security guard. These jobs are traditionally low paid and you just can't afford to entrust your life or the lives of your family members to them. The responsibility of securing your vehicle while overseas is yours and yours alone.

Checking Your Vehicle – What to Look For

Your vehicles should always be checked when they have been left parked on the street, in a public garage, in a parking lot, or even in your own driveway. If the vehicle is publicly accessible, a search must be conducted prior to entering it. You should absolutely refuse to enter or start your vehicle until you have conducted at least a cursory search. (No, having your spouse start the car for you is not a good idea.)

As You Approach

Your vehicle search should begin as you approach your car, having a clear view of both your vehicle and the area surrounding it. As you approach, you should be looking for evidence that someone has tampered with your vehicle. Pay attention to anything suspicious in appearance or out of the ordinary. Any loose wires hanging from the vehicle, unknown cylindrical objects on or near the vehicle, or anything else that looks out of place should arouse your suspicion. If you happen to see something that appears out of place or suspicious to you, don't touch it or handle it in any way. Back away from your vehicle, call the police, and let them handle it.

Around and Under

When conducting your search, first look around and under the vehicle. Start from the front of the vehicle and look at the hood and grill area. Look for smudges or dirty fingerprints on the hood. Look behind and underneath the front bumper. Walk around the vehicle and look at the tires, wheel covers, body panels, window moldings, doors and door locks. Look for pry marks, fingerprints and smudges on the doors and windows. Look in the wheel wells and on the ground in front of and behind the tires. While you are walking around the vehicle, and without touching the vehicle or opening the doors, look into the interior for anything out of place.

The Rear

Work your way to the rear of the vehicle, looking at the bumper area and side body panels. Pay particular attention to the trunk. Again, you are looking for wires hanging out of the vehicle, fingerprints, smudges, pry marks, and anything else out of the ordinary. Don't forget to check out the exhaust pipe. Take a good look underneath the vehicle as well. Look for dirt or mud that has been knocked loose from the undercarriage. A good flashlight can be an invaluable tool in helping you see objects that may be attached to the undercarriage, lying on the ground underneath the car, and in other concealed areas.

Now the Other Side

Continue around to the other side of the vehicle and repeat the procedure. Once you are certain that the vehicle hasn't been tampered with, unlock and slowly open one of the doors. As you are doing this, be careful to notice any wires or anything unusual near the door. Carefully examine the interior of the vehicle, looking on the seats, carpets and at the overhead lining. Look in the glove box, console and all interior compartments of the vehicle. (You can intentionally leave these compartments open when you park your vehicle to make them safer and easier to check). Using a flashlight, check under the seats and dashboard.

Your Trunk and Hood

Carefully open the trunk and the hood. Look in the engine compartment, particularly around the battery and near the firewall. Examine the trunk area and look in the spare tire well and all other compartments as well. If everything appears normal, then and only then should you consider it safe enough to drive.

Who Else Drives Your Car?

Your vehicle should be searched whenever someone else has driven it. Be particularly careful who you allow to have access to your vehicle. Only permit people you trust and who have been "vetted" to work on, maintain, or otherwise have access to your vehicle. Locking your vehicle gas cap, hood and trunk are good precautions, as well as a having a good alarm system on your car. It should go without saying that all of your vehicles should be kept locked at all times. You must keep in mind, however, that even the best security mechanisms and alarms can be defeated. Do not place your trust in them alone for your security.

When parking your vehicle at work, or in any public location, try to park in a well-lighted and highly traveled area. The best option is to find a relatively secure parking garage with an attendant and/or a security guard. This does not absolve you, however, of the responsibility of conducting a search of your vehicle prior to entering it. The weakest link in any security system is the human factor. Don't trust a $5.00-per-hour security guard or parking lot attendant with your life.

If your vehicle has been parked in a reasonably secure area, you may not want to conduct quite as thorough a search, but you should at least do a cursory search each time you approach the vehicle, glancing underneath the car and taking a quick look at the trunk, hood and interior before entering. This cursory search takes only a few seconds to complete and should become part of your daily security routine. Taking the time to do this could very well save your life or the life of a loved one. ❖

"It is better by noble boldness to run the risk of being subject to half of the evils we anticipate than to remain in cowardly listlessness for fear of what might happen."

~ *Herodotus*

CHAPTER 11

THE ATTEMPTED ABDUCTION:

SUBMIT OR RESIST?

Handling an Attempted Abduction

Kidnapping as a terrorist tool has received widespread public attention in recent years. Tourists, businessmen, government employees and even military and police officers have been kidnapped and held hostage by terrorist and criminal enterprises. Kidnappings conducted by terrorist groups are definitely on the rise worldwide and show no sign of abating anytime soon. Colombia, Russia, Mexico, The Philippines, India, Yemen, Pakistan, Kyrgystan, Tajikistan, and of course, Iraq and Afghanistan are countries where terrorist kidnappings are rampant. (Any country with "stan" as a part of its name is a place you should avoid if possible).

"Do I submit or do I fight?"

There has been much debate concerning the issue of whether you should submit to the demands of a terrorist intent on kidnapping you or whether you should resist. There are clearly two sides to this issue. Those who advocate surrendering to the terrorist demands and will-

ingly subjecting themselves to capture, argue that by cooperating, you are increasing your chances of being set free at some point in the future when either the demands of your abductor are met or the terrorists get tired of holding you. Some of the hostages abducted in Lebanon in the 1980's were eventually set free, but only after spending several years in captivity. There have been other recent instances in which terrorist groups have released their hostages "unharmed" after holding them for a period of time. However, the current trend seems to be heading in the opposite direction. Seeking maximum publicity and "shock value", today's terrorist is more likely to behead their hostage than to release him.

I cannot tell you what to do if you suddenly find yourself faced with the possibility of being abducted and spending time as a guest in a terrorist "safe-house". This is largely a personal decision similar to the decision a woman must make if she finds herself about to be raped. The dilemma she faces is whether to submit to her rapist or to fight back. You will find many so called "experts" who advise women to go ahead and submit, hope for the best, and above all, not to fight back. Their rationale is that by resisting, she might make her attacker angry and run the risk that he might beat or even kill her. Some "experts" will tell the victim to fight back only if she thinks she has a good chance of escaping, but if the odds seem overwhelming, to go ahead and submit. Lastly, there are a few who encourage women to fight back with every fiber in their being and with every ounce of courage they can muster.

The same dilemma holds true when confronted with the question of whether to submit to the demands of a terrorist group intent on abducting you and holding you hostage. This is largely a personal decision based on your beliefs, personality and level of confidence in your ability to defend yourself. Some people are, by nature, more compliant and phlegmatic than others. They have no desire or propensity to fight back and would rather die than physically resist their abductors. If this describes you, it might help to understand the rationale behind this attitude.

Doubts and Fears: Your Worst Enemy

"No passion so effectually robs the mind of all its powers of acting or reasoning as fear." ~ Edmund Burke

Like many other people, perhaps you have an innate fear of being involved in a physical confrontation. Many people have never been in a violent or physical confrontation and have no idea what to expect. I grew up in the '50s and '60s in an environment where "fighting" among boys was relatively commonplace. "Schoolyard fights" were a regular occurrence and I was involved in several of them (most of which I summarily lost). While I do not advocate fighting in school or anywhere else for that matter (unless it is a matter of self-defense), I did learn that I could take a punch and it wouldn't kill me. Taking a punch is not that big a deal and I survived most of these confrontations with no more than a bruised ego. Contact sports were big back then as well. Several times a week most of the neighborhood boys would gather for a sandlot football game that occasionally evolved into a wrestling match, fistfight, or a free-for-all.

By the time I had graduated from high school I had been involved in several physical confrontations and had survived them all, more or less intact. Today's environment is totally different. In this day and time of "zero tolerance" in the schools, most boys graduate from high school without ever trading punches with another. Make no mistake, I believe that is a good thing and I don't advocate fighting unnecessarily. I never wanted my own children to fight unless it was a case of self-defense or a situation where they were defending a weaker person who was being bullied. The good news is that we live in a "kinder and gentler" environment today. The bad news is that very few people grow up having learned the skills necessary to defend themselves. This becomes painfully apparent when you find yourself in the position of having to use physical skills to remove yourself from a dangerous situation and in an alien environment. When faced with a violent confrontation and without knowledge of basic self-defense skills, you are far more likely to go into "condition black", which was discussed in an earlier chapter.

Another reason people may hesitate to fight back is lack of knowledge in defending themselves. Most people don't know how to fight back. They lack the rudimentary skills necessary to defend themselves in a violent confrontation. The good news today is that there is a plethora of self-defense courses offered by martial arts schools, police departments and private individuals. Karate, Tae Kwon Do, Ju jitsu, and other martial arts schools are in abundance in almost every community. There are innumerable books and videotapes available, as well as a wealth of information on the Internet on how to protect yourself. As a former Karate instructor, I am encouraged by the number of children enrolled in martial arts classes today, as well as adults who take up martial arts training later in life. I believe that everyone should possess some basic knowledge of defensive tactics. Even if you never have to use these skills, the knowledge that you are able to defend yourself when necessary builds self-confidence. Terrorists and criminals have a way of reading your demeanor and can usually tell by your "body language" whether you are confident in your ability to defend yourself. This is similar to the way a dog can sense your fear of him. The dog is more likely to bite you if you show fear and the terrorist or criminal is more likely to attack you if you demonstrate a lack of self-confidence. Numerous studies conducted among incarcerated criminals revealed that the way a potential victim carries himself makes all the difference in whether that person is selected as a victim. Taking self-defense and martial arts classes is an excellent way to build up that self-confidence. Another added benefit of attending martial arts classes several times a week is getting in good physical shape. Being physically fit leads to self-confidence and is clearly a major factor in helping to survive a physical confrontation or other emergency.

Having a black belt in martial arts does not guarantee your never becoming a victim. The odds of surviving a physical confrontation or an attempted abduction, however, are significantly increased when you have defensive tactics training; and the more trained you are, the better you will fare. On the other hand, beware of becoming complacent and putting too much confidence in your defensive tactics. I clearly recall one of my students who was enrolled in a defensive tactics class. This class was comprised of government employees being deployed to high threat areas. This particular woman was going to a post in Africa, notorious for having a high number of rapes, car-jackings, and other assaults. She proudly announced that she had a fifth degree black belt in karate and was convinced she could protect herself from rape. In fact, she claimed there wasn't a male in the room, instructor or student, who could get her down on the floor. At that point one of my assistant instructors, a man of average height and weight, proceeded to throw her on the mat and pin her arms and legs in a matter of seconds. Faced with the fact that she was helpless to do anything, she immediately burst into tears. From that point on we had her complete, undivided attention, as well as that of her classmates.

The point I am trying to make here is that having extensive training in the martial arts will not automatically "save you". I am a huge proponent of the martial arts and have been both a student and an instructor for many years. I have a black belt in American style karate, a red belt in Tae Kwon Do, and have studied Judo, Jiu Jitsu and boxing. Nevertheless, I will be the first to admit there is much more to self-defense than having some nice colored belts tied around your waist. Having the proper "mindset" plays a crucial role in the probability of your becoming a victim. If I had to choose between having a black belt and having a survival mindset, I'd choose the mindset every time. The best combination is to have both the training and the mindset necessary to survive a confrontation. Possessing good self-defense skills in conjunction with a survival mindset is an almost unbeatable combination in an emergency situation. I strongly urge everyone to enroll in some type of martial arts or self-defense training and to get in the physical shape necessary to handling a confrontation. Most importantly, however, develop a mindset that says, "I will win the fight and survive any confrontation that comes my way".

Many people hesitate to fight their attackers because they believe that they are physically unable to do so. Fighting and escaping is hard work. Depending on the situation, you may be required to fight off one or more attackers simultaneously and then run several blocks to escape from the "kill zone". Most confrontations last only a couple of minutes at most, but this can seem like an eternity if you are out of shape. You don't have to be a super athlete to survive an attack, but it does help if you are at least in minimally good shape.

Again, attending a martial arts class a couple of times a week can help get you into good physical condition and provide you with some useful self-defense skills, significantly increasing your confidence level. Many people, however, feel intimidated just walking into a martial arts school, much less signing up for the classes. I know because I was there once myself. There is absolutely no reason to feel intimidated, as most good martial arts schools (and there are thousands of them), have a wealth of experience handling students just like you. No one will laugh or make fun of you, because everyone in that school was in your place once. I've found that most instructors and senior martial arts students are more than willing to help you obtain good self-defense skills. After you get over your initial awkwardness, usually at about the three to sixth-month period when you test for your first belt, you will find the study of martial arts to be a truly rewarding experience. An added benefit to learning your defensive tactics skill is getting in good physical condition.

If you choose not to enroll in martial arts or self-defense class, at least do something to get yourself in shape. Walk, run, ride a bike, swim, lift weights, do aerobics or yoga. Do whatever you prefer, but do something. An extra benefit to getting healthy is the self-confidence you will gain by being in good physical condition. This alone is reason enough to devote an hour or so a day to your physical conditioning.

Fear is often another reason people fail to take action in a life-threatening situation --fear of what? Several fears play on our psyche to convince us that taking action is unwise. Some of these fears are:

- **Fear of the unknown.** Most of us are not used to violent emergencies. Unless you are a police officer, fire fighter, or combat soldier, you probably don't live with danger as part of your daily routine. Most people go through their lives not having to resort to violence to survive. There are, however, some situations that can only be resolved through the use of force and violence on your part. Once you come to grips with that reality, you can better prepare yourself to face a violent emergency, such as a terrorist attack. Expect the unexpected and be prepared to transform yourself from "prey" into "predator". If you have given serious thought and consideration to what you would do in an emergency; if you have played the "when this happens, then I will react in this manner" game, you should be mentally prepared for whatever happens. Think tactically. Tactical thinking ("when/then") leads to developing good tactical solutions. Developing good tactical solutions leads to confidence on your part, and confidence leads to less fear of the unknown. If you prepare for the "unknown" in your mind, it is no longer an unknown equation. You now expect it to happen and you know exactly what you are going to do when it does ("when/then"). By thinking tactically, you are able to transform the "unknown" into the "known". This is also known as "visualization" and has been used for decades to prepare athletes for competition. If an athlete can visualize a certain play and visualize how he will successfully react to it, then he has convinced his mind that he can pull it off. The same principle can work for you. Visualize what could happen, and how you are going to react to it. Be sure to visualize yourself as the victor, having done everything you can do to survive. Above all, do not visualize or worry about failure because failure is not an option.

- **Fear of failure.** What if I do something and it doesn't work? This is a legitimate question and it could happen. If you try something and it doesn't work, do something else, and keep doing it until you find something that does work. Don't give up! Do not surrender to the terrorists or submit to their demands. At the very least, make them fight for what they get. As I stated earlier, most terrorists are cowards who tend to pick on the weak and unprepared. The last thing they want to do is to get involved in a fight. They simply want to complete their mission with as little hassle as possible. If you do fight, there are no guarantees that you will win. Sometimes you get the bear and sometimes the bear gets you. There is one guarantee, however, and that is if you do give up the fight and give in to the terrorists, you will fail. Again, failure is not one of your options.

- **Fear of harming someone.** There are many people who simply do not want to cause harm or inflict pain on another person. Whether it is due to personal conviction, religious training or simply an aversion to hitting someone, they can't seem to bring themselves to cause injury to another human being. To begin with, you cannot allow yourself in this situation to regard terrorists as "human beings". You have to look at them as "sub-human beings" that are out to harm or kill you and your family. This is not a "fair" fight and you shouldn't think of it as one. This is the time to transform yourself into a ruthless and cold-blooded aggressor being single mindedly focused on getting out of the situation alive.

I once had a student in a firearms class who told me that she would never shoot anyone, regardless of the situation. This person was being transferred to a very dangerous part of the world and was taking her ten-year-old daughter with her. Despite reports from that area indicating that Americans were being targeted with increasing frequency and crime was at an all time high, she remained the most uninterested and unmotivated student in the class. She saw no reason for firearms training and was there only because being "weapons qualified" was a pre-requisite for going to that particular country. Stating it mildly, she had a poor attitude about the course and about guns in general.

I gave my best effort to convince her she needed to take this training seriously, but my pleas fell on deaf ears. Finally, in desperation, I asked her what she would do if someone were breaking into her house while she was at home. Surprisingly, she replied that she believed it was best to let them alone and allow them to take whatever they wanted. I asked her, "what if they wanted you?" She replied that she would submit to them and hope for the best, but would never use a firearm to protect herself. I then asked, "what if they wanted your daughter?" The change in her demeanor was immediately noticeable. Clearly, I had hit a nerve with this woman. Her emphatic reply was, "I would do whatever I had to do to save my child, including killing that *&%#@* bastard!" She then went on in graphic detail, stating what she would do to anyone who tried to harm her daughter. I could tell she meant it and would indeed do whatever it took to protect her child, to include taking a life. I recommended that she use this scenario to her advantage throughout the remainder of her training. She agreed and began using this visualization and I was amazed at the dramatic change in her attitude.

Considering where this student was being assigned, that situation could very easily have become a reality. Visualizing this scenario gave her a valid reason to become serious about her training and she went from being the worst student in the class to being the best, both in skill and in attitude. In fact, by the end of the course and passing with flying colors, she became somewhat of a "gun nut", wanting to learn all she could about "man-stopping" rounds and calibers, where she could buy a gun of her own and get additional training. I almost pity the poor schmuck who tries to mess with this lady.

- **Fear of consequences.** In our litigious society today, everyone is afraid of what will happen to him or her if, when trying to defend himself, he seriously injures or kills another person. Will he be arrested, indicted and prosecuted? Will he find himself in jail? Will he get sued? In the case of a government employee, will he get fired? The answer to all of the above questions is, possibly yes. Any and all of the above could happen, but is worrying about it worth your life? Even well-trained police officers have been known to "freeze up" and fail to react in scenarios where deadly force is clearly authorized. Often the results are disastrous for the officer. They "second guess" themselves and hesitate in situations where deadly force is clearly authorized. They let their fear of possible reprisals by their superiors, the public, or the legal system keep them from pulling the trigger.

Unfortunately, their failure to take action sometimes results in the loss of their own lives. You know the old saying, "It's better to be tried by twelve than carried by six". In the first place, terrorists are not likely to "sue" anyone. Let's say, however, innocent victims get caught up in the attack. Perhaps, in your effort to "ram" your way out of a terrorist roadblock you accidentally run over an innocent bystander. While tragic, keep in mind that you did not start this fight -- the terrorists did. Any injuries or deaths of innocent civilians can be tied directly to the terrorists' actions, not yours. None of this would have happened if they had left you alone.

In your attempt to escape from your attackers, there could be collateral damage and innocent people could be hurt. In the middle of a terrorist attack is not the time to worry about that. Obviously, you should do everything possible to prevent innocent casualties, but your first priority is the safety of you and your family. Do whatever it takes to get out of the kill zone and survive. Again, you didn't ask for nor start this mess, so collateral damage is not your fault. You cannot expend the time and energy required worrying about the consequences when you are trying to save your life or the lives of your family. In most countries the law of self-defense allows you to do whatever is necessary, up to and including deadly force, to protect yourself or your family from death or serious bodily injury. Save your life and your family first and worry about the consequences later. You can hire a lawyer or get another job, but your kids can't get their father or mother back if you fail to act.

- **Fear of more terror by the terrorists if they don't cooperate.** Recently I watched an old movie in which a couple of escaped convicts took a family hostage. The actress playing the part of the mother in the movie tried to convince her phlegmatic, poor excuse of a husband to fight the convicts. Clearly not wanting to do anything, his nervous response was, "Let's not try anything. It might make them mad." The end result of the movie, which was based on a true incident, was the entire family being brutally murdered. I cringe whenever I see this movie. I just can't imagine a husband or father not doing everything in his power to protect his family.

In a terrorist situation you could die in the process, but at least do something. I have news for you -- the terrorists are probably going to harm you anyway. They are not there to invite you to tea. They are there to (a) kidnap you; (b) kill you; or (c) kidnap you and then kill you. None of these are particularly good options, so you may as well go down fighting. I believe you actually stand a much better chance of survival if you fight back than if you just sit there at the mercy of the criminal or terrorist and do nothing. Even if I knew the terrorists only wanted to hold me for ransom, which is impossible to know, I would still fight back. I value my freedom and I am not going to willingly let anyone take it from me. Some things are worth fighting for, and I personally believe my freedom is one of them. You don't know what the terrorists intend to do with you, despite what they might tell you. In addition to being cowards, terrorists are liars. If they say they aren't going to harm you, don't believe them. They obviously want you to cooperate as this makes their job a lot easier. Their track record, however, is not good when it comes to keeping hostages alive and unharmed. Do not let them take your freedom or your life. Do not make it easy for them. Do the unexpected and fight back. You might just find that launching a violent counterattack is enough to make them quit and break off their attack.

In 1966, an itinerant drifter by the name of Richard Speck methodically and brutally raped and murdered eight student nurses in Illinois. One student nurse was able to hide and was spared, eventually testifying against Speck in a court of law. The point I'm making is that there were nine women against one man. The victims outnumbered their attacker by a ratio of nine to one. Granted, that man was armed with a knife, but I have to wonder what would have happened had the women turned the tables on Speck and violently attacked him with whatever "weapons" they could get their hands on. Most of them might have been able to survive this confrontation, but they let fear paralyze them and they failed to take action. I am sure that Richard Speck was expecting an easy day of raping, terrorizing, and murdering the student nurses. What he was not expecting, however, was a violent, aggressive and ruthless counterattack meant to disable or kill him. A violent counterattack may have just disconcerted Speck enough to cause him to break off the attack and leave. On the other hand, the victims might have died anyway. At least they would have extracted a price from their attacker and they wouldn't have made it easy for him. It's up to you whether you choose to fight back or to submit, but I, personally, am not going down without one "helluva" fight.

The question is this -- If you do what your abductors want, will they release you unharmed? To be sure, there have been a few instances of terrorist groups releasing their captives "unharmed", depending on what your definition of "unharmed" might be. Richard Speck certainly had no intention of releasing his captors unharmed. We have seen terrorists hold hostages for months, even years, before releasing them. In Lebanon during the 1980's there were several examples of hostages being held and released by their captors after a prolonged stay, sometimes of several years duration. Today's terrorist, however, seems more interested in separating you from your head than in releasing you. The typical terrorist today is less interested in making demands for hostage exchanges or for media coverage and seeking the release of "political" prisoners. He is much more interested in obtaining maximum terror value, by beheading his victim and showing it on the Internet or on the Al-jazira news network. In today's world terrorists are much less likely to negotiate. Their goal is to obtain a high body count and maximum shock value.

I can't make the decision for you, telling you to submit to terrorist demands by going with them or to fight back and try to make an escape. This is largely a personal choice. Some people are naturally compliant and non-violent and wouldn't dream of offering resistance, regardless of the outcome. If your decision is to submit to the terrorists, I wish you luck. I hope you survive. Even though I can't tell you what to do, I can tell you what I would do. I would use everything in my being to prevent them from taking me. I like my freedom and I am not going to allow anyone to take it from me willingly. Even if I knew the terrorists would release me after a set period of time, which in reality no one could know, I would still fight like hell. The audacity of someone assuming they can take my freedom and dictate where I go and what I do is enough to make me fighting mad. For this reason alone I would resist with every fiber of my being.

There is another reason to resist a terrorist abduction attempt. In the majority of terrorist-related abductions, the victim usually doesn't make it back alive. If past behavior is indicative of future behavior, there's an excellent chance that once you go with them, you're not coming back. They aren't taking you to a nice place. Bad things happen when your abductor gets you on his turf. He wants you to go with him for a reason -- so that he can do what he wants with you, when he wants to do it and without witnesses. By the time you get to the terrorist's safe haven, it's too late to fight back. The deck is stacked heavily in favor of the terrorists. They can now isolate you and do whatever they want.

If you let them take you to their turf the control is theirs. Instead of dealing with one, two or three terrorists, you may now be in the middle of a terrorist camp with hundreds of terrorists and their sympathizers. The chances for escape are slim indeed. They now have absolute and total control over you and there isn't much you can do about it. They most certainly will lock you in a cell or a room and may very well handcuff, blindfold, drug you or all of the above. They may chain you to the wall or otherwise secure you so that any hope of escape is dashed. At this point they are free to torture and kill you at their leisure.

So is there an alternative? The alternative is to fight back at the very onset of the attack with everything you have until you see an opportunity to escape, getting off the "X". Fight back aggressively and with maximum force and violence. Try to make as much of a "scene" as possible. The last thing the terrorist wants is to attract attention. His goal is to accomplish his mission with as little attention drawn to him as possible. He wants to grab you and get out of there with minimal hassle.

The time for you to act is immediately after the attack begins. Don't hesitate. Take action immediately. Obtain the element of surprise by doing the unexpected. Your attackers expect you to submit meekly and willingly to their demands. The minute you do, you have lost the fight and your fate is in the hands of the terrorists. The mere fact that you have the audacity to fight back may just surprise them enough to temporarily immobilize them. This will buy you some time and aid in making your getaway. Even though faced with seemingly insurmountable odds, your best option is to resist with all your might, and keep resisting until you can safely escape from the "kill zone".

When faced with extricating yourself from an attack you can do several things, depending on the situation. You can either run or drive off the "X", which is by far your best option. If you find yourself having to fight, do so only long enough to facilitate your escape. Think of it as a "hit and run" tactic designed to distract your assailant and enable your escape. The one option that you absolutely cannot do is to freeze, doing nothing. Fight or flight are your only two options. If you do have to fight, use every weapon at your disposal. ❖

"The weapon of the brave is in his heart."

~ Anonymous

IDENTIFYING AND UTILIZING YOUR WEAPONS

A weapon, according to Noah Webster, is defined as, "an instrument or device used to injure or kill"; and "any means of attack or defense". This definition covers a lot of territory. A weapon can be something as complicated as a firearm or something as simple as a part of your body (hands, feet, etc.) with which to ward off an attack.

Without a doubt, if you can legally carry a firearm and if you know how to effectively and safely use a gun for self-protection, this is your best option. If you are unable to do so or choose not to carry a firearm, you have other "weapons" at your disposal.

Let's take a look at what weapons are available to you.

Firearms

As a professional firearms instructor, I am definitely a strong advocate of the right to carry and use firearms as a means of self-defense. Obviously, a firearm in trained hands is a powerful tool in fighting off a terrorist attack. If you are considering arming yourself, or if you are thinking about employing armed security officers to protect you and your family, there are some issues that

should first be considered.

Your initial concern should be one of legality. While it may be legal in the United States to carry firearms if you have a weapons permit (at least in most states), it is not legal in most foreign countries, especially if you are a resident alien. Prior to living or working overseas you should become intimately familiar with the weapons laws in that country. In the event you are unfortunate enough to reside in one of the anti-firearms countries, you have two options. You can break the law and carry a gun anyway (remember the old *adage*, "it's better to be tried by twelve than carried by six"), or you can hire someone who is authorized to carry a firearm. There are problems with both of these options. If you possess and carry a weapon illegally and are caught, you could face stiff fines and an even stiffer jail sentence. I do not recommend this option. Who wants to do time in a Third World prison? The second option, which is to hire someone who can legally carry a weapon to protect you, is also fraught with danger.

During my career in the CIA I had the opportunity to work with and train security officials in over thirty foreign countries. This amounted to hundreds of individuals, most of whom were police, military, intelligence and other government agents generally considered to be the elite of their organizations. Of the approximately one thousand foreign nationals I've been involved with, both operationally and in training, I can probably count on two hands the number of them I would trust with my life. Don't get me wrong -- there are some fine law enforcement and military organizations abroad, and some outstanding people. With a few exceptions, however, those being predominately Westernized nations, none of their weapons training standards come close to the standards imposed upon US law enforcement, military, and intelligence officers. Those Third World countries where the terrorist threat is highest, ironically have the most poorly-trained officers. Police, military and security officers in Third World countries receive very minimal firearms training, if they receive any at all. They are not the trained professionals you see in the US and other Western nations, and you would certainly want to think twice about entrusting your security to them.

Hiring Professional Protection

If you do decide to hire a security "professional" to protect yourself, your family, or your employees, please observe a few precautions and ask the following questions:

Who is this person I am entrusting with my life? Is he a professional military, police or intelligence officer, or is he simply a private security guard? Does he come recommended by someone I trust? Has he preformed this type of duty before? If so, when and with whom? Was he successful?

Has his background been thoroughly investigated? Is he really who he says he is? Does he or any of his close relatives have ties to any extremist or fringe groups? Does he possess the background he claims to have? Did he provide references and have you checked them? Does he have a police record or has he ever been the subject of a terrorist-related investigation? Does he have any credit or money problems? (This is an important question to ask -- you don't want to hire someone who is susceptible to bribery. Terrorist groups, like intelligence agencies, look for individual weaknesses to exploit). Does he have a drug or alcohol problem?

What is his level of training? By whom was he trained and how long ago? How much experience does he have in the security and personal protection field?

Is he legally authorized to carry firearms in his country? If he is, what kind of weapon does he carry and is he qualified to use that weapon? Who trained him and certified him with that particular weapon? Is he carrying his firearm concealed or out in the open? If he is carrying his weapon concealed, where does he keep it and can he get to it if he quickly needs it? The reason for asking these questions is due to an experience I had while on assignment in a Third World country.

While there, I was assigned a "bodyguard" for the duration of my stay. This bodyguard worked for a federal law enforcement agency in his country, approximately equivalent to our FBI. On my first day in the country he picked me up at my hotel. As we were driving to our destination, I asked him if he was armed. He replied that, indeed, he was. I asked him if I could see his gun, and at that point he pulled to the side of the road and began rooting around under his seat. After what seemed like several minutes, but was probably only about thirty seconds, he proudly produced an ancient, Egyptian-made Helwan pistol. Even fresh out of the factory, the Helwan is an inferior pistol; but this one had obviously been carried in a humid jungle climate for years, appearing in desperate need of being cleaned and serviced. When I tried to open the action on the gun to see if it was loaded (it was not!), it took me several tries, as the action was almost rusted shut. Had there been an attack on me, there was no way this officer could have retrieved his gun and loaded it in time to thwart the attack. The country I was visiting at that time was a virtual hotbed of terrorist and criminal activity; and Americans, especially CIA officers, were at extreme risk. As a matter of fact, while I was on that very assignment, a narco-terrorist group abducted seven U. S citizens and was holding them hostage. The agent assigned to protect me was, according to his superiors, one of the best in his organization. I can only imagine what the others were like. For obvious reasons, I obtained a weapon and provided for my own security during that stay.

Is the person hired to protect you a citizen of that country or an expatriate from another country? There are many former foreign military personnel that operate private security services in Third World countries. Some of these individuals are the best of the best, highly trained, and they definitely know what they are doing. They don't come cheap, but you get what you pay for. How much is your life or the lives of your family members or your employees worth?

Make absolutely certain that any security professionals you hire have a solid background with a reputable organization. You may want to delve a little deeper, assuring they aren't organization "rejects", possibly involved in some misdeed.

Some of the best military units in the world are the US Army Special Forces and Rangers; US Navy SEALS; US Marine Corps Force Recon; British Special Air Service (SAS) and Special Boat Service (SBS); and Australian Special Forces. There are other good units, of course, but individuals who have served in one of these organizations will be well trained. There are also some excellent security companies run by former FBI, US Secret Service and CIA officers, not to mention Scotland Yard and Royal Canadian Mounted Police (RCMP) officers. You can hardly go wrong contracting with any of these security services, although I've found that the US Secret Service officers are particularly skilled in providing personal protection. They are, after all, in the business of high-level dignitary protection.

Carrying Your Own Firearm

The other option you have is carrying a firearm yourself, assuming that it is legal for you to do so. If you make the decision to carry a firearm, do yourself a favor and get some training, and I'm not talking about going out in the backyard with Uncle Harry and plinking at beer cans! Get yourself some legitimate training from a well-known and recognized firearms instruction school.

The very first thing you obviously need to do is to buy your firearm. There are many good handguns, rifles, carbines and shotguns suitable for personal protection. Of course, the type of weapon you get depends on the environment in which you will be operating. If you are in a war zone, you will probably want a rifle or a carbine. A shotgun is a good weapon for home protection, and a handgun is easily concealable (although not as effective as a rifle or a shotgun in terms of "man-stopping" power).

Whatever firearm you decide to purchase, long gun or handgun (and you may decide to get one of each), make sure it's of good quality. There are many good, reputable firearms manufacturers who make quality weapons. Try several of them and choose what best suits your particular needs. You should feel completely comfortable with the weapon and it should be one that is relatively easy to deploy quickly and efficiently. The caliber of the firearm should be sufficient to provide adequate man-stopping power, but not so large that you have difficulty controlling the weapon when it is fired.

After selecting your firearm, it is imperative that you get the best training possible in how to safely and effectively use it. There are several reputable firearms training schools in the US and abroad, and you should be able to find one that suits your needs as well as your budget. The two important considerations when choosing a school are: (1) they must have a good safety record and (2) they must teach "tactical" firearms. If self-defense is your goal, you don't want a school that teaches "target shooting" or sport shooting to the exclusion of "combat" shooting. You want to attend a school that teaches tactical combat shooting. This kind of training will prepare you for a real life confrontation. All good firearms schools incorporate a system of training that moves the student in logical progression from "beginner" to "gunfighter". This will take a minimum of one week, but preferably two weeks. Weapons safety should be stressed throughout the course and the terminal objective should be to take you to a level of competence where you are comfortable carrying a firearm 24 hours a day, seven days a week. By the end of the course, you should be able to safely and effectively employ your firearm to save your life, should it become necessary. Regular follow-up training is critical in maintaining your skill level with a firearm. Like most things, shooting skills deteriorate without practice, so plan for a few days on the range every year. Ideally, you should take some advanced firearms courses from a reputable school and continue to work on your skills as long as you carry a weapon. Tactics change and it definitely pays to stay current regarding new developments in the firearms tactical arena.

Remember, owning a firearm is a huge responsibility. You walk a fine line when you are keeping your weapon ready to deploy at a moment's notice and at the same time keeping it secure from unauthorized people. Your family should know you have a weapon and be aware of where you keep it; and they should be taught to respect all firearms, treating them with care. It might be worth your consideration to enroll your spouse and older children in a firearms training course. At the very least, they should receive serious instruction in the safety of firearms.

Other Weapons at Your Disposal

Using Your Vehicle as a Weapon

If you decide not to use firearms or employ a bodyguard for your defense, there are other things you can do to significantly increase your chance of survival in an attack. As discussed in earlier chapters, if you are in your vehicle and an attack suddenly occurs, keep in mind that a 3000-pound weapon is at your disposal. Don't hesitate to use it. Ram your way through the attack, running over anyone who gets in your way.

If you are on foot, you will most likely have other weapons at your disposal. These personal weapons can be as benign as a pen or pencil; an umbrella; or a rolled up newspaper. You don't have to be a martial arts expert to defeat an attacker. Although I studied and taught martial arts, I will be the first to admit that many of the techniques taught are largely ineffective in a "street" situation. Some martial arts techniques and styles are more specific to "sport" applications than to self-defense. Having said that, I do believe that training in the martial arts will help you learn some basic techniques to increase your chances of surviving in an emergency situation, as well as help you to get in "fighting shape".

Using Your Body as a Weapon

Even if you are "unarmed" in the traditional sense, you have a number of "personal weapons" at your disposal. Knee and elbow strikes to the face, head or groin area can be extremely effective in stopping an attacker. Striking your opponent with a "hammer fist" to his nose or jamming your thumb in his eye socket can do wonders, causing him to worry about his own survival. Repeated kicks and punches in those highly sensitive areas can make your assailant re-think his plan of attacking you.

Using Your Creativity as a Weapon

The point I'm trying to make here is the importance of doing something. Think outside the box. Use everything at your disposal to fend off an attack. Take a look around you. Regardless of where you are -- in your home, your car or on foot, almost assuredly you will see several things to use as weapons in an emergency. Again, you don't have to be Bruce Lee to successfully fight off an attack. Use anything you can get your hands on and fight back hard, fast and with fury. Show no mercy and don't stop fighting until you can get away. Above all, don't give up. Once you give up, all is lost. Do whatever it takes to get through the attack and out of the "kill zone".

Fighting back at your attackers will require you to do something you are probably not used to doing -- becoming extremely violent. Three things will win the fight: speed, surprise and violence of action. In essence, you must strike fast, do the unexpected, and use extreme violence to win the fight and get away. In the words of Teddy Roosevelt, "Don't hit at all if you can help it; don't hit a man if you can possibly avoid it; but if you do hit him, put him to sleep". I say "amen" to that.

Fortunately, a violent personality is not the norm for most people. Most of us are basically peace-loving people who abhor violence. When faced with a violent emergency, such as a terrorist attack, however, we must transform ourselves into a ruthless and violent personality. If ever there was a time to have a "Jekyll and Hyde" persona, this is it. During a violent confrontation (remember, you didn't start this), you must resort to overwhelming and unrelenting violence if you expect to survive. You must do whatever it takes to win the fight and get away from the kill zone. That may mean running over a terrorist with your vehicle, gouging his eye out or any other number of violent options. Do whatever it takes to survive the confrontation. I'm acquainted with a few women who, in fighting off an assailant, used pens, pencils and other objects, jamming them into the attacker's eye socket, quickly ending his will to fight! This may seem like an extreme course of action, but these victims did survive.

It's always a possibility you may be forced to take another person's life in order to save your own or the life of a family member. You must always remember that you didn't start this fight -- the terrorist did. By his choosing to attack you, the terrorist in essence will be making the decision to risk his own life and you will be doing only what it takes to survive. ❖

"Act decidedly and take the consequences. No good is ever done by hesitation."

~ Thomas Henry Huxley

PROTECTING YOURSELF ON THE ROAD

More Americans are "on the road" than ever before. Despite the high cost of fuel and the increased threat of terrorism, Americans like to stay on the go. Both domestic and international travel is at an all time high and shows no indication of abating anytime soon.

Given this fact, it is no wonder that the majority of terrorist attacks take place while the victim is traveling from one place to another. You are far more vulnerable and a far easier target when you are away from home and away from your familiar surroundings. Whether you travel for business or for pleasure, there are steps you can take to help protect yourself and your family. You should be knowledgeable regarding the terrorist threat in each of your destinations, as well as the steps you can take to avoid becoming a victim. Particularly when traveling in dangerous or semi-dangerous areas, be alert and aware of your surroundings at all times.

Additional things you can do to increase your chances of survival are:

- When driving, remain alert and aware of your immediate surroundings. Always drive defensively and be prepared to respond to changing situations around your vehicle.

- Do not publicize your travel plans. Tell your travel plans only to those who have a need to know. Treat documentation regarding your travel itinerary as "classified" information, and secure it in a safe place.

- Advise close friends or family members of your intended routes of travel and the approximate time you plan to arrive at your destination. Establish check-in procedures with your family, friends or employees, carrying a cell phone with you at all times.

- When possible, travel only on lighted, well-traveled main thoroughfares and avoid isolated back roads. If you can avoid traveling alone, do so. Avoid traveling in any known dangerous areas of your city.

- Try and allow yourself an avenue of escape when driving. Avoid allowing yourself to be "boxed in" by other vehicles. Travel in the lane that gives you the most room for escape. Always look for a "way out" if evasive action is necessary.

- When parked at a stoplight, stop sign or intersection, allow enough room between your vehicle and the car in front of you so that you can make an escape if necessary. Don't pull up closely to the bumper of the vehicle in front of you.

- Keep all doors locked and windows up to prevent unauthorized entry into your vehicle.

- Park unattended vehicles in a well lighted, secure area, keeping your car locked while parked. If your vehicle is so equipped, keep the alarm on.

- Keep your vehicle in good running condition, and wear your seatbelt at all times. In the event of an attack you may have to take evasive maneuvers, such as ramming another vehicle or driving at a high rate of speed. The seatbelt will help keep you from getting killed or injured in an intentional ramming maneuver and will keep you from sliding all over the seat during high speed, evasive driving. Don't make the mistake of thinking you will remember to put your seatbelt on at the time of the incident -- you won't. I have a friend whose car was intentionally rammed by a terrorist vehicle in Afghanistan. The terrorist, who was not wearing a seatbelt, was thrown through the windshield of his car and died at the scene. My friend was securely buckled up and survived with only minor injuries. Wear your seatbelt.

- If you can, use local license plates on your vehicle. Stay away from "vanity" plates or anything else that could distinguish your vehicle from others. For the same reason, avoid driving a vehicle that stands out among the other cars on the street. You should drive a vehicle that allows you to blend in with the local populace, if possible. Terrorists in places like Iraq, Afghanistan and Pakistan have reported that Americans are easy to identify because their vehicles stand out from those of the locals. Try to blend in as much as possible. Knock a few dents in your car and hang a pair of fuzzy dice from your mirror!

- Pay attention to your surroundings when driving. Do not allow yourself to get distracted by other passengers in your vehicle, the radio, or anything else. Always be on the lookout for surveillance. Know where the chokepoints are and be especially vigilant when approaching one. Pay attention to other vehicles and pedestrians around you and play the "when/then" game. Report any unusual activity to the authorities immediately.

- Avoid traveling in any "problem" areas that are hostile to Americans, or places known to have political or civil demonstrations on a regular basis. Avoid high crime areas.

- Conduct a route analysis or security survey of the routes and locations you frequently travel or visit. Identify "safe havens" -- places you can retreat to in an emergency. Some good safe havens are police stations, military installations, government buildings, the US Embassy or the embassies of other countries, hospitals, and similar locations.

- Always keep your gas tank at least half full. You don't want to be making your escape from a terrorist attack and run out of gas.

- It should go without saying, but do not pick up strangers or hitchhikers, regardless of the circumstances. Don't stop to help anyone. Use your cell phone to summon assistance for them, but don't stop your vehicle. Be aware of "diversionary" tactics that terrorists may use to try and get you to stop, such as someone trying to flag you down for assistance

- When traveling commercially, move through the inspection and check-in areas as quickly as possible, staying in security-controlled areas.

- On buses, planes, trains, etc. attempt to sit near an exit. Know how to open the exit doors.

- When traveling on public transportation, avoid flashy, ostentatious displays of money, jewelry and other personal effects. Try to fit in with the locals and become anonymous. Do not attract undue attention to yourself. If this is not possible, consider taking another mode of transportation.

- When using taxis, vary the pick up and departure points. Be familiar with your route so you will know if the driver is taking you there by the most expeditious route. Always call for a taxi, or have the concierge at your hotel call a taxi for you. Avoid randomly flagging one on the street.

- If you have a "pool" of vehicles in your agency or office, try to rotate the vehicles so that you don't become associated with any one vehicle.

- Always examine your vehicle before entering it. Look for evidence of tampering or any unusual objects on, under or around your vehicle. If you see something suspicious, do not handle it. Call the authorities immediately.

- Be aware of individuals loitering near your vehicle. If you sense that something is wrong, it probably is. Listen to your sixth sense and go back inside your home or building until the authorities have checked it out and it is safe to leave.

- Above all, when traveling, do not be time and place predictable. Vary your routes, times of arrival and departure, stops, and mode of travel as much as possible.

The Twenty Rules for Counter Terrorist Driving

1. Prepare your car for evasive maneuvers by keeping it maintained and in good running condition.
2. Know all possible routes between home and work or other locations you frequent on a regular basis.
3. Vary your routes.
4. Be aware of your location at all times.
5. Know the locations of "safe havens".
6. Be alert when entering and exiting your vehicle.
7. Arrange your car mirrors for maximum visibility to the rear.
8. Never leave your car keys with anyone you don't know and trust and don't keep your house keys on your car key ring.
9. Time your driving to use the minimum number of stops.
10. Be alert to anything that causes you to make an abnormal stop.
11. If forced to make an abnormal stop, drive around it as quickly as possible.
12. Do not stop to help anyone.
13. Be extra alert when approaching "chokepoints".
14. Play the "what if" game. Continually be in the planning process.
15. Pay attention to other vehicles around you.
16. Do not stop at the same places at the same times.
17. Make sure a trusted person knows your itinerary.
18. Use major roads when possible. Avoid side streets.
19. Always watch for surveillance and report any unusual activity at once.
20. If attacked, take control of the situation. Get off the "X" and out of the kill zone as quickly as possible. ❖

"To be on the alert is to live; to be lulled into security is to die."

~ Oscar Wilde

STAYING SAFE AT HOME

Threats to Your Home's Security

Your home is the one place where you should feel safe. It should be a sanctuary for you and your family and a place to relax, away from the everyday stresses of life.

Your home, however, is the one place that terrorists know, without a doubt, where you can be found. Even a minimal amount of surveillance will let them know when you and your family are home.

Your common, everyday burglar (not known for being overly intelligent) is an expert at determining when you are at home and when you are away. How much more so is the terrorist, having many more resources at his disposal. Terrorists have been known to conduct extensive surveillance of a prospective victim, sometimes for weeks or even months, without the victim's having a clue that his home was being watched.

It is imperative that the security of your residence be a high priority and it is mandatory for you take proactive steps to ensure that your home remains your inviolate castle.

The Improvised Explosive Device (IED)

Improvised explosive devices, commonly known as IEDs, are increasingly becoming the favorite terrorist method of attack. Improvised explosive device is simply another term for "homemade bomb". Many of these devices can be made using normal, readily available household items that can be purchased in any hardware or home supply store. The bomb that took down the Alfred Murrah Federal Building in Oklahoma City was made of fertilizer and fuel oil.

Although homemade, and usually quite simple in construction, terrorist IEDs can do extraordinary damage. They are nothing to take lightly. If you suspect that you have received an IED by mail or any other method of delivery, do not handle it. Get everyone safely out of the area and call the police. Important safety tip: do not use your cell phone or a radio in the immediate vicinity of what you believe is a bomb or IED. The electrical impulses may set it off.

Abandoned vehicles are a favorite hiding place for bombs. If you see an abandoned vehicle parked near your residence, place of business or while you are driving, notify the police or security. Look for suspicious devices left unattended in your driveway, the parking lot of your office, on your doorstep, or other similar locations.

Your Mail and the IED

Often, improvised explosive devices are disguised as packages, books or letters. You, your family and employees, including all domestic workers, should be familiar with security procedures for handling mail. Following are some basic guidelines:

- Do not accept unexpected packages or parcels without a return address.
- If an unexpected package is delivered, verify the sender before accepting it.
- Examine all mail, parcels and packages to determine if they have been tampered with. Visually inspect them for the absence of a return address or unfamiliar return address. Be alert to packages arriving by international mail; having excessive postage (this is a big clue); letters weighing more than normal; items marked with the words "confidential", "personal", "eyes only", or "to be opened only by ---". Be wary of wires or similar material protruding from the package, grease spots on the letter or package, and anything out of the ordinary.
- Immediately isolate any suspicious letters, parcels or packages. Absolutely do not pass the package around or let other people handle it. Slowly set the package down in a "safe area", getting everyone out of the room as quickly as possible. Close the door to the room and do not allow anyone to enter until the arrival of the police or bomb squad.
- Evacuate the immediate area and notify the authorities.

Telephoned Bomb Threats

In the event that you, a member of your family or staff receives a bomb threat via telephone, there are some specific procedures that should be taken. Upon receiving a telephonic bomb threat, remain calm and listen carefully to what the caller says. You should gather as much information as possible. This information can be used to help track down the source of the call and counter the threat. If you can, try and record the exact words of the caller. Attempt to get answers from the caller to the following questions:

1. When is the bomb set to go off?
2. Where is the bomb located?

3. What kind is it and what does it look like?
4. Who are you? (The caller may identify himself as part of a terrorist group, which will greatly aid the police in his capture).
5. Why are you threatening us?

You should make every attempt to identify the caller by listening for certain characteristics. Is the caller male, female, adult or child? Is the voice remarkable in some way (accent, loud, soft, deep)? Is speech fast, slow, slurred, obscene, calm, educated? Did you hear any background noise, such as street or traffic sounds, airplanes, other voices in the background or any sounds that may give an indication where the caller is located? Did the caller seem familiar with your residence, office or building by describing characteristics of it?

Gathering as much information as possible not only aids the police in the identification and capture of the suspects, but can also aid the bomb squad if they have to deactivate the device. That is why it is so important to attempt getting the caller to tell you what kind of device he has planted. Some bombs have pressure switches and others are activated manually or electrically. There are many ways to build a bomb and any information you can get will help the bomb squad detect and disarm it. The information you get from the caller may mean nothing to you, but it might mean a great deal to the bomb-squad technicians. Do not discount anything he or she says, and report it all.

Above all, treat every bomb threat as legitimate. There should be no differentiation in your procedures for handling what may seem to be a hoax call and what is a real threat.

Protecting Your Home

Most of the following "twenty common sense rules for residential protection" are, indeed, common sense and you should make it a priority to incorporate them into your "security posture". You will notice that these rules involve spending little or no money to incorporate. They require only a change in your behavior.

Twenty "Common Sense" Rules for Residential Protection

1. Be alert for any signs of unusual activity around your residence. Look for signs of surveillance on your person or your property.
2. Don't carry your car keys and house keys on the same ring and do not have your address affixed to your house keys.
3. Avoid the use of any type of identifying descriptors on your mailbox, door, gates, etc., or anything which could expose your status.
4. Never give your address to unknown individuals.
5. Keep a cell phone in the area of your residence that you have designated as a "safe haven".
6. Do not react to a telephone call from an unknown person who alleges that a member of your family has been involved in an accident, injury or some other type of emergency, until you have verified its legitimacy through a secondary source, such as a hospital or police department.
7. Avoid becoming involved in local disputes. If a stranger tries to involve you in a dispute, leave the area immediately.
8. When departing your residence, leave an interior light and a radio or television on to give the impression that someone is home.
9. When leaving your residence for an extended period of time, arrange to have all deliveries stopped.
10. Be particularly alert when arriving and departing your residence and be suspicious of anything that appears to be out of the ordinary.
11. Prior to entering or leaving your residence make it a habit to stop and observe anything unusual or out of place. If you see anything of a suspicious nature, do not enter or leave. Immediately notify the authorities.
12. Closely examine all mail received at your residence, particularly that which is unsolicited or comes from an unknown source.
13. Assume a low profile in your neighborhood. Get to know your neighbors and solicit their help in keeping a watch on your property. They will probably know better than you what or who is unusual or out of place in the neighborhood.
14. Repairmen and other service people should come by appointment only. Be sure to check their identification and verify that they are who they say they are. Do not leave them alone in the residence unsupervised.
15. Be alert to any suspicious persons working around your residence. Terrorist groups have a history of utilizing a "cover", such as public utility workers or road repair crews, enabling them to gain access to their victims.
16. Do not frequent the same establishments at the same time each day.

17. Do not provide unknown persons or callers information about yourself, your family, your friends, or your work associates without first establishing their bona fides and their need to know this information.
18. Be alert to sudden, unexplained absences of local nationals who are normally present in your neighborhood. It's possible they are aware of pending trouble of which you have no knowledge.
19. If you have a firearm, make sure you get the proper training in its use and storage. Brief your family members on its location and your plans to use it in an emergency.
20. Prepare and keep in your possession a card with relevant medical and emergency contact information that can be used in an emergency situation or in the event you are unable to communicate. Each family member should have one of these cards.

The Safety of your Physical Residence

This residential security questionnaire is very similar to the one provided for U.S. Government employees residing abroad. Each question is designed to elicit a "yes" response. Your goal should be to eliminate all "no" responses as you work to improve the security of your home and family. A one hundred percent "yes" response does not make you and your family terrorist proof, but it does significantly improve your security posture.

The Exterior
1. Do you have a fence around your property and is it in good repair?
2. Are the gates adequate and in good repair?
3. Are the gates properly secured during both day and night?
4. Are there any poles, trees, boxes, etc. that might help an intruder scale the fence?
5. Have you eliminated or cut back on shrubbery around the windows and doors of your residence?
   Note: Shrubbery provides an excellent hiding place for criminals and terrorists. Look at your property with an eye toward eliminating those hiding places.
6. Do you leave exterior lights on at night?
7. Do your exterior lights illuminate all areas around your residence?
8. Do you check regularly to see that the lights are working properly?
   Note: Be alert to any lights that are regularly removed or damaged. This may be an indication that criminals or terrorists are planning an attack.

Doors
1. Do you have deadbolt locks on your exterior doors?
2. Are they in good working order and do you use them?
3. Can any of your door locks be accessed by breaking out a glass window or panel located on or near the door?
4. Do you have more than one lock on each exterior door, and if so, do you use them both?
5. Can all of your exterior doors be securely locked (basement, garage, porch, etc.)?
6. Are your locks the best available and in good working order?
7. Do you know and trust everyone who has a key to your house?
   Note: You should change the locks every time you move into a new residence.

8. Are all unused doors permanently secured?
9. Are all locks securely mounted to both the door and the doorframe or wall?
10. Is your spare key in a secure location?
    Note: Under the doormat, on a sill above the door, and in a flowerpot are not secure locations!
11. Are exterior door hinge pins secured against removal?
12. Are the door hasps installed so that the screws cannot be removed?
13. Are the hasps and staple plates mounted so that they cannot be pried off?
14. If you use a padlock on doors, gates, etc., do you lock it in a secure place when it is not in use?
    Note: Criminals and terrorists can easily replace your padlock with one of their own, thereby giving them easy access to your residence or out buildings.

Windows
- Are all unused windows permanently closed and secured?
- Are window locks properly installed and securely mounted?
- Do you keep your windows locked when shut?
- Are those windows located on the ground floor and in the basement locked?
- Are all ladders and other objects that can be used for climbing locked up?
- Do you have a rod or bar in your sliding glass doors to prevent them from being pried open?

Garage
- Do you lock your garage at night?
- Do you lock your garage when you are away from home?
- Are your garage doors and windows equipped with locks?
- Are the garage door locks in good working order?
- If you have other out buildings such as sheds, etc. are they properly secured when not in use?

Apartment Residences

Dangers of Apartment Living Overseas

Many people living and working abroad reside in apartment house-type dwellings, which present some unique security issues. Generally, you are safer in a single family home, as you can control ingress and egress from your home much easier than you can from an apartment building. Living in an apartment also means that you probably won't know all of your neighbors. The transient nature of residents in apartment buildings makes it impossible to determine the identities of all your neighbors. Are they generally law-abiding citizens or might they be members of a terrorist or criminal enterprise? If not actual members of a terrorist group, might they be sympathetic to a terrorist cause and therefore easily "co-opted". Could a terrorist or foreign intelligence agency use them to help conduct surveillance on you and your families? Keep in mind that a terrorist group looking at you as a possible target could rent an apartment in your building (ideally next door to you). This would provide an ideal situation for conducting surveillance on you and in planning the operation. Police officers and federal agents frequently rent units adjacent to a suspect they are investigating, in order to build a case. They use these rooms or apartments to either conduct surveillance or to place listening devices.

In many countries local terrorist organizations are much like the old time mafia or big city political bosses of yesteryear. They control the neighborhoods and everything going on in them. Even residents who don't necessarily agree with their policies and tactics are often too afraid to say "no" when approached and asked for their assistance.

The apartment manager, building superintendent or engineer, security guards, or maintenance people could also be members of a terrorist organization or be co-opted by them. What better asset could a terrorist group have than a person with a key to your apartment? Foreign intelligence agencies have been employing this method for years as a means to spy on resident aliens in their countries. Remember, in some areas of the world the majority of the populace reveres terrorists as "freedom fighters". They are sympathetic to their causes and will gladly assist them when asked. Living and working safely in an environment such as this is challenging, at best.

Another thing to consider when living in an apartment building abroad is that you are living among all types of people, many of whom are foreigners from other nations. Terrorists have no qualms about blowing up a building to get one person, even though many other innocent people may be killed and injured in the process. You may not even be the target they are after. Someone else in the building may be the subject of a terrorist attack and you are simply caught in the crossfire, an innocent victim. A bomb planted by a terrorist intended for someone else does not discriminate. When it is detonated, if you are unfortunate enough to be in the vicinity, you are just as dead as the intended victim. Witness the US embassy bombing in Nairobi, Kenya and Dar-Es-Salaam, Tanzania in 1998. For the sake of killing a few Americans, Al-Qaeda was willing to sacrifice hundreds of innocent Kenyans and Tanzanians who were working in or near the embassy at the time of the blast. The bomb was not intended for them. They were simply in the wrong place at the wrong time.

Natural disasters and fires are other things to be concerned about in many apartment complexes abroad, particularly those in Third World countries. Fire codes and regulations are not nearly as strict in most foreign nations as they are in the US and in other Western countries. Enforcement is nil and many buildings are so ancient that they have no safeguards against fire whatsoever. Buildings in Third World countries are usually of poor construction. In a natural disaster such as a flood or earthquake, they become death traps. I was in Cairo, Egypt once when a "minor" earthquake occurred. Several apartment buildings collapsed, resulting in the loss of many lives. Had this same earthquake occurred in California, it would have hardly made the news.

If you do decide to opt for apartment dwelling overseas, there are some important precautions you should take. Prior to signing a lease, be sure to ask the following questions:

- ♦ **Location:** Is the apartment located above ground level, but below the tenth floor? Ground level apartments are easy pickings for burglars and other undesirables. The windows and doors are easily accessible and sometimes shrubbery obscures visibility, thereby making a perfect hiding place for terrorists and criminals. You will also want to stay below the tenth floor because the fire apparatus of most cities does not reach beyond ten floors. (As an extra precaution, while overseas you may want to consider apartments between the second and seventh floors, for added fire and natural disaster safety).

- ♦ **Security Personnel:** What kind of personnel security does the building have? Do they have security guards? If so are they armed? If they are armed, are they trained sufficiently in the use of their weapons? Are they paid reasonably well? Have they been vetted to ensure they are not criminals or members of a terrorist group? Are they full or part-time security guards? In many countries police officers moonlight as security guards. This can be bad or good depending on the country in which you reside. Generally speaking, police officers are much better trained that the average security guard. That does not mean, however, that they can't be compromised by a terrorist organization. Do not be over confident just because the building hires a security guard. They generally scrape the bottom of the barrel to get someone who is barely competent, at best. Remember, the security guard is not responsible for the security of you and your family, you are.

- **Building Security:** Does the building have good physical access control? Is the front door to the lobby locked? If so, who has access to the keys? Are the locks changed on a regular basis? Does the building employ video cameras for security? Where are they located? Front door, rear doors, hallways, exterior alleys, elevators, etc.? Is anyone watching the monitors? If so, who? A security guard, receptionist, or doorman?

- **Alarm System:** Does your apartment have a security alarm system? If not, you might want to invest in a portable one you can place on the windows and doors. They are relatively inexpensive, and work pretty well.

- **Elevators:** Where are the elevators located? If they are in the lobby, are they under visual control of the receptionist, doorman or security guard?

- **Safety at Your Front Door:** Does the front door to your apartment have a peephole? Is your apartment alarmed? What kinds of locks are on the doors? Does the apartment management provide good deadbolt locks? If not, you should buy them and have them installed. Are the exterior doors to your apartment solid core doors? Do not move into an apartment that has hollow core exterior doors. They are extremely vulnerable to a break-in. Are the door hinges mounted so that the pins cannot be removed?

- **Windows:** Do all windows have functional locks? Even though you might live several stories up, don't assume that the bad guys can't get into your apartment via a window. Police and military units practice free climbing and rappelling to get into windows above the ground floor. There is nothing stopping terrorists and criminals from doing the same.

- **Sliding Glass Doors:** Are all sliding glass doors secured with "charley bars", as well as with good locks? Be careful of any residence with bars on the windows. While they provide excellent security, they may hinder you from getting out of a window in a fire. They also will hinder you from using the window as a secondary escape route in a home invasion or terrorist attack.

- **Stairs and Fire Escapes:** Do stairwells and fire escapes have any security devices? Are they alarmed and/or monitored by security cameras?

- **Your Keys:** Who has a key to your apartment? Were the locks changed when you moved in?

- **Balcony and Patio:** If you have a balcony or a patio to your apartment, is it accessible to others?

- **Lighting:** Is sufficient lighting available inside the building (stairwells, hallways, elevators), as well as the exterior (doorways, sidewalks, alleys, parking lots and garages)?

- **Alternative Entrances:** Does your apartment building have alternate points for arrivals and departures? Do you always have to go in the front door, or are there additional entrances you can use? Multiple entrances are both good and bad. They are good because you can vary the ways you enter and leave the building, thereby eliminating a major chokepoint. They are bad because multiple entrances are more difficult for security to monitor and control. If I had to choose, however, I would pick a building with multiple entrances and exits. I don't like chokepoints.

- **The Safe Room:** Is there a suitable room in your apartment that you can use as a safe room? Can it be strengthened with extra locks and are you able to keep a telephone or other communication gear in the room?
- **Your Neighbors:** Are there other Americans, Westerners or embassy personnel living in your apartment building? While it is good to have a few Westerners in your building, you want to make sure that the building is not designated exclusively for Americans and other Westerners. These types of buildings are of particular interest to terrorists. With only one bomb, they would obviously be able to kill or injure a maximum number of Westerners and Americans, giving the terrorists high value for their effort. In fact, a building of this type is referred to by terrorists as a "high value target", much as an embassy would be. If terrorists can penetrate an embassy (Kenya and Tanzania) or a highly protected military building (Kobar Towers), they should have no problem attacking an apartment building. If there are local nationals residing in your apartment building, the terrorists may be less likely to target that building and risk arousing the anger of local citizens.

The "Home Invasion"

On 27 February 1976, seven armed terrorists abducted American businessman, William Niehous, from his residence in Caracas, Venezuela. Niehous, who was vice-president of Owens-Illinois, was kidnapped in front of his wife and three sons, who were tied up during the incident. Niehous was held in a safe house for several months, until the terrorist's demands were finally met. Three of the terrorists turned out to be individuals who had been hired by Niehous to perform yard work around his residence.

Have you thought about what you would do if someone were to break into your home while you were present? How would you protect yourself and your family in the event that one or more people were attempting to gain access to your home? In my experience, most people don't have even the most basic plan to deal with a home invasion. (Most of them don't have a plan in the event of a fire either, but that's another book). Their plan, if they have one at all, usually consists of calling the police and hoping they could handle the situation. That might work if you live next door to a police station. In the United States, even in jurisdictions with an excellent police response time, the police would probably be too late to help. In the several minutes it would take for them to get to your residence, a desperate criminal or a dedicated terrorist could do a lot of damage. Police reaction time in most foreign countries, however, is far worse. Depending on where you live, you may or may not have reliable police protection. In some locations you are lucky if they show up at all. In any event, you should not depend on the police getting there while the attack is ongoing. On television the cops always get there just in the nick of time and rescue the terrified family. In real life it doesn't usually work that way. Every police officer worth his "salt" prays for the day he can catch a burglar or home invader in the act. Cops live to catch criminals red handed. It rarely happens. It is far more likely that by the time the police get there, the deed is done and the officers' job is reduced to taking a report and calling in the detectives to conduct the investigation.

Burglaries of occupied residences are increasing in frequency in the US and have always been a problem in most Third World countries. In fact, society has given a new term for this phenomenon – "home invasion". Wikipedia defines home invasion as "entering a private residence and occupied dwelling with the intent of committing a crime, often while threatening the resident of the dwelling". When I was a street cop back in the 70's and early 80's, the term "home invasion" was unknown, at least where I worked. Burglaries of occupied residences were extremely rare. Most burglars broke into a home for the sole purpose of committing a theft. This being the case, most burglars committed their acts when the residents were away from home and there were no witnesses to identify him.

Terrorists, on the other hand, are not concerned about getting arrested and going to trial. Their intent is not to steal your valuables, rape or rob you. What they want is you and possibly your family. Their intent is either to kill or to kidnap you or a family member. If you live in a part of the world prone to terrorism and kidnapping, you must make a plan to deal with the possibility of a home invasion. "Calling the police" is not a viable plan. Calling the police and hoping they show up in time to intervene is wishful thinking at best and absolute denial at worst. You and you alone are the person primarily responsible for the safety of your family. Even if you can afford to hire security officers to provide you and your family with protection 24 hours a day, 7 days a week, this does not absolve you of your responsibility. Security officers or "bodyguards" are notorious for being compromised by terrorist organizations. What would you do if your security guards are killed or otherwise disabled? What if they simply decide to run away? This has actually been known to happen in past incidents. If that becomes the case, you are on your own and you had better have a plan.

Your Plan

Formulating a basic plan of action is an essential step in protecting your family during a home invasion. As in formulating your plan to counter an attack on your vehicle, you should also keep your "home invasion" plan as simple as possible. Be sure to brief your family on the plan. Rehearse it several times, working out the kinks and assuring yourself that your family is completely familiar with it. Neither you nor your family members should have to stop and think through a complicated plan during an attack. All of you should be able to react immediately and automatically, just as you have done, hopefully, with fire drills. You should have a secondary and tertiary plan in the event the primary plan does not work, and you should be prepared to adapt to changes in the situation as they occur. Keep the plan as simple as possible.

Obviously, the more people living in your home, the more complicated your plan will be. If you have a spouse; children, especially young ones; elderly parents; or a handicapped person residing with you, you will have to devise a plan that will allow you to safely get to them and lead or carry them to safety. If your children are older and everyone is physically capable of responding, then you may want to devise a plan where they come to you. Whatever your plan, keep it simple, review it often in order to refresh your memory, and revise the plan if necessary. If you have a friend in law enforcement or have access to a US embassy security officer, you may want to have them take a look at your plan and get their input.

Your plan should incorporate a pre-selected escape route out of the house (window, door, etc) for every member of your family, as well as a pre-arranged meeting place away from the residence that will serve as your rally point. If you have a neighbor you can trust, his residence may be a good place for that. Try to keep your rally point easily accessible, one where they can get to quickly. Having an escape route out of the residence is mandatory, not only in the event of a home invasion, but also in the event of a fire. Have at least two ways of escape, a primary and a secondary means. If you have second-story bedrooms, it would be advisable to consider investing in a few escape ladders that can attach to the interior of your windowsill and roll out of the window as a means of escape. Do not, however, place a ladder or any other device on the exterior of your home. This would be equivalent to putting out a "welcome mat" to a terrorist or criminal. If you do purchase one of the "roll up" ladders, make sure you and your family practice deploying it and actually climb down the ladder. In the midst of an emergency is not the time to find out that the ladder is not adequately secure or long enough to reach the ground.

The Safe Room

In addition to having a plan of escape from your residence, I also strongly recommend that you have a plan in which everyone retreats to a "safe room" inside your residence. A safe room is a predetermined and secure location in your home set up specifically to serve as a retreat in the event of a home invasion.

Preparing Your Safe Room

The safe room can be an actual room or it can be a walk-in closet, attic, or similar area. The idea is to make the intruder's job more difficult and to buy some time to give the police or security services an opportunity to get to your home. Terrorists want to get in and accomplish their mission quickly and with little chance of detection. Your chances of survival are significantly increased if it takes them longer than they had planned to execute their mission. US Government employees living abroad have long been familiar with the concept of a safe room, and there have been examples of individuals and families utilizing their safe room to stay alive. The following are some criteria that every safe room should meet.

- If possible, the safe room should be an interior room, without windows and with one entry door. A walk-in closet adjacent to you bedroom is ideal. Keep in mind this will be an area that you and your family can retreat to in the event of other emergencies, such as hurricanes, tornados, and riots.

- You should install a solid core, outward-opening wood or steel door to your safe room. Reinforce the door and the doorframe as much as possible by installing heavy-duty hinges, screws and strike plates.

- Install a good dead-bolt lock on the door to your safe room. If the safe room is a closet within a room, you should install a similar deadbolt lock on the room door as well as on the closet door. This makes it doubly hard for the bad guys to get to you. A keyless deadbolt is best, since you don't have to worry about losing or misplacing the key. If you have a keyed deadbolt, be sure to take the key into the safe room with you.

- The safe room should be easily accessible to all members of the family. It may become too dangerous for a family member to get to the safe room. In that event they should be instructed to try and escape the residence and report to the "rally point", their pre-designated secondary safe area. In some cases you might want to have more than one "safe area" in your home. If you reside in a two-story home, having one upstairs and one downstairs would be best. You also might want to consider a secondary safe area in your children's room.

Furnishing Your Safe Room

Your safe room should include a fully charged cell phone containing pre-programmed emergency numbers. In the probable event the telephone lines to your home will be cut, your cell phone can literally be your lifeline.

Many families living abroad like to use radios to stay in touch with their neighbors or with the American Embassy. If you decide to store a radio in your safe room, be sure you keep extra batteries available for it.

Additionally, in the likely event you lose your electricity, you should have two good flashlights (an extra in case of malfunction) and spare batteries for these as well.

A good, fully equipped first aid kit containing several bandages (suitable for applying direct pressure to a wound) is also highly recommended.

If you own a firearm and know how to use it, I strongly recommend keeping one in your safe room. Obviously you should take precautions to safeguard the weapon, particularly if you have children or there are children who have access to your home. Your gun should be readily accessible to you, however, and you should have extra ammunition available. Most important, you need to be ready, willing and able to use it. After all, if someone has broken into your home and has made it as far as your safe room, their intentions are obvious -- they are after you and your family. If they make it through the safe room door, consider them fair game.

If you choose not to keep a firearm in your home, at least consider investing in a non-lethal weapon, such as pepper spray. Although hardened terrorists will not be intimidated by something as benign as pepper spray, it may very well defeat the common criminal, or allow you and your family an opportunity to escape. It is best to have some sort of weapon, even if it is only a baseball bat – something is always better than nothing!

Ideally, you will have something to use as "cover" in your safe room in case there is gunfire. Cover is anything that can stop a bullet. A heavy safe, a large piece of furniture, or any heavy item can serve as cover. If you are in your bedroom, getting behind the bed or a large dresser is probably your best cover. You will want to get your family and yourself as securely behind cover as possible. Even if you don't get in a gunfight with the terrorists or criminals, police or other rescuers may. In many cases, due to high stress and confusion, they will not be aware of where their rounds are going. The last thing you need is to be shot by one of your rescuers. Stay low and behind cover as much as possible. When you call the police or local security services, be sure and tell them where you are located in the house. It is also important, if you are armed, to let them know. Whatever you do, don't approach the police or security services with a gun in your hand. In all of the excitement you could easily be mistaken for a bad guy. Stay with your family until the police get there and you know it's safe to come out, and then do so without your gun and with your hands visible to the police officers.

The "bug out bag"

There is one item that I would always recommend to our employees who were going overseas, whether it was job related or pleasure. I suggested that they assemble what I refer to as a "bug out bag", and that they carry this bag with them on their trip. I used to recommend carrying a "bug out bag" only for those employees going to high threat areas, such as parts of Africa and the Middle East. With today's international terrorist, however, almost anywhere overseas is a potential danger area.

A "bug out bag" is simply a small bag (canvas, leather, etc) that you have packed with items you may need in an emergency, especially if you have to "bug out" of your residence or office in a hurry. It would probably be preferable to have two of these bags – one to keep at your residence and another at your place of work. These simple items may very well be the key to your survival if you have to make an escape from a dangerous area and get to a safe location. What items should you carry in your "bug out bag"?

- **A small handgun (if you can legally do so).** If you carry a handgun and do not choose to carry it on your person, a "bug out bag" is a good place for it. The kind of handgun you carry is up to you, but I recommend at least a .38 caliber revolver or a 9mm semi-automatic pistol. Most of the major gun manufacturers make some excellent small, compact, lightweight pistols and revolvers up to .45 caliber. Be sure to carry several extra fully-loaded magazines.
- **A good flashlight.** The technology in small, hand-held flashlights today is amazing. There are many models on the market that provide excellent illumination and have hours of run time. Choose a small, lightweight one, making sure you carry extra batteries. You don't want to find out at the very moment you need your flashlight that your batteries are dead.
- **Cash and a credit card.** Chances are, in the event of a terrorist incident or another emergency, you will need money for transportation, food, and other necessities. Having cash on hand is also good in the event you need to bribe someone. There are very few places in the Third World where you can't get everything you need by bribing an official with a few dollars. You may also need money to pay a cab driver or another form of transportation to transport you to a safe area.
- **A good map of the area.** Obtain a small, compact map of the area in which you are operating, living or working. If you find yourself in an area in which you don't have good familiarization, a map is an invaluable resource.
- **A small multi-tool type knife.** The knife company, Swiss Army Knives, as well as other knife and tool companies, makes a small device known as a multi-tool. These devices generally have a knife blade, a pair of pliers, a file, tweezers, and other gadgets that may come in useful in an emergency. In addition to the various tools this device contains, it has a knife blade which can be used a weapon in an emergency.
- **A foldable "space" blanket.** You can buy these "space blankets" at any camping supply store. They are small, foldable Mylar blankets that can easily fit in your pocket and are used in survival situations to keep you warm. Most of the space blankets I have were given to me at the finish line after I had completed marathon races. These compact blankets are excellent for helping to retain body heat. If you find yourself having to spend the night outside, one of these inexpensive items can save your life.
- **Waterproof matches.** Again, nice to have if you find yourself spending the night in the woods.

There are other items you may store in your "bug out bag", depending on the area in which you are operating, living and working. You may want to consider a small bottle of water and some food items. Power Bars and other such foods are excellent items to keep in your bag -- they last forever and can provide you with sustainable nutrition in a compact form. Again, the part of the world in which you find yourself determines what will go in your "bug out bag". In you are in a largely urban area, what you will carry is vastly different from what you will need in the jungle, desert or similar rural environment. Personal preference also plays a part in what you carry. The main thing is to have one that suits your needs and is ready for any emergency. Being victimized by a terrorist group or having another type of emergency is not your fault. Failure to prepare for it is.

Devising Code Words

Devise a code word that you can use to communicate to your family what it is you want them to do. For instance, the word "blue" could mean to rally to the primary safe area, while the word "red" could mean to evacuate the residence. The reason you will want to use a code word is to (a) keep unnecessary talking to a minimum and (b) not alerting the bad guys to your plan. If you were to say, "Go to my bedroom" or "Crawl through the window", it would simply alert them to your intentions. Don't tip your hand to the bad guys. Use code words whenever possible. If you have small children, you can make a game out of it when rehearsing your plans. Use a stopwatch to time them, seeing how long it takes them to get to the safe room or to exit the residence and get to the pre-determined rally point. Practice these drills over and over and try to improve their response times. While rehearsing your plan, you will be building "muscle-memory" in yourself and in your family through repeated repetitions. That way, if you have to execute your plan for real, it will be almost second nature to them. Your family will react automatically without having to do a lot of thinking, which is counterproductive and takes up valuable escape time.

Keeping Your Children Safe

The security of yourself and your family at home is only as strong as the weakest link -- and sometimes the weakest link are your children. I'm not too worried about something happening to me because I have enough confidence to believe I can take care of myself. Something happening to my children or grandchildren is another matter altogether. Think about it. If a terrorist wanted to inflict maximum terror on a family or a society at large, there is no worse thing he could do than to attack the children. That is precisely what a group of Chechen terrorists did on 1 September 2004 when they stormed a school in the town of Beslan, North Ossetia, Russia. For three days they held over 1200 children and adults hostage, eventually killing 344 people, of whom 186 were innocent children.

Living and working overseas has its own set of problems, not the least of which is providing for the safety and security of your family. If you are a potential target of a terrorist group, then you must assume that your family is as well. Your spouse and children should be fully briefed on what to do to detect, prevent and defeat a terrorist incident. There are certain safeguards and security measures they should take and it is your job to ensure that they know what to do. You are the principal person responsible for their safety and security.

First of all, your family members should be aware of the situation regarding crime and terrorism in the area in which you reside. Do not try to shield them from the reality of living abroad. The world can be a dangerous place, and they need to be aware that there are bad people out there who, given the opportunity, would harm them. In many ways your family is just as much a target as you are, maybe even more so, since criminals and terrorists consider them a "soft" target (i.e., an easy target having very little security). Following are some of the precautions you should take to prepare your children for the worst:

- Make sure your children know the location of the "safe room" in your home and how to safely and quickly get there in an emergency. The older children may be able to get to the safe room on their own, but you may have to go and get the younger ones. Also, make sure they know the "code word" you will use when you want them to retreat to the safe room. Just as you

would, hopefully, practice a fire drill in your home, make sure to practice an "emergency response drill" with your family. You can even make a game out of it. Use a stopwatch to time them to see how long it takes them to run from their bedrooms to the safe room. A little competition between the kids (and the adults) can be fun while also teaching them a valuable skill. (Although this is serious business, try not to come across as too serious. There's no sense in frightening your children to the point of making them paranoid).

- Identify a safe location outside of your home where the family can rally to if staying in the home is not an option (a "rally point"). Suppose you are the victim of a home invasion in the middle of the night. You will probably retreat to your safe room; however, it may be too dangerous for family members in other parts of the house to get to the safe room. The bad guys might be blocking the way. In that case, you have hopefully identified a secondary escape route, possibly out of a window or another doorway, where your children can safely escape. They can then go to a rally point well away from the main house and wait until it is safe to return (usually after the police get there). Ideally, this rally point would be a trusted neighbor's house (be sure to brief your neighbor on your plan!). It could also be an outbuilding on your property, a nearby public building (hospital, police station, etc.) or another safe location that you have pre-identified. It wouldn't hurt to have a tertiary rally point location, just in case the safe room and the secondary safe areas are unavailable for some reason. For instance, the safe room could be "Safe Area Number One", your detached garage could be "Safe Area Number Two", and your neighbor's house could be "Safe Area Number Three". You could have pre-arranged words or signals for each safe area and a plan that details how to get to each one quickly and safely.

- Tell your children that during a home invasion you may have to come to their room and get them. They should retreat to a safe area inside their own room, possibly in a closet or under a bed. It is important that you identify the safe area beforehand so that you aren't tearing through their bedroom frantically looking for them while the bad guys are charging up the stairs. Keep a fully charged flashlight beside their bed, and if they have a cell phone, tell them to take it to their safe area with them.

- Instruct your children what to do in the event that you are in your car when a terrorist tries to run you off the road, stop you at a roadblock, or begins firing into your vehicle. Children should be instructed to always keep their seat belt securely fastened in case you have to make high speed, evasive or ramming maneuvers with your vehicle. They should also be told to get down as low in the seat as possible, keeping their heads below window level, in the event terrorists begin shooting. The car windows should also be up to prevent anyone from throwing an explosive, such as a Molotov cocktail or an IED into the car. Should the car be disabled, you should tell them to exit the vehicle as quickly as possible and to rally around you. Once you have accounted for all of your family members, you should then make your way quickly out of the "kill zone" and to a safe location.

- Your children should be told to report any "strange or unusual behavior" in your neighborhood, around their school, at their playgrounds, on their routes to and from home, etc. Of course they should first be briefed on what constitutes "strange and unusual" behavior. Most parents do a good job of telling their children what to look for in terms of "stranger danger", and other such things. However, the typical terrorist who is conducting surveillance on you or your family will probably not exhibit the same characteristics as the ubiquitous "stranger" that kids are told to avoid. Children should be encouraged to report any unusual behavior they observe, particularly if someone is asking them personal questions about themselves, their parents, or any other members of their family. Because they are generally friendly and talkative, kids can unknowingly be a good source of intelligence for terrorists who are planning an operation against you or you family.

- Children should be instructed to keep doors and windows secured, and not to disable alarm systems. They should never admit unknown persons into the home, nor should they answer questions from a "solicitor" who appears at the door, even if this person appears benign, unthreatening or official. Remember, one thing terrorist groups must do before conducting an attack is to gather intelligence. They also may conduct "probes" of your residence to try and determine where the weak links in your security are. What better way to gain access to the home than getting a child to open the door for you? Tell your children to beware of people who may be masquerading as utility workers, distressed motorists looking for help, or even police officers or other officials. You should instruct them that, when in doubt, do not open the door for anyone, and alert an adult in the home immediately.

- Insist that your children travel in groups, or at least in pairs, whenever they leave the house. There is safety in numbers.

- Instruct your children to use heavily traveled streets and to go to playgrounds, parks, etc. that are not isolated. Tell them to avoid alleys, dark streets, and similar potential danger areas.

- Your family should not be "time and place predictable" either. If you, your spouse or an employee takes your children to and from school or other appointments each day, make sure that they are not "time and place predictable". They should have a couple of different routes to school, and vary those as much as possible. Even varying your departure and arrival times by a few minutes can help to defeat a possible terrorist attack. Timing is everything in planning a terrorist incident such as a route bomb or a kidnapping, so if you can disrupt the terrorist's timing you stand a good chance of defeating the attack before it occurs.

- Your children should be advised to absolutely never accept a ride from a stranger or to go with a stranger anywhere on foot. Tell them that if they are approached in such a manner, they should throw down their books and backpacks and run, making as much noise as possible while doing so. This should be easy for them, as running and making a lot of noise comes naturally to children!

- Make sure that, when leaving home, your children tell you where they are going, who they will be with, and when they will return. Many older kids, as well as, some younger ones carry cell phones. For a few dollars you can obtain tracking devices that are embedded in their cell phones that monitor the location of your children. You should strongly consider purchasing one, particularly if you live and work overseas.

- If you live in a foreign country, teach your children some useful phrases in the native language. Make sure they know the location of the nearest police station and hospital and how to get there.

- Enroll your children in self-defense classes.

As to the self-defense classes, let's face it, there are criminal predators out there, both in the United States and abroad and they target children for the purpose of victimizing them. Terrorist groups also target children. What more effective way to inflict maximum terror upon a society than to target its children? For these reasons you should teach you children how to protect themselves. I am a big proponent of kids learning some type of martial art or defensive tactics. Not only does learning a martial art teach them how to defend themselves, but the good schools also teach them discipline and respect for others. Additionally, it is a good way for kids to stay in shape while simultaneously learning something useful. If you, as a parent, have good martial arts and defensive tactics skills, then by all means teach your children at home.

There are good martial arts schools all over the world, many of which specialize in teaching children and are very good at what they do. The style of martial arts you select and the school you choose should be one that you and your child are totally comfortable with, and that would most likely be one that caters primarily to children. I have studied several different styles of martial arts and taught them extensively, and I can tell you that there are pros and cons to all styles. There is no "perfect" martial arts or defensive tactics system out there, regardless of what the owner may tell you (his main focus could be getting you to sign a fat contract). The perfect system for you and your child is the one that your child likes. After all, if it's not fun for your child, he will not want to go (my wife and I raised five kids, so ask me how I know that!). I have seen parents spend enormous amounts of money to sign their children up for karate class, only to discover that the child does not like it and refuses to go. Again, the important thing is that your child enjoys going to class, learns some basic self-defense skills as well as discipline, and gets in good physical condition. This last criterion is not to be taken lightly. In an emergency situation your child may have to either (a) fight, (b) run, or (c) run and fight to save his or her life. This requires being in good physical condition. The kid who sits around eating Ding Dongs, staring at video games or the computer all day is not going to be in good enough shape to protect him or herself in an emergency. This fact also applies to adults who sit around eating Ding Dongs and watch TV, instead of working out.

If you can't afford to sign your child up for karate class or there is no martial arts school nearby, you can still teach them some basic self-defense moves at home. There are some excellent books and videos available today, and I recommend that you purchase some of these to aid you in teaching your child. Additionally, the Internet is full of advice on how to keep your children safe. Many local police departments have excellent self-defense programs for women and children, often at little or no cost.

Some basic techniques children and adults can use to fight off an attacker are: the eye gouge, a pencil or pen to the eye or soft tissue of the throat, an elbow to the attacker's nose, a knee to the groin, a kick to the shins or instep, using a comb to rake across the attacker's eyes, biting, scratching, yelling, and the best one, in my opinion, is running away while screaming at the top of their lungs. Some of these techniques (sharpened pencil to the eye) may seem like harsh methods to be teaching a child, but remember, we are talking about saving his or her life. When they are getting abducted by a terrorist or criminal is not the time for them to be gentle and to use their "inside voices". You must teach them to do whatever it takes to get away from the threat. They should be encouraged to do anything and everything to facilitate their escape and keep them alive. Once they have made their escape, they should be told to run and to keep running until they are completely safe and out of harm's way.

Again, the safety and security of your family is chiefly your responsibility. Prepare them for the worst and pray for the best. Sit them down and give them a "reality briefing" on the current terrorist and criminal situation in your locality. Don't "sugar coat" the situation. Tell it like it is. Denial does not serve a useful purpose when it comes to the security of your family. Go over some escape and evasion techniques with them. Although some of these things may seem "boring and stupid" to them at the time (especially if they are teenagers or pre-teens), they will thank you for it later.

In summary, the key to surviving a home invasion is what I refer to as the Three "Ps" -- planning, preparation and practice. Develop two or three good plans; prepare yourself, your family and your home; and practice diligently. Hopefully you will never need to implement your plan or use you safe room for an emergency. In the event that you do, however, you will be ready. You and your family stand a far better chance of survival by practicing preparedness.

State Department Recommendations for Residential Security

Regarding your residence, the U.S. State Department recommends taking the following precautions, especially when living abroad. Have a security survey done on your residence. Adopt all of the recommendations made by the Regional Security Officer or other official who will be conducting the survey. Make sure you have addressed satisfactorily each of the following items:

- Who lived in your residence prior to you?
- Did you consider security in selecting your residence?
- How did you select your residence? Did a local real estate agent assist you? Did you check on his or her reputation, reliability and trustworthiness? Terrorist groups are known to use real estate personnel and other individuals who are involved in the housing market to identify the houses of prospective targets.

- Did you change or re-key all locks after moving in? Do you maintain strict control of all residential keys? Do you keep a key "hidden" outside of your residence? (A tip: the bad guys know to look under the doormat or in a flowerpot for the spare key). Do you allow your neighbor to have a key to your home?
- Is your family briefed on what to do if a salesman, service person or other solicitor comes to your door?
- Are you and your family familiar with the local police? Do you know what types of uniforms they wear and what credentials they carry?
- Have you put into place procedures for accepting deliveries? Are suspicious or unexpected deliveries refused? Do you verify the identities of delivery people?
- Do you verify the identities of repairmen and service representatives? Are they closely supervised while in the residence? Has someone you trust recommended them to you? Do they schedule appointments or just show up unannounced? (Discourage them from showing up without an appointment.)
- Have family members been instructed not to unlock or open doors to persons they do not know? Are doors and windows always kept locked?
- Do you employ cooks, gardeners, maids or other similar individuals? Did someone you trust recommend them? Did they approach you and ask for a job or did you solicit them? Did they provide references and did you check them? Did you check police and security services records for involvement in any criminal, terrorist or subversive type activities?
- Do employees have unlimited access to the residence? Do their family members? Do they have a key to your residence?
- Have you had occasion to dismiss any employees? Did they have keys to your residence?
- Do you or your family members provide transportation to and from work for your employees? (I recommend that you refrain from this, as it is generally a dangerous practice. Pay for their bus or taxi fare instead).
- Do your employees have access to your travel schedules? If so, how far in advance do they have them?
- Is your residence left unattended during the day? Is it left unattended daily or only occasionally?
- Do you employ security guards? Are they from a private contractor or are they off-duty military or police officers? Do you pay them or does the company pay them?
- Do the security guards appear to be professional and well trained? Are they armed? Are they qualified with the weapons they carry?
- Is your name on mailboxes and other public locations where people can see it?
- Do you have a telephone? Do you have at least one cell phone? Do you have a listed or an unlisted telephone number?
- Have you received threatening phone calls or an unusually high number of "wrong numbers" or silent callers? Have you maintained a log of these calls? Have you reported them to police or security officials?

STAYING SAFE AT HOME

- Have you instructed your family members how to answer the phone and how to respond to questions from unknown callers? An unknown caller is someone whom you personally do not know and whose identity you cannot verify over the phone. Absolutely do not give out any information until the identity of the caller is established.

- Do you know your neighbors? Once you do get to know them, you can ask them to report any suspicious activity or persons in the neighborhood to you. You should also ask them to report anyone asking questions about you or your family.

- Do you and your family know where the nearest police station is? Have you identified other safe areas for your family to go in an emergency? (This is another good reason for getting to know your neighbors. A neighbor's residence can be a good place to retreat to in an emergency. Just be sure and fill them in on your plan. You don't want to get shot by your neighbor when you are banging on his door at three o'clock in the morning).

- Do you and your family know enough about the neighborhood to be able to tell when something is out of place? Do you notice strange people or vehicles in the neighborhood?

- Do you own a dog? A recent survey of incarcerated criminals determined that they were more afraid of encountering a dog during a break in than they were of a homeowner with a gun, an alarm system, or any other security device.

- Do you have a weapon in your home? Are you trained in its use? Are family members familiar with the location of the weapon?

- Are family members careful when discarding letters, personal papers and other similar materials to insure nothing is in the trash that would assist a terrorist in developing information about you? Material containing names, addresses, titles, business addresses, travel information, itineraries, maps, telephone and address books, or other such information should be shredded or otherwise disposed of to prevent terrorists from obtaining them. Police investigators will frequently search a criminal suspect's trashcan to develop information and evidence about him.

- Do you have a "safe room" or similar area in your home to which you and your family members can rally in an emergency? Does the room have adequate locks or other security devices? Is it windowless and easy to defend? Most important, is there a telephone or cell phone located in your safe haven? (The safe room is a good place to store your weapon, if you have one). ❖

"It is a good thing to learn caution from the misfortunes of others."

~ Publillus Syrus

STAYING SAFE WHILE YOU TRAVEL

Part 1: Your Hotel

In October 1977 Dutch Industrialist Maurits Caransa was abducted as he left his hotel club in Amsterdam, The Netherlands. He was held for five days before his release. The terrorists selected Caransa because he was deemed a "soft" target.

Americans and Europeans are traveling abroad more than ever now. Terrorist groups know this and they target Western businessmen, tourists and military personnel, knowing that people are generally more vulnerable while traveling than at home. Security in many foreign countries is clearly deficient, compared to the United States and Europe. In some Third World countries, members of terrorist groups and those who are sympathetic to them have infiltrated the police, security and intelligence services. Terrorists are often employed by or have sources in the customs and border control organizations of these countries. This information provides them access to the details of your itinerary -- exactly when you arrive and depart, as well as where you are staying. Someone wearing the uniform of a police, military, customs or intelligence officer of that country is not necessarily your friend, and to assume so would be foolhardy.

Most major terrorist organizations have excellent and very active intelligence networks. They have effectively placed operatives in every department and branch of the government in many Third World countries. In some countries terrorists and their sympathizers occupy prominent positions in the police, security and intelligence organizations of their respective governments. Some have even risen to top leadership positions in their country, including Chief Executive.

The primary person responsible for your security when traveling is yourself. The measures that you take at home to enhance your security posture should be significantly increased when traveling. All of the tips for driving and counter-surveillance apply even more on foreign territory, as you are on unfamiliar ground. In this chapter and the next one, I will discuss precautions you should take in the two locations where you will spend much of your time while traveling: your plane and your hotel.

How Safe Is Your Hotel?

Security in most foreign hotels today is virtually non-existent. Hotels are there to make money from businesspersons and tourists by providing lodging and, in some instances, meals and other services. Providing professional security is expensive and cuts into the hotel's profit margin. At best, most hotels have rent-a-cops, who are poorly trained and poorly paid. They really have no loyalty to their employer or to the hotel's guests, and are basically in the job because they can find nothing better. Most of these security guards are temporary and, at best, have only a few months of experience in security work. They are ill trained and poorly equipped; most are not even armed (which may be a good thing, depending on their level of proficiency). Terrorist groups have been known to infiltrate private security services by having their operatives obtain jobs with the security firms. What better way to conduct surveillance on a prospective target than to have an inside position as a security guard? Because most foreign security guards are extremely low paid, and often mistreated by management, they are fertile ground for recruitment by terrorist organizations.

Other hotel employees can be compromised as well by terrorist organizations. Desk clerks, bellmen, the concierge, maids, maintenance people, managers, and others can be agents or sympathizers of terrorist organizations, if not actual full-fledged members. These individuals can provide information to terrorists regarding your comings and goings, the type of vehicle you are driving, any security precautions you take, the room in which you are staying, information about your family members, and other relevant information. If they are actual members of the terrorist group, they can orchestrate and participate in an operation directed against you. A prime example of this was when Sirhan Sirhan assassinated Senator and Presidential candidate, Robert Kennedy, in 1968. He was an employee in the kitchen of that Los Angeles hotel.

What Precautions Should You Take?

Selecting Your Hotel

Generally speaking, the better the hotel, the better the security. When traveling abroad, spend the extra money and stay in the nicest place you can afford. It is not worth saving a few dollars at the expense of your safety and that of your family. Keep in mind, however, that terrorists tend to target hotels that cater only to Westerners. Try to select a hotel that has indigenous people, as well as Westerners staying there. Consider staying at a hotel away from the city's center. Most hotels targeted by terrorists meet one of two criteria: They are large, Western-owned hotels in the city or they are located in major tourist areas.

Interacting with Hotel Staff

Be very careful whom you trust on the hotel staff. It is best to have minimal contact with these individuals and not provide them with unnecessary personal information. The "friendly" desk clerk, concierge or other hotel employees are probably just trying to be courteous, but you can be polite without divulging too much private information.

There is one inviolate rule when dealing with hotel employees -- absolutely do not share your schedule or travel plans with anyone. This information should be shared only among those who have an absolute need-to-know. Terrorist organizations are in the business of collecting intelligence against their potential targets. The less information you give out about yourself, the better off you are. Resist the urge to respond to seemingly polite inquiries about your itinerary and travel plans. If you feel that you must reply, give them false information, or at least be vague in your answers. Confide your travel plans to no one except individuals most trusted, such as your spouse, business partner, co-workers, or others who have a need to know.

Your Room

Try to book a room between the second and seventh floors of the hotel, if possible. The bad guys can easily enter your room through ground floor windows, so try to stay away from first floor rooms. Avoid going above the seventh floor, due to the possibility of a fire or a natural disaster occurring. I was caught on the fourteenth floor of a hotel in Cairo, Egypt during an earthquake. Believe me, it was not a pleasant experience!

Stay in a hotel with rooms that are off of an interior hallway, rather than rooms that open to the outside. With an interior room, the bad guys at least have to come into the hotel, which makes it more difficult for them.

When in your room, lock all of the door locks. There are some excellent portable locks and small alarms that can be affixed to doors and windows. I strongly recommend purchasing one or two of these and using them when you travel. I have stayed in many hotels that had only one lock on the door, and that one didn't work properly. I felt a lot better because I had a lock that could be placed on the door. Although these locks are not as effective as a good deadbolt lock, they are better than nothing. Another inexpensive fix is to buy and carry a couple of rubber doorstops with you. They are very effective when wedged under your closed door. Also, consider who may have access to your room keys. Maids, desk clerks, maintenance people, and other hotel employees have copies of your room key, or access to master keys. And you never know who else might have a key to your room. Former hotel employees have been known to keep master keys to the rooms and use them to steal and commit other crimes against the guests.

If you are in a room with a defective or inefficient lock, alert management and try to get it repaired immediately. If this fails, wedge a chair under the doorknob. It's not very effective, but it's better than nothing, and it will at least buy you a little bit of time if someone is trying to break into your room.

When checking into your hotel, have the hotel secure your jewelry, extra money and other valuables in the hotel safe.

Immediately upon coming to your room, locate all the available exits from your hotel room. In an emergency you will not want to depend on the elevator. Find out where the nearest stairs are located and check to make sure the doors are not blocked. I have been in Third-World country hotels and seen the fire exit doors chained and locked. This was done presumably to keep thieves out, but it is also a danger keeping the guests from exiting the building in the event of a fire or other emergency. Keep in mind that the laws and regulations regarding safety are either non-existent, or not enforced in many countries. It is better to know that the stairways are blocked before you have to use them. Ideally, you will be able to identify a primary, secondary and tertiary escape route from your room. Test all of your escape routes by conducting a "walk-through" of them. Again, make sure that the exits to the stairwells are not locked or blocked. The last thing you want is to be trapped in a stairwell with a terrorist in pursuit of you or the hotel on fire. Count the number of doors between your room and the exits in case you have to feel your way there. In dark or smoky conditions, you will probably not be able to see well enough to make your way to the exit, and you might have to do it by feeling your way. If your floor is not too high up, consider using a window as a means of escape. Some hotel windows do not open, so you might have to pick up a chair or similar object and break the window. Do whatever it takes to escape. If you do have to leave your room for any reason, remember to take your room key and car keys with you.

Identify a safe area away from the hotel. If you have to evacuate you will need a safe place to go. Ideally you will be able to get to the American Embassy or consulate, or the embassy of a friendly country. Police stations, military installations, and other government buildings make excellent safe locations. Other hotels in the vicinity may also be an option, as well as hospitals, fire stations, and other public buildings. Wherever you identify as your safe area, be sure to conduct a couple of practice runs so you know the route and approximately how long it takes to get there. Identify a couple of different routes of escape in case your primary one is blocked or unavailable for some reason. Also, you might want to have a backup safe area to which you can retreat. In the event of a major riot or demonstration, the US Embassy may not be an option.

Be careful what you leave laying around your hotel room. Do not leave personal information, schedules, telephone numbers, or anything else that could help a terrorist determine your routine. Even seemingly innocuous things such as travel brochures and airline schedules can tip off a terrorist to your plans. Lock your briefcase, suitcases and other luggage to help prevent someone from looking into them. One trick I have used overseas is to put a "trap" on my luggage to see if it has been tampered with while I was away from my room. A "trap" is a small piece of clear tape, a piece of string, a small bit of cloth, or some other seemingly innocuous item that you place on the opening or latch of your luggage, briefcase, or other personal item. If you see that the "trap" has been disturbed, there is a good chance that someone has made an effort to gain entry into your luggage or briefcase. In many countries the local intelligence service will take a look around your room while you are away to see what they can find out about you. I have been the victim of this many times, but in intelligence work that comes with the territory. If a terrorist group has bribed or co-opted a maid to search your room for information about you, this is something you will want to know. You may not be able to do anything about it, but at least you will know.

When you leave your room, leave the lights and a television or radio on. There are two reasons for this. First of all, it gives the impression that you are in your room. Secondly, if you leave the TV, lights or radio on when you go out and they are off when you come back, then it is obvious someone has been in your room. In all likelihood it was just the maid, but you never know.

Beware of unusual or suspicious telephone calls to your room. Someone who is tracking you will call your room to determine when you are in. Be particularly suspicious if someone from the "front desk" calls and tells you that someone is in the lobby to see you (somebody you are not expecting);

your car has been in an accident in the parking lot, or some other similar scenario. This could be a ruse to get you out of your room and into an area from which you can be easily abducted. The police often use this tactic to lure crime suspects out of their hotel rooms so that they can more easily arrest them. This gets the unsuspecting person out of their familiar area and into territory that is out of their control. If you do get a call from someone who claims to be the desk clerk or other hotel employee, hang up, and call the front desk to verify the information. If the call is from a "police officer", you can call the police department dispatcher or a supervisor to confirm it. You can also call the front desk clerk to verify that there actually is a police officer looking for you. At the very least, you should be extremely cautious and conduct a brief counter-surveillance of the area prior to entering it. You could be walking into an ambush. There are a lot of criminals in jail because they fell for this trick. Be suspicious and take nothing for granted.

Keep a good flashlight next to your bed, as well as your cell phone. A good, bright flashlight can be a valuable tool in the event the electricity goes out due to power loss or natural disaster. If someone tries to gain access to your room while you are in bed, you can at least shine the flashlight in his eyes as a distraction while you make your escape. Some flashlights make very effective impact weapons as well. A good jab to the head, nose or eye will deter most attackers, at least temporarily. In Third World countries the electricity can go off for hours, if not days, so this is even more reason to carry a good flashlight. (And don't forget to take extra batteries with you -- you may not be able to find them in the country you are visiting.)

Don't make a habit of frequenting the hotel's bar or restaurant. Most travelers like to stay close to their hotel when dining or when going out for a drink. Terrorists know this and frequently target hotels that cater to Westerners. A hotel bar or restaurant is an ideal location for a terrorist to plant a bomb. I'm not saying you should never go to the hotel bar or restaurant, but I am saying to mix up where you go to eat and drink. Don't set a pattern by going to the same restaurant or bar at the same time every day. Americans tend to be creatures of habit, and if they find a place that they like and feel comfortable in, they often frequent that place many times. In most foreign cities there are some excellent restaurants that primarily cater to the locals. You are generally far safer in one of these than in an establishment that caters primarily to Americans and Europeans.

Who's Watching You?

Be on continual lookout for surveillance at your hotel. I have traveled to the former Soviet Union, and on every trip I was able to identify surveillance in the hotel lobby. The surveillance I experienced there was orchestrated by a local intelligence service, not terrorists. We were told to expect this, so we weren't at surprised, and I must admit that picking out a KGB officer was somewhat fun and not all that difficult. KGB officers were all essentially the same -- white males between thirty and fifty years of age, dark clothing, cheap sunglasses, and Russian-made shoes.

On the other hand, identifying surveillance from a terrorist group is substantially more difficult. Terrorist organizations may very well use your hotel staff to conduct surveillance on you. The maid who cleans your room knows exactly when you depart and arrive each day. The desk clerk sees you when you leave. Waiters and waitresses in the hotel bar and restaurant can be surveillants. The doorman, and even hotel security officers, could possibly be conducing surveillance for a terrorist group. Look for people "hanging out" in the lobby, particularly if they take an unusual interest in you. Most unsophisticated terrorist and intelligence organizations tend to use the same people over and over again to conduct surveillance. Pay attention to the people you see on a regular basis.

Notice faces, clothing or anything unusual about the person that stands out. A tip you should keep in mind: look at the shoes. Unlike Americans, most people in Third World countries tend to wear the same shoes every day. So if you see a guy in red high-top sneakers standing in the same spot every day watching you intently, that might just be a clue.

Look for people who don't seem to fit in with the regular clientele of the hotel. If you are in the Middle East, you are going to see many people who fit the American's idea of a "terrorist profile" -- young, Middle Eastern males. Obviously, that doesn't mean they're affiliated with terrorists, but how do you know? Spotting surveillance in this kind of environment is very difficult, even for experienced intelligence officers who are pros at this sort of thing. The reality is that you will probably not be able to spot surveillance, especially in a Middle Eastern country. That is why you must not be time and place predictable. Your only salvation is to be "predictably unpredictable".

I cannot emphasize the importance of being "predictably unpredictable". As you would do at home, while traveling abroad you should vary your travel routes and times, particularly if you are in an area that has a high threat level. In my opinion, being time and place unpredictable is your best defense against a terrorist attack while traveling. Due to a number of factors, you are usually more vulnerable when you are away from home. First of all, you are in an unfamiliar area, with strange (to you) customs, laws, and values. You are not as familiar with the streets and transportation systems. You don't know the location of the nearest police station or hospital. There is a good chance you don't speak the language. You are away from family, friends and familiar territory. You are not sure what is out of place and what is normal activity on your daily routes. These are some of the many variables you have no control over when you are away from home. This is why it is even more important to vary your routes and times. Try not to arrive or depart your hotel at the same time every day. Find an alternate entrance and exit to the hotel, using this from time to time. Don't always go through the front door. If you have a car, try not to park in the same location every day. Be observant to what is happening around your hotel. If you suddenly notice the absence of locals who usually are present in the hotel, it may mean that something "bad" is about to happen. In many countries, word of an impending bombing or other terrorist act tends to rapidly spread throughout the populace. If you see a sudden decrease in pedestrian and vehicular activity around your hotel, it may be time to change hotels. In fact, if you suspect that you may be under surveillance by a terrorist group, change hotels immediately. If I am going to be in a dangerous country for more than a week or two, I usually change hotels anyway -- and without advance notice. I simply show up at the desk, pay my bill, and go to another, pre-arranged hotel. The trick is to keep anyone who might be planning a terrorist or criminal operation against you off guard. Become predictably unpredictable. Do not set a pattern and keep your adversaries guessing. Hopefully they will get frustrated by trying to keep tabs on you and will go pick on an easier, more predictable target.

Try putting yourself in the mindset of a terrorist. Think, "If I were a terrorist planning an operation against myself, what would my vulnerabilities be? Where are the weaknesses in my security?" Identify your weaknesses and vulnerabilities and try to do your best to eliminate, or at least mitigate them. ❖

"Let's Roll!"

~ *Passenger Todd Beamer on September 11, 2001*

STAYING SAFE WHILE YOU TRAVEL

Part 2: In the Air

Wikipedia defines aircraft hijacking ("also known as skyjacking and aircraft piracy") as "the takeover of an aircraft, by a person or group, usually armed. In most cases the pilot is forced to fly according to the orders of the hijackers". That was the definition, at least prior to September 11, 2001.

September 11, 2001 was a wake-up call to all Americans. Prior to that infamous day in history, most hijackers who took control of a commercial airliner generally allowed it to land, holding the passengers and crew as hostages until their demands were met. Counter terrorist units all over the world were trained to "take down" a hijacked aircraft while it was sitting on the tarmac. During the 1970s, hijackings of commercial aircraft were so frequent that they rarely made the front-page news. During the 1990s, aircraft hijackings dropped off considerably, leading to more relaxed airline security.

Then came September 11, and the world as we knew it changed forever. The 9/11 hijackers had no intention of landing at an airport and negotiating with authorities. Their sole goal was a high body count and a massive loss of life, both in the air and on the ground. Pre-9/11 advice to passengers on a hijacked airliner was to remain calm, cooperate with the terrorists and, above all, don't fight back. With the sole exception of United Airlines Flight 93, which crashed in a field in Pennsylvania, that is exactly what the victims did on that terrible day. I don't get on an airplane today without thinking of the passengers on those ill-fated flights. Would I have done anything differently had I been on one of those aircraft? I'd like to think I would have. In light of that tragedy, however, I am now more convinced than ever that I would fight back with everything in my power. Those passengers on United Flight 93 who fought back were heroes in every sense of the word. They did not succeed in saving the aircraft and themselves, but at least they prevented the plane from crashing into a building as the hijackers had planned. This surely would have resulted in an even greater loss of life. Their willingness to resist the hijackers also sent a serious message to any terrorist considering hijacking an American airline. The message? –"You just might get your ass kicked if you try!"

Note: Interestingly, the use of hijacked planes as missiles by terrorists was not a new concept on September 11, 2001. This type of skyjacking had been attempted twice before, in 1974 and 1994, with disappointing results for the "hijackers-to-be". Due to the "success" achieved by the terrorists on 9/11, I fear we have not seen the last of terrorists attempting to use a hijacked aircraft as a suicide missile.

Who Is Protecting You When You Fly?

Transportation Safety Administration (TSA) Federal Air Marshals are highly trained, well equipped law enforcement officers who are ready, willing and able to handle an in-flight situation regarding an armed person or persons. The problem is there aren't nearly enough Federal Air Marshals to go around. There are so few that it is impossible to assign one to every domestic flight, much less to the international ones. To compound the problem, most foreign carriers have no on-board security officers. Ultimately, the chance of a Federal Air Marshal being on a plane in the process of being hijacked is extremely slim, leaving only you in charge of your personal safety.

You might ask the question, "Hasn't pre-boarding security improved considerably since 9/11?" The appearance of security has improved. However, if you consider the following scenario, I think you will see that in some ways we may be even worse off.

Many of us have read of the encounter described by columnist Annie Jacobsen and published in WomensWallStreet.com on July 13, 2004. There are experts who argue against the validity of her report, but I have chosen to include excerpts of her article, outlining her view of what happened on her flight from Detroit to Los Angeles on June 29, 2004:

"On June 29, 2004, at 12:28 p.m., I flew on Northwest Airlines flight #327 from Detroit to Los Angeles with my husband and our young son. Also on our flight were 14 Middle Eastern men between the ages of approximately 20 and 50 years old. What I experienced during that flight has caused me to question whether the United States of America can realistically uphold the civil liberties of every individual, even non-citizens, and protect its citizens from terrorist threats.

On that Tuesday, our journey began uneventfully. Starting out that morning in Providence, Rhode Island, we went through security screening, flew to Detroit, and passed the time waiting for

Stay Alert, Stay Alive

our connecting flight to Los Angeles by shopping at the airport stores and eating lunch at an airport diner. With no second security check required in Detroit, we headed to our gate and waited for the pre-boarding announcement. Standing near us, also waiting to pre-board, was a group of six Middle Eastern men. They were carrying blue passports with Arabic writing. Two men wore tracksuits with Arabic writing across the back. Two carried musical instrument cases – thin, flat, about 18 inches long. One wore a yellow T-shirt and held a McDonald's bag. And the sixth man had a bad leg – he wore an orthopedic shoe and limped. When the pre-boarding announcement was made, we handed our tickets to the Northwest Airlines agent and walked down the jetway with the group of men directly behind us . . .

. . . Once on the plane, we took our seats in coach (seats 17A, 17B and 17C). The man with the yellow shirt and the McDonald's bag sat across the aisle from us (in seat 17E). The pleasant man with the goatee sat a few rows back and across the aisle from us (in seat 21E). The rest of the men were seated throughout the plane, and several made their way to the back.

As we sat waiting for the plane to finish boarding, we noticed another large group of Middle Eastern men boarding. The first man wore a dark suit and sunglasses. He sat in the first class in seat 1A, the seat second closest to the cockpit door. The other seven men walked into the coach cabin. As "aware" Americans, my husband and I exchanged glances and then continued to get comfortable. I noticed some of the other passengers paying attention to the situation as well. As boarding continued, we watched as, one by one, most of the Middle Eastern men made eye contact with each other. They continued to look at each other and nod, as if they were all in agreement about something. I could tell that my husband was beginning to feel "anxious".

The take-off was uneventful. But once we were in the air and the seatbelt sign was turned off, the unusual activity began. The man in the yellow T-shirt got out of his seat and went to the lavatory at the front of coach—taking his full McDonald's bag with him. When he came out of the lavatory he still had the McDonald's bag, but it was now almost empty. He walked down the aisle to the back of the plane, still holding the bag. When he passed two of the men sitting mid-cabin, he gave a thumbs-up sign. When he returned to his seat, he no longer had the McDonald's bag.

Then another man from the group stood up and took something from his carry-on in the overhead bin. It was about a foot long and was rolled in cloth. He headed toward the back of the cabin with the object. Five minutes later, several more of the Middle Eastern men began using the forward lavatory consecutively. In the back, several of the men stood up and used the back lavatory consecutively as well.

For the next hour, the men congregated in groups of two and three at the back of the plane for varying periods of time. Meanwhile, in the first class cabin, just a foot or so from the cockpit door, the man with the dark suit – still wearing sunglasses – was also standing. Not one of the flight crewmembers suggested that any of these men take their seats . . .

. . . After seeing 14 Middle Eastern men board separately (six together, eight individually) and then act as a group, watching their unusual glances, observing their bizarre bathroom activities, watching them congregate in small groups, knowing that the flight attendants and the pilots were seriously concerned, and now knowing that federal air marshals were on board, I was officially terrified. Before I'm labeled a racial profiler or – worse yet – a racist, let me add this. A month ago I traveled to India to research a magazine article I was writing. My husband and I flew on a jumbo jet carrying more than 300 Hindu and Muslim men and women on board. We traveled throughout the country and stayed in a Muslim village 10 miles outside Pakistan. I never once felt *fearful. I never once felt unsafe. I never once had the feeling that anyone wanted to hurt me. This time was different.*

Finally, the captain announced that the plane was cleared for landing. It had been four hours since we left Detroit. The fasten seat belt light came on and I could see downtown Los Angeles. The flight attendants made one final sweep of the cabin and strapped themselves in for landing. I began to relax. Home was in sight.

Suddenly, seven of the men stood up – in unison – and walked to the front and back lavatories. One by one, they went into the two lavatories, each spending about four minutes inside. Right in front of us, two men stood up against the emergency exit door, waiting for the lavatory to become available. The men spoke in Arabic among themselves and to the man in the yellow shirt sitting nearby. One of the men took his camera into the lavatory. Another took his cell phone. Again, no one approached the men. Not one of the flight attendants asked them to sit down. I watched as the man in the yellow shirt, still in his seat, reached inside his shirt and pulled out a small red book. He read a few pages, and then put the book back inside his shirt. He pulled the book out again, read a page or two more, and put it back. He continued to do this several more times.

I looked around to see if any other passengers were watching. I immediately spotted a distraught couple seated two rows back. The woman was crying into the man's shoulder. He was holding her hand. I heard him say to her, "You've got to calm down." Behind them sat the once pleasant-smiling, goatee-wearing man.

I grabbed my son, I held my husband's hand and, despite the fact that I am not a particularly religious person, I prayed. The last man came out of the bathroom, and as he passed the man in the yellow shirt he ran his forefinger across his neck and mouthed the word 'No.'

The plane landed. My husband and I gathered our bags and quickly, very quickly, walked up the jetway."

Is this a work of fiction? No, these events did occur. As I mentioned earlier, there are some who think the author's interpretation of this encounter may be somewhat skewed, due to her emotional involvement. Obviously, there is no way we can know for certain what those Middle Eastern nationals were thinking or planning during the flight. Nevertheless, there is a very real possibility events of this nature have occurred and will continue to occur in this country, as U.S. airport screeners are prohibited from "racial profiling" of any kind. Regardless of whether all the details described above are completely accurate, intelligence has revealed that before the 9/11 attacks, terrorists did perform "dry runs" of their operations on domestic and international flights. Indeed, we have a long way to go before we can safely "fly the friendly skies" again.

Do not make the mistake of assuming that the Transportation Security Administration or airport security is doing a thorough enough job of protecting you and your family. In many ways they are hampered more now than before 9/11, due to complaints and lawsuits filed by ethnic groups who claim to be victims of "racial profiling". Although I am absolutely against racial profiling of any kind, I am in favor of "terrorist profiling". If the government you trust and with whom you entrust the lives of your loved ones, is not doing the job of "terrorist profiling", that responsibility must lie with you.

While there is little you can do about "terrorist profiling" once you have become airborne, there are a number of things you can do prior to boarding a plane, helping you to reduce your chances of finding yourself on a "high risk" flight.

What Can You Do?

To begin with, use a US carrier if at all possible. As we graphically saw on September 11, 2001, US carriers are certainly not immune from being hijacked and security, by far, is not as effective as it should be. Even so, you are far safer on a US carrier than on most foreign carriers, particularly those of Third World countries.

Use discretion in selecting the airports you fly into and depart from. Most airports in Third World countries, particularly in Africa and South Asian countries, are notoriously weak in terms of their security. Some of these airports are even transit ports for terrorists because they know they won't be closely scrutinized in those locations. In some countries the terrorists virtually "own" the airports, due to the many terrorist sympathizers employed there.

While on the topic of airport security, I have found profound differences in the precautions taken by airport security in the United States and by those in Europe. As an example, I remember an occasion when I was flying round trip to Africa, with a stopover in Frankfurt, Germany going over and a stopover in Amsterdam, Holland on my return trip. This was prior to September 11, but I was shocked even then at the differences I found in the attitude the Germans and Dutch held toward airport security, compared to that of American airports.

In the U.S. airports it appeared to me as if the airport screeners were bored and mechanically performed their jobs, security appearing to be a low priority. Even after 9/11, although we pay lip service to security, such as removing our shoes during the screening process, it still seems that no one is actually taking security that seriously. We remove our shoes, we empty our pockets, but doing something that might actually work, like profiling of passengers, is off limits. We demand that our security personnel remain "blind", lest they discriminate. We are far more concerned with being politically correct in this country than with the safety of our own citizens.

Comparatively, the attitude toward airport security in most Western European countries is very different from that in the United States. In Germany, the first thing I noticed when I stepped off the plane was the armed police officers with automatic weapons and attack dogs. They were everywhere. Security was tight. In Amsterdam, Holland, an officer armed with a submachine gun questioned me extensively prior to my boarding the flight. Although I had an official US Government passport, I was questioned just like the other passengers. We all got the same treatment. That kind of intense questioning by an officer, armed with an automatic weapon, has got to give serious pause to any terrorist contemplating hijacking an aircraft under those circumstances.

When planning your trip, opt to fly non-stop, if at all possible. It is a known fact that the riskiest times during a flight, from a safety standpoint, are take-offs and landings. Obviously minimizing these will diminish your risk. From a security viewpoint, the fewer stops your plane makes, the less opportunity there will be for terrorists boarding your flight.

Avoid layovers, if at all possible. If you must have a layover while traveling internationally, consider doing so in a country with a reputation for tight security. England, Germany, Australia and Japan, among others, have excellent reputations for security in their airports. Especially avoid layovers in Third World countries. As I mentioned earlier, many Third World airports, particularly in the Middle East and Africa, are transit points for terrorists, due to their lax security.

Try not to stand out as an American citizen. As much as you can, blend in with the local populace. Don't be conspicuous by wearing expensive clothing, jewelry or flashing a lot of cash. Pay attention to what is going on around you in the airport terminal and in the waiting areas. If you see people waiting to board your plane and they appear suspicious or are behaving in a strange manner, consider taking another flight. At least alert a security officer if you think something is amiss.

Keep your carry-on bags and luggage in your possession at all times. Do not give anyone an opportunity to slip a bomb or a weapon inside your bag.

Hijacked! "What now?"

Your worst nightmare has become reality – your plane has been hijacked. The scenario may go something like this: You are on a domestic flight. The crew has just turned off the "Fasten Your Seatbelt" sign and you have begun to relax. All of a sudden, several men seated in the coach section of the aircraft jump up from their seats, stand in the aisle and start yelling commands in broken, heavily-accented English to the other passengers.

Due to the myriad unknown factors involved in your scenario, I can't tell you unequivocally what you should do if you find yourself in this position. I can give you some guidelines that I would adhere to and recommend that you consider. Keep in mind that what you do should depend on your level of training, what the situation is inside the cabin and the cockpit, the number of hijackers, how they are armed, among other variables.

Should you find yourself on a hijacked aircraft, your first goal would be to gather as much information about the hijackers and the situation as possible. Without information (intelligence) you will not be able to make a fair and accurate assessment of the situation and you will be hampered in your efforts to mount a counter attack. Ask yourself the questions "Who, What, When, Where, Why and How?" and use the answers to these questions to help you formulate a plan of action.

Some variables to consider are:

- **Who are they?** Do the hijackers appear to be a contingent of highly organized extremists with a well thought out plan, or does there appear to be only one disoriented, unprepared, mentally disturbed individual? How old are they? Why is this important? Because many of the 9/11 terrorist hijackers were young males, mostly in their 20s and 30s. We now know that most of them were totally inexperienced in conducting terrorist operations and most likely were scared out of their minds. When confronted with youthful terrorists, you can use the terrorists' fear, youth, and inexperience to your advantage.

- **What are their demands, if any?** Does it appear that they intend to negotiate or are they keeping quiet about their demands? If they don't appear to be making any demands, this can be a bad sign. Their intentions may be to crash the plane into the ground or a building. On the other hand, having terrorists who are ranting and raving about demands doesn't necessarily mean they intend to negotiate. The terrorists that hijacked the aircraft on 9/11 tried to calm the passengers by telling them that they would be okay, indicating that the plane would land and the passengers would be released when some unspecified demands were met. If terrorists allude to some vague demands, don't believe them. Their plan is most likely to put you at ease so you won't be a problem to them. People believe what they want to believe, which is usually the best-case scenario they can imagine. You are far better off if you face the reality of the situation. They very likely don't have any intention of letting you go. Formulate your plan based on the assumption that they won't release you. Do not allow yourself to be lulled into a false sense of security.

- **What are the their tactics?** Have they taken over the cockpit or just the cabin? Is one of the terrorists flying the aircraft or are the pilots still in control? How much of the aircraft is under their control? Do they have control of the entire plane, just the coach section, or just the first class/business class sections?
- **When was the hijacking initiated?** On the runway or in the air? Early in the flight or mid-flight?
- **Where was the aircraft when it was hijacked?** If you are over the Pacific Ocean you may handle the situation differently than if you are over the Continental United States, where the pilot can quickly land the plane at an airport.
- **Why is the aircraft being hijacked?** What are the terrorists' motives and what do they want to accomplish? If they are spouting something like, "all infidels must die", or "today we will see Allah", it might be a clue that they have no intention of letting you out of this alive.
- **How are the terrorists armed?** Although it would certainly be better if they were unarmed, they will likely be armed, at least with rudimentary weapons. The 9/11 hijackers were armed with ordinary box cutters. Will you be able to disarm the hijackers? I have extensive training in the martial arts and have spent many hours practicing gun and knife disarming techniques. I have no doubt that I could take a weapon away from one of these "bullies" and would gladly turn it against him and his buddies. Let me stress strongly, though, that it takes many hours of training and practice to accomplish this. I wouldn't advise trying this without substantial training, unless I had a couple of other people to help me tackle the terrorist and wrestle his weapon from him.
- **Do they have Improvised Explosive Devices?** They may have something that looks like a bomb strapped to their waist, but it may be only a counterfeit device. If one of the terrorists has something that looks like a bomb or he claims it is a bomb, this complicates things considerably, but don't let this stop you from developing your plan.
- **How many hijackers are there?** Obviously one hijacker would be better than twelve. It helps to get a handle on how many people you are dealing with and how many of your fellow passengers might be willing to help in an attempt to retake the aircraft.

Once you have obtained sufficient intelligence and assessed the situation to the best of your ability, you are now ready to formulate a plan of action. Be careful that you don't fall into the "paralysis of analysis" trap, taking too long to gather intelligence or devise a plan. Gather your information and develop your plan as quickly as possible. The best time to launch a counterattack is in the initial stages of the hijacking. It is in the initial stages of the hijacking that the terrorists are most vulnerable to a counterattack. The initial stages of an aircraft hijacking are generally marked by uncertainty, chaos and confusion on the part of the hijackers. The terrorists are apt to be disorganized, scared and extremely agitated. They have not had the time to put their plan into action and consolidate control over the aircraft, and are thus at their most vulnerable point in the operation.

There are two schools of thought as to when the counterattack should begin. One thinks that you should wait until the terrorists become tired and their level of alertness has lowered before launching your counterattack. The passengers on the four airplanes on September 11, 2001, did not have that option (and if you wait too long, you and the other passengers will also be tired and unable to effectively respond).

The second school of thought advocates initiating a counterattack as soon as possible following the onset of the attack, so as to take advantage of the terrorists' initial disorganization and confusion.

Then, of course, there is always the third option of doing nothing and hope the hijacking will be resolved peacefully. While there is some validity in this viewpoint, recent aircraft hijackings have indicated that contemporary terrorists have no intention of engaging in negotiations to attempt a peaceful resolution to the hijacking. Their goal is a high body count and maximum terror value.

Many security "professionals" will tell you to take the third option. They will say to do nothing, be compliant, give in to the terrorist's demands and wait to be rescued. This option may have had some validity in the past, but the tragedy of 9/11 has changed that, at least in my opinion. The American public admired the victims in United Flight 93 who fought back. Their bravery in the face of insurmountable odds should be an inspiration to us all. Yes, they died, but at least they went down fighting. Surely they saved many more innocent lives on the ground. We'll never know how many lives would have been lost if the terrorists had succeeded in crashing that plane into a building.

I certainly don't subscribe to the school of thought that advocates doing nothing. Of course, much depends on your particular situation, and no one can make that decision for you. I will say, however, that if I am ever on a hijacked aircraft and have any reason to think the terrorists' plan may include killing passengers, I will be doing something. If you think the possibility is high you are going to die and there is even a slim chance your plan may succeed and you and your fellow passengers may live, what do you have to lose? Ask yourself what your chances of survival would be if you choose to do nothing.

Planning Your Counterattack

Let's say you have now studied the situation and have gathered your intelligence. Finding the situation to be very likely deadly, you have decided that something must be done. If your decision is to launch a counterattack against the hijackers, you need to be prepared.

If you have made the decision to fight back, you could always jump up and begin fighting the hijackers on your own. I would not recommend that approach and your chance of success would be minimal, at best. A much better idea would be to take a few minutes to develop a plan of action. I must caution you, however, not to over plan, falling into the trap of "paralysis of analysis".

I have included the following suggestions that could very well make the difference between living and dying.

- **Have a plan.** A poor plan vigorously executed is better than a well thought out plan only halfway executed. Your plan does not have to be elaborate and probably shouldn't be. Simple is better in this case. Have a secondary plan in case the primary one doesn't work, and don't be afraid to improvise and adapt as the situation develops. Your plan should take into consideration that you may have to act alone. So be it. Hopefully, you will be able enlist others to help you carry out your plan. If not, be prepared to act alone.

- **Enlist others in your fight.** There is nothing like having several big, strong men to fight on your team. Ideally, your fellow passengers will include some Marines, Army Rangers or Navy SEALS. If that's the case, you can trust me when I say they are thinking exactly the way you are thinking. They're not going down without a fight. In the more likely event that your co-passengers are typical Americans, traveling for business or pleasure, they will still be capable of helping you.

When selecting passengers to help you, exercise caution. Some passengers may be prone to develop what is called the "Stockholm Syndrome". This term originates from a 1973 bank robbery in Stockholm, Sweden, in which several bank employees were held hostage for six days. The "Stockholm Syndrome" refers to a phenomenon in which the hostages became emotionally attached to their captors and actually began sympathizing with them. Other passengers may try to stop you from doing something because of their fear, attempting to garner favor with the terrorists and possibly even reporting your plans to them. This is similar to the "Stockholm Syndrome", but while hostages with the Stockholm Syndrome act out of some perverted loyalty to their captors, these particular hostages act purely out of fear. Their sole intent is to save themselves, even at the expense of others. Typically, these people don't actually sympathize with either the hijackers or their fellow hostages. Neither of the above are uncommon occurrences in hostage situations. This is one very good reason why it is important to act quickly in a hijacking; it gives your fellow passengers less time to 'bond" with the terrorists.

Give each of the participants in your plan something specific to do during the counterattack. Most people don't have a clue what to do in a situation of this nature, so you, being prepared for an emergency situation, may have to give out specific assignments and instructions to them. Otherwise, the chaos that ensues will give a distinct advantage to the hijackers. Make sure that everyone involved in your plan knows exactly what to do.

- **Look for weapons you can use.** It is amazing what items you can come up with to use as weapons if you have to. The plastic knife and fork the stewardess gave you at lunch can be an excellent weapon, as can your ballpoint pen or a sharpened pencil. A plastic knife or fork, or a pencil or pen forcefully and aggressively jabbed into the terrorist's eye can do wonders for getting him to rethink his plans. A scarf or necktie can be used as a garrote (a device for choking or strangling). Even a magazine rolled up tightly can be used as an impact weapon. The keys in your pocket or purse can be used to strike at the terrorist's face and eyes. Your own body can be a very effective weapon, although it does take a minimum of training to know how to use your body effectively. An elbow or palm heel strike to the nose can be devastating if delivered with maximum force and aggression. A knee strike to the groin can bring even the toughest terrorist to his knees; again, it must be delivered correctly and with power. Even a head butt to the nose can be extremely painful. Be creative. Think outside the box. When you first get on the plane, look around and think about what you could use as a weapon if you needed one.

Executing Your Counterattack on an Aircraft

"When you get into a tight place and everything goes against you, 'til it seems as though you could not hold on a minute longer, never give up then, for that is just the place and time that the tide will turn".

---Harriet Beecher Stowe

Once you have gathered intelligence and made an assessment of the situation, enlisted the assistance of your fellow passengers, and formulated a plan of action, it is time to execute a counterattack. Timing is important. By now you should have observed the terrorists' actions long enough to see if they have a pattern. This will help you in the timing of your counter attack. Maybe one of the terrorists has a habit of coming into the coach area every few minutes to visit his buddy. If you are conducting the assault unilaterally (by yourself), you may want to plan your attack to occur at a time between these visits, when a hijacker is alone and easier to overpower. If you have several other passengers helping you, you then may want to conduct your assault when the terrorists are together so that you can take them all out at once. Whatever your plan and whenever you decide to execute it, there are three inviolate rules that you must follow.

First, it is critically important that, once you commit to the counterattack, you follow through to the end. Even if no one goes with you, you must continue the assault. Forget everything else and totally focus on the job at hand. Stick with your plan as long as it is working and be ready to adapt to changing circumstances. Above all, do not stop the assault until you are either victorious or out of the fight altogether. Once you commit, there is no turning back

Second, use maximum force and all-out aggression. This is the time for serious business. I understand that many people are squeamish about taking a sharpened pencil and jabbing it in someone's eye. Unfortunately, this is exactly what you must do if you want a chance of making it through alive. Think maximum violence. Use whatever weapons you can find and show no mercy. Remind yourself that you didn't start this fight; the terrorists did, so do whatever it takes to neutralize your adversary. (Webster's definitions of neutralize: *to make ineffective; destroy or counteract the effectiveness of, etc.*). In other words, destroy your adversary and do it quickly. Utilize speed, surprise and extreme "violence of action", to "shock and awe" your enemy. Once you begin the counterattack don't stop until you are absolutely positive the terrorist is eliminated and can no longer be a threat to you and your fellow passengers. The hijackers must be unsuspecting that anything is about to happen (surprise), it must be a lighting fast "blitzkrieg" attack (speed), and it must be overwhelmingly violent (violence of action) in order for it to succeed.

Finally, and most importantly, don't quit until you have gained total and unconditional victory. Remember that terrorists are, by and large, cowards. That is why they predominately pick on innocent civilians. Believe me, they do not want a violent confrontation with you. In the planning of most terrorist operations, the possibility that their victims might rise up against them is not seriously considered. The passengers on Flight 93 being the exception, most terror victims comply meekly and willingly with terrorist demands. The terrorists don't expect a sudden surprise and violent uprising from the "sheep". Transform yourself from a sheep to a wolf, and you do the terrorizing. It amazes me the number of people who, finding themselves in life threatening situations, simply give up and die. If they would keep fighting they just might find that victory and survival could be just around the corner. Persevere, even if it looks like you are losing and the situation seems hopeless. You never know when the terrorist is getting ready to give up, so keep fighting with maximum force and extreme violence of action, and don't stop until you have obtained total victory. ❖

"Strength does not come from physical capacity. It comes from an indomitable will."

~ Mahatma Gandhi

SAFETY IN THE PUBLIC DOMAIN

Are you thinking that just because you aren't a U.S. government official or a member of the U.S. armed forces, you will never be the target of a terrorist attack? Think again. Increasingly, tourists are being targeted by terrorist organizations worldwide. The impact of a terrorist incident on the economy of a country dependent on tourist dollars can be devastating. Terrorists know this, and for this reason frequently target tourist destinations for their attacks. I have included in the following list some of the better-known attacks that were conducted at tourist sites:

- Islamic terrorists set off bombs at the popular tourist site of Sharm el-Sheikh on Egypt's Red Sea. The July 22, 2005 attack killed 88 people and wounded over 200 others when the terrorists employed two suicide car bombs and one improvised explosive device that was planted in a bag.

- On November 9, 2005, Al-Qaeda claimed responsibility for a series of coordinated bombings of three hotels in Amman, Jordan. The explosions occurred at the Grand Hyatt Hotel, the Radisson Hotel, and the Days Inn, killing 60 people and injuring 155 others. US and other Western military personnel, government employees and tourists regularly frequented all three of the hotels.

- Terrorists opened fire on a tour bus at the Egyptian Museum in Cairo wounding two passengers. At the same time another terrorist ignited a bomb behind the museum that wounded another five tourists. On April 7, 2005, a terrorist suicide bomber exploded an improvised explosive device packed with nails in an historic Cairo shopping bazaar, killing two tourists and wounding 18 others.
- Terrorists executed bombings in the Red Sea resort areas of Taba and Ras Shitan, killing 34 tourists and wounding in excess of 100 others, mostly Israelis.
- A bombing in Bali, aimed specifically at tourists, killed some 100 Australians in 2002.
- Terrorists armed with automatic weapons killed 62 tourists in Luxor, Egypt in November 1997.
- Islamic extremist terrorists shot and killed six German tourists and three others at the Egyptian Museum in Cairo, Egypt on September 18, 1997. (Ironically I had visited that museum a couple of months prior to the shootings while on a trip to Cairo and noticed the visible lack of security, thinking, "This would be a good place for a terrorist attack". Apparently, I was not the only person who noticed this).
- On April 18, 1996, terrorists opened fire outside a hotel located near the pyramids in Egypt, killing 17 Greek tourists and one Egyptian. An additional 15 people were wounded in the attacks.
- On November 9, 1995, terrorists opened fire on passengers of a train carrying tourists to southern Egypt. A Dutch man and a French woman were shot.
- Terrorists firing on a train carrying tourists in Egypt seriously wounded two Argentineans and four Egyptians.
- Four people were killed, including two German tourists, during a terrorist attack in the Red Sea resort of Hurghada, Egypt on September 27, 1994.
- A gun and bomb attack on December 27, 1993 seriously wounded eight Austrians and eight Egyptians on a tourist bus in Cairo.
- June 8, 1993. An improvised explosive device exploded adjacent to a tour bus on the main road to the pyramids in Cairo, killing two Egyptians and wounding 22 people, including five British tourists.
- On October 7, 1985, four terrorists from the Palestine Liberation Front hijacked the cruise ship, Achille Lauro, while in the Mediterranean Sea. One American passenger, wheelchair-bound Leon Klinghoffer, was shot and his body thrown overboard.

These are only a few examples of tourists who are routinely targeted by terrorist groups. One of the major goals of terrorist organizations worldwide is to damage a country's financial infrastructure by attacking their tourist industry. A side benefit to the terrorist organization is that they get to kill Americans and Europeans, thereby discouraging them from traveling abroad.

Pre-Trip Intelligence Collection

Before you move or travel abroad, make it a point to become an amateur "intelligence officer". By this, I mean you should make it a point to gather as much information as you can about the country to which you will be visiting or moving. It will be in your best interest to become as familiar with the terrorism issues in your region as you can prior to your arrival. This will assist you in developing a security plan for your family and yourself, giving you a fair assessment of the true situation in that country.

There are two basic ways to gather intelligence – overt and covert. The covert method is used by intelligence agencies worldwide to obtain information through the method of spotting, assessing, developing and recruiting "assets" or, for want of a better term, spies. Covert intelligence collection is illegal in every country and it generally requires a trained intelligence officer to facilitate. Because it is usually considered to be "classified information", intelligence obtained from covert operations is not readily available to the public.

Covert intelligence collection is the method you will use to gather your "intelligence" on a particular country, area or region. Covert intelligence is also facilitated by intelligence agencies all over the world and utilizes "open source" information. Covert intelligence is generally derived from books, magazines, newspapers, the Internet and any other legal sources readily available to the public. Anyone living in a free society has access to this type of "open source" information.

Before traveling or moving to a foreign country, visit your library and check out all the books you can find on the country you will be visiting, especially the books dealing with the political and security situation in that region of the world. Read major newspapers for articles relating to that country. Don't think that looking at the front page will provide all the information you'll need. Because most Americans aren't all that interested in the news in Kyrgystan, many of the articles may be buried in the back of the newspaper, taking up only a couple of columns of space. If you, however, are getting ready to go to Kyrgystan, that "back page" information can be invaluable to you. A vague reference to the emergence of a terrorist group in one of the provinces of that country may have a profound impact on your life. Stay informed.

The Internet is also a valuable tool for conducting "intelligence" research. Try to find everything written within the past few years on the political climate and stability of the country and region to which you are traveling. There are people who, thinking they were going on a relaxing vacation have found themselves in the middle of a violent African revolution or found themselves blindfolded and tied to a tree somewhere in the jungles of South America. Do your homework. Read what is going on in that area of the world. If you are transiting through another area in route to your final destination, brush up on the situation there as well.

Talk to other people who have recently traveled or resided in the country to which you are going. Get their first-hand knowledge and opinion on the situation and pay attention to what they tell you. Rely upon them to give you advice for safe hotels, safe areas in which to live and parts of the city or country you should avoid. Find out where the "bad areas" are before you get there and steer clear of them. Other people can also provide you with names of people who can assist you there – reliable service workers, maids, cooks, drivers, and others who have personal knowledge.

Read up on the history and culture of the area. Become familiar with the particular customs, etiquette and social norms of the country. Review current maps of the cities in which you will be staying and of the general countryside. Gain some area knowledge before you get there. It's always helpful to learn at least a few phrases in the native language prior to your arrival there.

Avoid blindly placing your trust in the information provided by that country's local embassy or consulate. After all, they do have an interest in promoting tourism, business and commerce in their country. They may tend to "color" the situation to appear less dangerous than it really is. Instead, log on to the U.S. State Department's website and find out what your own intelligence agencies have to say about the situation overseas. The information you will get will be much more reliable, relevant and up to date.

Once you have obtained general information about the country, it is time to get specific intelligence on terrorist and criminal groups and their recent activities in that area of the world. When conducting your research, ask the question, "who, what, when, where, why and how".

Who: Who are the terrorist/criminal groups operating in your area? Who are they targeting as potential victims – politicians? Businesspersons? Americans and other Westerners? Their own citizens? The wealthy? Christians, Jews, Muslims?

What: What types of terrorist acts are they committing? Assassinations? Kidnapping for ransom? Kidnapping to murder? Bombings? Drive by shootings? Air or sea piracy? What tactics do they employ in their attacks? What is the local government doing to prevent terrorist attacks? Does the local government have a good track record of solving terrorist incidents and dealing harshly with the perpetrators? What is their record of rescuing hostages?

When: When was the last terrorist act? Do the terrorists appear to be active only at specific times of the year or are they committing acts year-round? Are they active only at night or at any hour of the day? Is there a pattern to their attacks?

Where: Where are the terrorist acts being committed? Where are the danger areas in your city, province, region or country?

Why: Why are they committing terrorist acts? Is it for political reasons or are they random criminal acts? Is it directed against their government or the population at large? Are they committing terrorist acts in order to influence U.S. policy or to provoke an incident? Why does this particular terrorist group appear to be successful?

How: By what methods are they committing their terrorist acts? What is their "modus operandi"? Do they prefer using "chokepoints" while the victim is mobile or do they specialize in attacking their victims at home or at work? How frequently are terrorist attacks occurring in this country or region?

The Assessment

An assessment is another critical piece of the intelligence puzzle. An assessment is essentially a "situation report" on the country in which you are planning to reside, work or travel. After you have obtained as much open source intelligence as you can, it is now time to conduct an unbiased and critical assessment on the situation in that country and its political climate. The assessment is an honest evaluation of all that is currently happening in the country and what you predict may happen, based on your research and on the intelligence you've collected.

Assessments are not written in stone. They continually change, based upon the developing situation in your country and in the region at large. Collecting intelligence and assessing the current terrorist threat should be an ongoing process and should continue as long as you are in that country. The longer you live and work there, the more sources of intelligence you will develop and the more accurate they will be.

Continue to develop your "sources", paying attention to what they tell you. Take your assessment of the situation seriously. By now you know better than anyone how the terrorist situation in that country may personally affect you, your family or your employees. Take the proper corrective measures based on your assessment and adjust your security posture accordingly. That may mean that you increase your security status, take additional precautions or even cancel or postpone your trip. Remember that you are responsible for the safety of your family. Take no unnecessary risks.

The Vigilant Tourist

Tourist sites, particularly in the Middle East, are favorite targets for terrorist groups. I have visited some of the more popular tourist sites in Egypt, and I can tell you from personal observation that security at these sites is poor to non-existent. Once again, it is your responsibility to provide for the safety of your family and yourself. This becomes much more difficult overseas, as you most likely don't know what activity is normal and what is out of the ordinary. There are some precautions you can take, however, to increase your chances of not becoming a terrorist victim while on vacation.

- ◆ **Don't be a "tourist".** This may be difficult to do in some areas, but it is to your advantage to try to blend in with the local populace as much as possible. I currently live in a popular tourist area and can usually spot a tourist a mile away. They are usually walking and looking at a map or a tourist brochure and have a camera draped around their neck. They could be carrying a backpack or fanny pack. Usually they are so engrossed in their own activities that they are totally oblivious to what is going on around them.

I have also served as a police officer in a popular tourist area and I can definitively tell you that the bad guys flock to these areas with the belief that tourists are an easy mark. Tourists assume that just because they are visiting a nice place they won't be victimized. They are usually on vacation with their family and are not as vigilant as they should be.

The reality is there is generally more criminal activity in tourist areas per capita than in non-tourist areas. If anything, you need to be more alert when you are on vacation than when you are at home. Why? First of all, on vacation you are more apt to carry more cash than usual and other valuables such as jewelry, cameras, etc. on your person. Second, you are usually in an area unfamiliar to you and probably have little knowledge of the vicinity. You aren't aware when you have inadvertently wandered into a bad area of town. And finally, if you are the victim of a crime and the suspect is apprehended, you are not as likely to travel hundreds of miles to return to testify in a trial. The bad guys know this. So do terrorists, which is one reason that tourist destinations attract these predators. Leave your cash in a hotel safe, or better yet leave it at home and carry credit cards and travelers checks. Hide your cameras, jewelry and other valuables on your person. You might even consider purchasing some indigenous clothing in order to blend in with the locals. You may be a tourist, but try not to look like one.

- ◆ **Avoid standing in lines** at tourist attractions, theaters, restaurants, and other public venues, if at all possible. Research of past terrorist incidents indicates that terrorists like to pick areas where high concentrations of people congregate. If you find yourself in the middle of a crowd, stand off to the side or to the back until the crowd thins out. This may be a time where "following the crowd" does not pay off.

- ◆ **Pay attention to your surroundings.** Try not to get too focused on looking at the tourist sites at the expense of being aware of what is going on around you. In each of the terrorist incidents listed above, there were indicators that something wasn't right prior to the attack. Terrorist attacks don't usually "come of out of nowhere". Look around you. If you see a "tourist" or a local that is more interested in watching you than in looking at the attractions, keep an eye on him. If you see two or more people talking in a conspiratorial manner, or making eye contact and gestures to each other, your security antennae should go up. Is there a car, truck or motorcycle in an area where traffic is prohibited? Pay attention to your "sixth-sense". Does something seem unusual or out of place? Look at the people around you. If most of the crowd seems to be laughing, smiling, and having a good time, but there are a couple of people standing to the side looking just a little too serious, keep an eye on them. If the weather is hot and you observe a person or two who are dressed in long coats, be aware. If anything looks unusual or out of place, start moving away from the immediate area and identify a location where you can go for cover and safety if you need it. Use all of your powers of observation; keep your eyes open and pay close attention to your environment and the people around you.

- **Do not be time and place predictable – again.** Have you heard this before? Yes, and you'll hear it lots more before finishing this book! At the risk of being redundant, this is a most important rule. Avoiding "routines" while on vacation is every bit as important as it is at home and work. Although the travel agency or tourist company may set your schedule, there are things you can do to avoid being too time and place predictable. Resist the urge to always join your group. At the tourist sites, hang back from the crowd, keeping to yourself as much as possible. If there is an attack, the terrorists will aim their weapons or bombs at the greatest concentration of people in order to obtain the maximum body count. Since I'm not particularly fond of being in crowds anyway, it's easy for me to avoid the more crowded attractions. I like "going my own way" when I find myself in a crowd of tourists. This might be one of those times where "safety in numbers" does not apply. Hang back from the crowd and keep your eyes open for anything out of the ordinary. ❖

"Survival is triumph enough."

~ Harry Crews

HOSTAGE SURVIVAL

The main purpose of this book is to provide you with information that will enable you to avoid becoming a target of terrorism. It is obviously far better to detect and avoid an impending attack before its onset than to try to survive one after it has occurred. If you do become a victim of a terrorist incident, it may be because you have omitted some precautionary steps, such as forgetting that you must be time and place unpredictable, or perhaps missed some "pre-incident indicators" -- warning signals that occurred prior to the attack. It could be, through no fault of your own, that you were just in the wrong place at the wrong time. Regardless of why and how it may happen, your single most important goal should now be to survive – get off the "X" and out of the "kill zone" as quickly as you can.

What if you are taken hostage?

To be sure, every hostage situation is different. Terrorists don't play by strict rules of behavior. Nevertheless, the hostage inevitably experiences a wide range of emotions. His fears, frustrations and concerns are very real. The shock of realizing that he is a hostage and that his future is uncertain will play a definite role in his reaction to the situation from a psychological standpoint. Although the situation may look bleak, it is not hopeless. The very first rule, above all else, is – don't give up!

Escape and Evasion

Terrorists have a method by which they logically plan and conduct an attack. Likewise, hostages should have a logical and cohesive method by which they can plan and conduct an escape. "Hostage methodology" is the term we will use to describe this method.

Immediately upon becoming a hostage of terrorists, you should mentally put yourself in the "escape mode" -- that is, start looking for avenues of escape. Generally, the best time to execute an escape is within those first few minutes of your capture. This is the point where there is maximum confusion and minimum control by your captors. An ideal time should be the period from the moment of your capture until you arrive at the permanent holding facility. This could be minutes, hours or days in length. Typically, the terrorists will be somewhat disorganized during this transient period. If at all possible, you should be looking for every opportunity to escape; it's at this point that the terrorists are most vulnerable. They are still in unfriendly (to them) territory and are in the midst of trying to avoid being captured themselves. They are trying to evade the police and security forces that are looking for them. At this point the terrorists have their minds on other things and are most likely in a state of disorganization and confusion. They are anticipating that the initial shock of the attack and your subsequent capture will keep you subdued until they can get you to a more secure area. Use this brief period of pandemonium to your advantage and look for opportunities to escape.

Once the bad guys get you to their secure facility, the cards are heavily stacked in their favor. You may be miles away from civilization and in the middle of hostile territory. You will most certainly be in an unknown location. The terrorists can call in reinforcements to guard you, can lock you in a cell or some other type of holding facility, can drug you, chain you to the floor, or any number of things to maintain control over you. This makes your chances for escape at this point much more difficult. All is not lost, however. Never, never give up hope of escape or rescue. There will most likely be other opportunities for escape if you are patient, observant and active in formulating a plan of escape. The first few days after your capture will be very difficult and may present no opportunities for escape. Your captors will be paying close attention to you and it is at this time that they will be most alert and diligent in their duties. It will be during this time they will most likely be using their best men to guard you.

As time passes, however, your captors will probably become more lax in their security. In any society, guarding prisoners is a tedious and boring task. No commander gives his best and brightest troops the mind-numbing assignment of guarding prisoners. After a few days or a couple of weeks, the terrorists will begin to assign the younger and more inexperienced troops to perform your guard duty. Eventually these lads will slip up, and when they do, you will want to be ready.

In order to be ready to spring into action when the right time comes, you need to know how to logically plan and execute your escape. As in planning any operation, there are certain steps you should take to increase your chance of success.

The first question you will have to ask yourself is this -- "Should I try to escape or should I wait it out and hope my captors release me?" This is largely a personal decision and every person must decide the best alternative for him or herself. What you decide to do will be based on several factors:

- Your physical condition. Obviously, if you are seriously wounded or injured, you may not physically be able to escape.

- Your level of training and experience. If you have a background in weapons, martial arts, survival skills, or you have spent time in the Army Rangers, Special Forces or similar organizations, you will be far better equipped to escape than most people.

- Your fitness level. Escaping may mean hiking for days through the wilderness or other difficult terrain. In a situation of this type, the person in good physical condition is at an advantage and is "ahead of the game".

- Your moral convictions. Escaping may mean that you will have to take another person's life. If you are unable do this, morally or psychologically, you may have no choice but to wait, hoping your captors release you or that friendly forces rescue you.

- Your psychological and emotional condition. Being taken hostage will almost certainly be psychologically devastating. Escaping will probably mean that you will be faced with and must overcome other traumatic experiences, yet unknown. You may have to hide out on your own for an extended period of time. You may have to make your way through enemy territory that, in itself, can be extremely stressful. You stand the risk of getting recaptured, with the distinct possibility of your captors making it even harder for you. All these issues are things you will have to deal with in making your decision to stay or attempt an escape.

There are two schools of thought on the topic of affecting an escape. The U.S. military teaches that a soldier is duty bound to attempt to escape captivity, if at all possible. Other experts in this area advocate waiting it out and hoping for either rescue or release. For a number of reasons, I am on the side of the military in this argument.

To begin with, most terrorist organizations operating in today's environment are not interested in negotiating for the release of a hostage. In most instances their goal is to inflict maximum terror and to obtain a high body count. Today's terrorists are more likely to behead their hostages than to negotiate for their release.

Additionally, if the terrorists don't kill their hostage, they may keep him in captivity for months, even years, before he is released. Obviously the decision to stay or attempt an escape is largely yours. As for me, I am certain that I would do everything in my power to escape.

Keep in mind that although a terrorist may say he will eventually release you does not mean that he will. He might be telling you that simply to appease you, quelling your urge to attempt an escape. Never let yourself fall into the trap of trusting what your captors say. Why should you? Terrorists are proven liars.

If you are taken hostage, there are steps you can take to mitigate the "psychological effects" of a hostage situation. Following are some recommendations that will enhance your ability to survive the incident, either by escape or your eventual rescue.

- Take charge of your emotions. Fear can sometimes have an overwhelming and paralyzing effect on you. Try to control your emotions as much as possible and maintain your composure. Attempt to organize your thoughts and pay attention to what is happening around you. Try to gather as much information as possible about your situation, such as where you are being taken, who your captors are, the direction and routes in which you are traveling, and other pertinent information. Anticipate the possibility that your captors may try to drug you or somehow disorient you. They may blindfold you in an attempt to make you feel isolated and alone.

◆ **Be observant**. Immediately upon your capture you should begin the process of gathering information, or intelligence, about your situation. When you are taken to the location of your captivity, closely study the environment. Ask yourself questions regarding your captivity:

Where are you being held? Is it in a rural or urban environment? Who are your captors? Are they young, old, do they seem to know what they are doing, or do they appear to be inexperienced at the "hostage taking business"? Do they appear to be part of a well-known, organized terrorist group, or are they "freelancers"? What are their demands, if any? Are they negotiating for a ransom, a release of prisoners, or are they simply attempting to make a statement? In what type of facility are they keeping you? What type of building are they holding you in, a private residence, apartment house, etc.? Are there bars on the windows and locks on the doors? Have the terrorists secured you in some fashion by using handcuffs, chains, ropes, etc.? If so, do they take them off sometime during the day or at night when you are asleep? Do your captors seem to have a routine regarding their arrivals and departures? Do they set a pattern in when they eat, pray, change guard, etc.? How many of them guard you at any given time? Are your guards younger members of the group and, therefore, less experienced? Do they appear to be acting unilaterally, or are they part of a much larger operation? Are there other hostages nearby? If so, who are they?

If you have access to newspapers, radio, television or any other media outlet, use this to your advantage as well. In other words, gather as much intelligence about your situation as possible. Not only can this information prove helpful, but this will also give your mind something creative to do. Keeping your mind active is the best way to forestall depression and despair.

- **Formulate an honest evaluation of your situation.** Try to be objective, assessing your situation as honestly and realistically as you can. The worst thing you can do is to give up hope of ever being rescued, but try not to be unrealistically optimistic either. The track record of most governments in rescuing hostages is pretty poor. In the majority of instances, finding a hostage is like finding a "needle in a haystack" -- almost impossible. The odds are overwhelmingly in favor of the terrorists at this point. Give yourself an honest "sit rep" (situation report) based on the information you have gathered and use this to help formulate a plan of action. Intelligence collection is a never-ending process. Because your situation is fluid and ever changing, there is always new intelligence to consider. Keep developing your "assets", gathering as much information as possible. There is no such thing as "too much information" in a hostage situation.

- **Develop a plan of escape.** General George Patton once said, "A poor plan vigorously executed is better than a well-thought out plan executed half way." It doesn't have to be, nor should it be, a complicated plan. Consistently work on and think about your plan. This will keep your mind occupied, giving you some control over your life. Of course, if you ever see an opportunity to escape, take it without hesitation. You should be constantly on the alert for any opportunity to escape, and because you have planned for it, you will be ready if and when the time comes. If you are being held with other hostages, be extremely careful with whom you share your escape plan. If it's someone you trust implicitly, then work together, as two heads are better than one. Solicit his or her suggestions. However, keep in mind that hostages have been known to inform on their fellow captives so that they can ingratiate themselves to their captors. In some cases they may even begin to identify and emphasize with the terrorists, thereby becoming an ally of your captors (and an enemy to you). This phenomenon, known as the "Stockholm Syndrome", was addressed in an earlier chapter. It is better to keep your plan to yourself until you are certain of the loyalties of your fellow captives. Trust no one initially. The terrorist may have "planted" an informant in your midst to try and gain intelligence about you.

- **Engage your captors.** Avoid the appearance of overt hostility toward your captors. Although you may understandably be angry with them, try to develop some type of rapport. Attempt to develop a dialogue with them. It is human nature, even among terrorists, to want to talk. Use this to your advantage and try to obtain as much information about them as possible, being careful not to give away too much information about yourself. By all means, stay away from political or ideological discussions or any topic that may trigger their anger. Try to obtain information about your captor's habits and patterns. Terrorists, like most people, prefer to follow a routine in their daily life. Learn what their routines are and use this knowledge to your advantage. Develop a "friendly" rapport with your captors. This is different from becoming friends with them. Your goal is not to actually "befriend" your captors, but to establish a level of trust that will help them to feel comfortable with you. Once this comfort level is established, they may come to trust you enough to let their guard down, possibly providing an opportunity for escape. Meanwhile, obtain all the information you can, with the intention of using this information in planning your escape. Be especially careful, while building this trust level, not to give away too much information about yourself to your captors. They will also be looking for information they can use against you, your family, co-workers, employers or others with whom you associate. Unfortunately, the terrorists will eventually learn a good deal about you through the news media. If they read the newspapers, watch television or listen to the radio, they will obtain substantial personal information about you. Keep a good balance by not being foolish enough to play the "name, rank and serial number" game, but being careful not to give the farm away either.

- **Stay in shape.** Eat, drink, exercise and try to maintain your strength. You will need all of your resources if and when the opportunity arises to escape.
- **Rehearse.** Although it will probably be impossible to physically rehearse your escape, you can certainly use mental imagery to prepare yourself. Mental preparation is one of the main the keys to success. Once you have developed your plan of escape, mentally rehearse your plan over and over until it becomes second nature to you. Sports psychologists tell us that mental preparation (also known as visualization) for a game is just as important as physical preparation. Visualize yourself being successful. Think about what could go wrong and mentally prepare yourself to overcome these obstacles. Prepare yourself by continually focusing on and mentally rehearsing your plan.
- **Preparation.** Begin gathering any items you will need to help facilitate your escape. You are going to have to be somewhat creative in gathering the tools you will need, because Aunt Martha won't be showing up with a file hidden in her cake. Begin to look around and assemble any items you think may be helpful in your escape. Think of ways you can go about collecting food and water to take with you, particularly if you anticipate a long walk back to safety. Depending on the degree of freedom you may be allowed, try gathering any clothing you have together, keeping these items handy so you'll be able to go at a moments notice. Also, assemble anything that can be turned into a weapon. Think outside the box. Prison inmates have long been adept at making weapons out of ordinary, every-day items. If you have a toothbrush, you can sharpen it and use it as a knife. You can do the same with a pen or pencil. Any metal object, such as a small piece of a mattress box spring, can be removed and fashioned into a weapon. Sticks can be sharpened and even a large rock can be used as a bludgeon (think caveman here!). Look around you. There are probably several objects within arms reach that could be classified as a weapon of some sort. Think like a prison inmate (because that's what you are!).

In an ideal situation, you would find a way to get your hands on one of the terrorist's weapons. Before attempting that, you must be confident in your ability to effectively operate this weapon. The terrorist weapon of choice is the AK-47 rifle or some variant thereof. If you will be going into an area where the bad guys carry AK-47s (and that would be most areas of the world), it would behoove you to learn how to use this weapon. At least learn how to load it, put it into battery, take the safety off and fire it. I read an account recently of a hostage who, during the course of his captivity, had several opportunities to grab one of his captors' AK-47 rifles, but chose not do so. Why? First of all, he had never fired a rifle before, much less an AK-47. Secondly, he did not possess the nerve or the will to kill his captors. Even if you don't know how to shoot an AK-47, you can always use it as a club. If you don't have the will to shoot and kill your captors, however, then learning how to shoot an AK-47 does you no good. If you can steal it and take it with you, it may prove useful as a bartering tool later on. Trade an AK-47 for a ride back to civilization.

- **Pre-operation preparation.** When I was in counter surveillance training, my instructors always told me to "put my adversaries to sleep". In other words, don't do anything that might heighten their suspicion and give them reason to watch you more closely. This applies to a hostage situation as well. Your goal is to get your captors to trust you by being totally compliant and trustworthy. Be the "good" hostage. This may be difficult for some of you "Type A" personalities, but it really is in your best interest to cooperate with the terrorists, at least initially. Although I advocate, as far as security is concerned, not setting a pattern in your daily activities and not being time and place predictable, this is not the case when you are a hostage. You must set a pattern in your daily routine – one that is completely unchanging and predictable, day in and day out. Your objective is to bore your captors to death. Remember, the terrorists who are most likely to be your guards in the latter stages of your captivity will probably be the youngest and most inexperienced of the group. They will most likely be somewhat naive, trustful, and easily bored (not to mention, fairly dumb). Set your daily routine in such a manner that you become someone who is extremely boring to watch. Put them to sleep. Give your captors a false sense of security. Make them believe that you are the type of compliant, phlegmatic, milk toast person who would never dream of attempting to escape. Be the most boring and predictable person on earth. And while you are doing this, continue to look for an opportunity to escape. Keep your eyes open. Your time will come, and when it does, you will be ready.

- ◆ **Don't give up!** Above all, stay positive and focused on your escape plan. Don't give up, and don't let yourself get demoralized. This is what the terrorists are hoping for and expect to happen. Deny them that satisfaction.

Upon seeing your opportunity to escape, seize it immediately. Do not hesitate (remember, "he who hesitates is lost"). Utilize speed, surprise and violence, if necessary, to affect your escape. Try to stick with your plan as much as possible, but remain flexible to any sudden changes in the situation. Have a primary, secondary and tertiary plan, and don't be afraid to substitute if the situation dictates. Adapt, improvise and overcome, and absolutely don't give up or stop until you are safe. Escape may mean having to take a life. Whether to do so or not is a personal decision, but remember that the terrorists have absolutely no regard for your life. You may have to steal a car, harm someone, or do something else that is totally out of character for you. If you don't feel that you can do this, then you might as well resign yourself to either a life of captivity or death (unless someone rescues you), because those are your alternatives.

Once you are free of your captors, go to the nearest police station, military post, U.S. embassy, consulate or other place of safety. Surprisingly, there are instances where for whatever reason (hunger, fear, or getting lost), the captives have voluntarily returned to their captors after having escaped for a brief period of time. If you escape and then decide to return to your captors, you will have most likely signed your death warrant. As for me, I would rather die as a free man than live as a captive. If you have the mindset that no matter what happens you will survive -- you probably will. If, however, you have the defeatist mindset and believe you will not survive, then chances are pretty good you won't.

Besides the obvious and, in my opinion, unacceptable choice to comply with your captors and submit to their demands, there are two other possible outcomes to your captivity: Escape and rescue.

Making The Escape

You've found the opportunity you have waited for and have executed your escape! Your next step will be to make your way to a safe haven. You are not safe until you well away from your captors and in a location where they cannot find you.

How you affect your escape depends on whether you are being held in a rural or an urban area. Obviously, both present unique challenges and require different skills. You could be held in a rural area consisting of a desert, jungle or mountainous environment. You may be a long way from civilization. You will want to know whether the local populace is likely to be friendly or hostile to you. How equipped are you to survive in a hostile environment? How trained are you in jungle, desert or mountain survival techniques? What is the weather like in that particular area? Where is the nearest highway? What other dangers might you face in the wilderness (dangerous animals, difficult terrain, rivers or swamps to traverse, altitude, etc.)?

You know your ability to survive in a harsh rural environment better than anyone. It will be your decision whether you want to take your chances by remaining with your captors or try to survive in the environment. If you think you can make it out successfully, go for it. You never know when you will stumble upon a friendly local that will render assistance or a military patrol out looking for you.

In an urban environment you face a different set of challenges. This is where your knowledge of the local area can save your life. There is a saying, "prior planning prevents poor performance", and this is certainly true in urban escape and evasion. Know the territory in which you live, work and travel. Invest in some good maps and travel books covering your area and study them thoroughly. Become familiar with the layout of the city in which you reside and spend some time driving around for "area familiarization". Know which neighborhoods you should avoid and which are safe and likely to be friendly. Make a note where the police and military checkpoints are, as well as buildings that could be used as safe havens. Collect as much area "intelligence" or area knowledge about your city as you can. The extent to which you know your area may determine whether or not you successfully escape and evade capture. If you do get captured, having area knowledge will enable you to better plan and execute your escape.

It also is a good idea to learn some key phrases in the native language and to become familiar with the cultural aspects of where you reside and work. The more knowledge you gain about your particular environment, the higher your chances of survival during an escape and evasion attempt.

Upon escaping from captivity, one of the first decisions you will have to make is whether to hold up in a relatively safe area, such as an abandoned building, or to take your chances out on the street. There are pros and cons to both, depending on your situation at the time. If you think the bad guys are out looking for you and you are in a hostile area, you may want to consider a "hide site" in an abandoned house, building, or similar structure, at least until things calm down. Depending on the environment in which you find yourself, you may want to conduct most of your movement at night. In that case you will want to hold up in a "hide site" during the day and use the darkness to conceal your movements as much as possible. Some areas are much safer in the daytime than they are at night, and in that case, holding up at night and moving during the day may be the better solution. I have visited in places where the police literally abandon the neighborhoods when the sun goes down and leave the streets to the thugs. Navigating through one of these neighborhoods to affect your escape should certainly be avoided at all cost.

Another good reason to try and find a "hide site" is to give you some time to re-group, assess your situation, and develop a plan of action. Take a discreet look around your site. You might see a police officer, military personnel or a house that you can go to for assistance. Keep in mind that you can't stay in your hide site forever. Once you have assessed the situation and developed a plan, be prepared to move.

The next issue you will have to address is that of transportation back to a safe area. Can you walk out? Do you have a car available to you? Can you ask for a ride from a local? Are you able to carjack or steal a car? (Don't rule that out!). Can you depend on public transportation, such as a bus, train, or taxi?

Regardless of your mode of transportation, be prepared to go through checkpoints on your way to a safe area. Depending upon the area, a checkpoint may be a good thing, a location where you can turn yourself in to the local authorities, gaining their assistance. On the other hand, checkpoints can be a very bad thing. Some checkpoints in Third World countries are not manned by the police or military, but are actually staffed by terrorists, criminals and other thugs, intent on controlling their neighborhoods and extorting money from people passing through. Be aware, that even if these checkpoints are manned by legitimate authorities, not all police and military will be friendly. The officers manning the checkpoint could just as easily turn you back over to your captors, particularly if they are sympathetic to them or are expecting a reward. Numerous tourists, businessmen, diplomats, and other travelers have been kidnapped, robbed or killed at checkpoints by terrorists and criminals (official and unofficial ones) in Third World countries. Unless you are approaching a checkpoint that you know is manned by friendly forces, you should avoid them if at all possible.

Approaching a Checkpoint

Do you know what to do if you approach a friendly checkpoint? How about a hostile one? Whether it is a friendly, hostile, or unknown, you will want to approach a checkpoint very carefully (especially if you are driving a stolen or carjacked vehicle). Generally speaking, the police and military officers manning these checkpoints are not the "sharpest tools in the shed". They also have loaded weapons and maybe an itchy trigger finger. I know of instances where my colleagues have been fired on while passing through supposedly "friendly" checkpoints.

Approaching checkpoints manned by US or other allied forces obviously means you are home free. Still, approach the checkpoint very carefully. Don't approach the checkpoint by driving at a high speed, acting like a crazed maniac. You don't want to get shot by our own troops who may have mistaken you for a car bomber or terrorist. The same advice applies to approaching a checkpoint on foot. Approach slowly and keep your hands clearly visible to the officers. In a vehicle, slowly approach the checkpoint with both of your hands on the steering wheel and in plain sight. Do exactly what the officers tell you to do and remain calm. Tell them who you are and where you have come from. Ask for their assistance and fully comply with all of their instructions.

What if you are approaching a hostile checkpoint? Obviously, your best option is to try to avoid hostile checkpoints if at all possible. Failing this, you can do one of two things. You can try to bluff your way though the checkpoint, which is somewhat risky, or you can try to ram your way through the checkpoint, which is even riskier! That doesn't mean you shouldn't ever try ramming your way through. Sometimes that may be your only option. If you do try to drive through the checkpoint without stopping, there are some survival techniques you will need to know.

Ramming a Hostile Checkpoint

As you approach the checkpoint, make sure your seatbelt is snugly fastened. Slow down initially, making them think you are going to stop. Put them at ease so that they don't suspect anything. Keep both hands firmly on the wheel and look for an opening where you want to aim your vehicle. Your vehicle will go where you are looking, so pick a spot that looks like you could get through, and as you slowly approach the checkpoint with a disarming smile on your face, put the pedal to the metal. Stomp on the accelerator and drive directly through the spot you previously identified. If anyone gets in your way, run over him. And keep going! Do not stop for anything. If you stop, the people manning the checkpoint are likely going to fill your vehicle full of bullet holes (and you along with it). You will be dead before your car stops rolling. They will probably open fire on you, but by the time it occurs to them that you are not going to stop, you should be moving at full speed. It is hard to hit a moving target, so keep moving!

Get down as low in the seat as you can to protect yourself from the gunfire and ram your way through anything that gets in your way. If the bad guys shoot at the car, the chances of hitting you are actually pretty slim. The engine block is a good "cover" and will stop most bullets. Other parts of the car, while not considered as "cover", will slow a bullet down considerably, if not stop it altogether, depending on the bullet caliber and where it impacts the vehicle. It is very difficult to hit a moving object, especially when that object weights three thousand pounds and is coming straight at you. This is why the element of surprise is so important. Many of the gunmen who man these checkpoints do not carry a round in the chamber of their weapons, thereby essentially carrying an unloaded firearm. It will take them a several seconds to figure out that you have no intention of stopping. At that point they will have to chamber a round into their weapon, take it off safe, bring it up and fire. By then they will, hopefully, be impaled on the hood ornament of your stolen 1975 Javelin.

Once again, when attempting to ram through a roadblock, do not stop for anything! Your vehicle may be shot up pretty badly. The radiator on your car may have been hit by gunfire, in which case it will be spewing steam. The tires may be flat and the gas tank hit (don't worry, gas tanks hit by gunfire only explode in the movies). Nevertheless, keep going. Continuing the forward motion of your vehicle is your only option at this point. If you stop, you are probably going to die.

The same principle of "speed, surprise, and extreme violence" applies to this situation as well. Surprise the people manning the roadblock by initially putting them off guard, speed through the checkpoint as quickly and aggressively as possible, and run over or through anything or anyone that gets in your way utilizing extreme violence. I have seen demonstrations where hundreds of rounds of ammunition were fired into every inch of an average passenger car. All of the tires were flat, the engine block and radiator hit, and the gas tank riddled with bullets. And I've seen a person get in that vehicle, start it, and drive away. Don't worry; the car will continue to move. Maybe not far, but it will go far enough to get you out of that checkpoint and down the street a half mile or so. That is far enough to get off the "X" and out of the kill zone. At that point you can abandon the car and continue your escape on foot. If you have to, you can steal or carjack another car. The point is, do whatever it takes to get away and keep moving forward until you are completely safe.

As soon as you have escaped, get as far away from your "prison" as quickly as you can. As soon as the terrorists realize that you've escaped, they'll probably come looking for you. If you are lost, try to find a "hide site" and hold up there until you get your bearings. Anywhere will do, as long as you are relatively safe there. You can then determine exactly where you want to go and develop a plan for getting there. But first you must start moving and keep moving!

Look for someone who can help you, such as a police officer or other authority figure. Be careful of military personnel unless, of course, they are American or other friendly forces. Some of the so-called "paramilitary" forces in Third World countries are either directly involved or sympathetic to local terrorist organizations. Even with legitimate police officers or soldiers, you will have a difficult time communicating with them if you don't speak their language.

Don't discount using bribery to aid in your escape. I haven't been to a Third World country yet where the officials could not be bribed. Indeed, bribery is not only acceptable in most Third World countries, but it is expected. Of course, the officials manning the checkpoint usually don't call it a bribe. It's a "permit" or a "tax" that is required to let you pass through.

Because your captors may have taken everything of value from you, you may not have much to offer them. But just about anything will suffice as a bribe. A watch, sunglasses (very popular in Third World countries), an article of clothing, and, of course, cash can be offered as a bribe. The point is, do whatever it takes to get around, through, or out of the checkpoint in one piece.

Attempt to get to a safe area, such as a government building, police station, the US Embassy or the embassy of a friendly country. The most important thing is, don't give up. You have survived the initial abduction and your time in captivity. You can certainly survive this.

You're Being Rescued --- What Do You Do?
(...or surviving in the middle of a gunfight)

Once the authorities discover that you have been taken hostage, they will most likely begin an attempt to find and rescue you. Almost every country in the world has teams of police, military or intelligence officers that specialize in "hostage rescue". Some of these teams are very good and some are pathetic. In some Third World countries the "hostage rescue" team has actually killed more hostages than terrorists during rescue attempts. I have worked with several of these teams and I can tell you that their attitude is, "so what if we kill the hostages, as long as we kill the terrorists in the process".

Most countries do not want the bad publicity that results if a foreign businessman, diplomat or tourist is taken hostage by a terrorist organization. Beheadings generally are bad for business. In the case of a diplomat, a hostage crisis could strain relations between countries. If a terrorist group operating in the country snatches a foreign businessperson, the resulting publicity could have negative repercussions in terms of foreign investment. Obviously, terrorist activity in any country has a negative impact on the financial well being of that country. Likewise, if too many tourists are abducted, the tourism industry of that country is going to suffer.

In the event that a terrorist group abducts you, the host country will most likely put their "hostage rescue" or counter terrorist teams on alert. Their first goal will be to find you. Depending on the country, this could take days, weeks, months or, as we have seen in some cases, years.

If the local authorities are successful in locating you, they will most likely organize a rescue attempt. Depending on the country, this can be very good or this can be very bad. The training, skill level and experience of foreign counter terrorist and hostage rescue teams vary widely. During my 28-year CIA career, I worked with dozens of foreign counter terrorist and hostage rescue teams. Many countries have excellent teams, made up of well-trained, experienced and dedicated police, military or intelligence officers. Some of them are every bit as good as their U.S. counterparts.

If a U.S. counter terrorist or hostage rescue team is on the way to rescue you, trust me, you are in good hands. The US Army, Navy, and Marine Corps have outstanding counter terrorist units that are, in my opinion, the best in the world. The FBI has an excellent Hostage Rescue Team and sev-

eral regional SWAT Teams that are outstanding. I would trust any of these units with my life. In addition, several foreign countries have well trained counter terrorist/hostage rescue units that are quite good at what they do. Britain, France and Germany have excellent units and the Israelis probably have the most experience in conducting hostage rescues and counter terrorist operations. There are other nations that have very good units that are solely dedicated to conducting counter terrorist-type operations. Some of these units have excellent track records of successful hostage rescues dating back many years.

There are other hostage rescue teams, however, that don't quite come up to the standards of a professional counter terrorist unit. I have been involved with some foreign counter terrorist teams that are made up of regular police officers or military personnel who are poorly trained, ill equipped, and totally unprepared to conduct a complex operation like a hostage rescue. In some foreign units the sole criteria for being accepted in the unit is to be related to a high-ranking government or military official. Skill, desire, training and experience are not necessary requirements to becoming a member of the unit. These people simply want the prestige or money of being in a "prestigious" military or police unit, and have no real desire to actually do the job or to get involved in the hard training required of such units.

On many occasions while working with these units, I would inquire why some non-performing "slipknot" was a member of this supposed elite unit, only to be told that he was the nephew, son or son-in-law of a person of importance. Usually this individual would be an officer in the unit, sometimes even the commander. So what do you think the other members of the unit were like? This is not a team that you want coming to rescue you. In some cases you are better off trying to rescue yourself than depending on an ill prepared and poorly trained team of "wannabe commandos".

In 1985, sixty hostages onboard a hijacked airliner died during a hostage "rescue" attempt that was conducted by the counter terrorist unit of a Middle Eastern country. In 1986, twenty-two hostages were killed when a South Asian country's security force stormed a hijacked aircraft after a 16-hour siege. Four Afghan terrorists kidnapped the US Ambassador in Kabul in 1979. The Ambassador was killed in a hail of gunfire, along with the four terrorists, when Afghan police conducted a rescue attempt. These are only three examples of incidents in which poorly trained and equipped counter terrorist units contributed to the deaths of the very people they were there to save. Keep in mind that, because the terrorists were also killed, these operations were considered a "success" by their respective governments. Some foreign governments consider a hostage rescue mission a success if the terrorists are killed, regardless of what happens to the hostages. Life is cheap in some Third World nations. Obviously, this is not the attitude of the US military and law enforcement community. In the US, a mission is considered successful only if the terrorists are killed or captured and the hostages rescued with minimum or no "collateral" damage.

Regardless of who your rescuers are, however, there are some things you need to know if you should find yourself in the middle of a rescue attempt, particularly if the bullets are flying. These are basically the same precautions I covered in Chapter 14 under the subheading, "Preparing Your Safe Room".

- ◆ **Immediately seek cover.** Cover is anything that will stop a bullet. Depending on the size and caliber of the bullet, several household items can be considered suitable cover. If you can get behind a large or heavy piece of furniture, such as a large desk, do so. A refrigerator or other large appliance may also serve as acceptable cover. At the very least, look for something solid to get behind. If it doesn't stop a bullet, it may at least slow it down and provide some bit of protection.

- ◆ **Get low, and stay low.** As soon as the rescue starts you should get down on the floor and stay there until you are directed to move. Get as low as possible, preferably behind some substantial piece of cover, and hunker down there. Whatever you do, don't stand up in the middle of the gunfight. Stay down until you are directed to stand by a member of the rescue party. The counter terrorist team will want you and any other victims to lie down on the floor, giving them a clear shot at the terrorists. If you are standing, there's a good chance you will be mistaken for a "bad guy". There's also the possibility of being hit by a stray bullet from either a rescuer's weapon or terrorist's weapon, neither one good options. Keep in mind that the terrorists may want to try and "take you out" as a last act of defiance. Stay low and try to hide or at least make yourself a difficult target to hit.

- ◆ **Do exactly what your rescuers tell you to do.** During the hostage rescue attempt, the assault team will be giving directions to the hostages. Follow their directions carefully. Once the shooting is over, they will probably give you some commands. Assuming you can hear them (there will be a lot of shooting, and maybe explosions from "flash-bang" type distraction devices), and understand what they are saying, follow their instructions carefully. Do not make any furtive or sudden movements, and keep your hands in sight at all times. Remember, it may be dark and smoky in the room, and for sure there will be a lot of confusion. The assault team may not immediately identify you as the hostage. The last thing you want is one of your rescuers to mistake you for a terrorist. Keep your hands in sight, and do exactly what you are told. This is not the time to argue or have a discussion with the rescue team. Depending on their

HOSTAGE SURVIVAL

level of training and experience, they may be nervous and jumpy. Don't make matters worse by being uncooperative. After all, they know a lot more about the situation than you at this point, so do what you are told.

◆ **Seek medical attention if you need it.** If you are hurt or injured, let one of your rescuers know, as it may not be readily apparent to them. During the actual assault they will be too busy to attend to your needs, so be prepared to assist yourself. If you have a gunshot wound, apply direct pressure on the wound to stem the bleeding. Keep the pressure on until medical personnel treat you. Most of the good hostage rescue teams have members with specialized medical training, and some even take physicians with them on their operations. Once the shooting is over, make your medical needs known to them, and receive treatment right away.

◆ **Above all, stay calm.** The last thing your rescuers need is a hysterical hostage to deal with in addition to everything else. Remember, they are there to help you, so keep your emotions under control and be prepared to assist them by providing important intelligence information if they request it. They will probably want to know if there are other terrorists nearby, how they are armed, if there are other hostages and other pertinent information. Be cooperative and answer their questions.

As I've stressed repeatedly, my main objective is to help you to avoid becoming a hostage at all. Unfortunately, the reality is that you can follow every guideline to the letter, cross every "t" and dot every "i" and still be captured. If, after doing everything you possibly can to keep yourself safe, and you still find yourself as a "guest" of the terrorists, stay calm, develop your plan, look for escape opportunities and above all, don't give up. Hang in there—your help could be closer than you think. ❖

CHAPTER 19

"You cannot run away from weakness; you must some time fight it out or perish; and if that be so, why not now, and where you stand?"

~ Robert Louis Stevenson

MAKING YOURSELF A "HARD" TARGET

When terrorists are selecting a proposed victim, one of the main criteria they use in determining their vulnerability is to consider whether he or she is a "soft" or a "hard" target. Obviously, the terrorists want to be successful in their mission, and the "softer" a target is the more likely they are to succeed. Your goal, therefore, should be to make your family and yourself "hard" targets. Becoming a "hard" target means that you must take proactive steps in developing your security and that of your family. The aforementioned suggestions regarding residential security, surveillance detection, route analysis, evasive maneuvers and development of the proper mindset are all positive steps you can take toward making yourselves "hard" targets.

There are other things you can do, however, that will also send a strong message to terrorists that you are a "hard target". The message you need to convey is that you are not one who will willingly submit to defeat, capture or submission. It is all about developing a certain attitude, or demeanor, and is worthy of discussion in this chapter.

If you look like a target, you will become a target. Your number one option for personal security is a lifelong commitment to making your family and yourself into "hard targets". Avoidance,

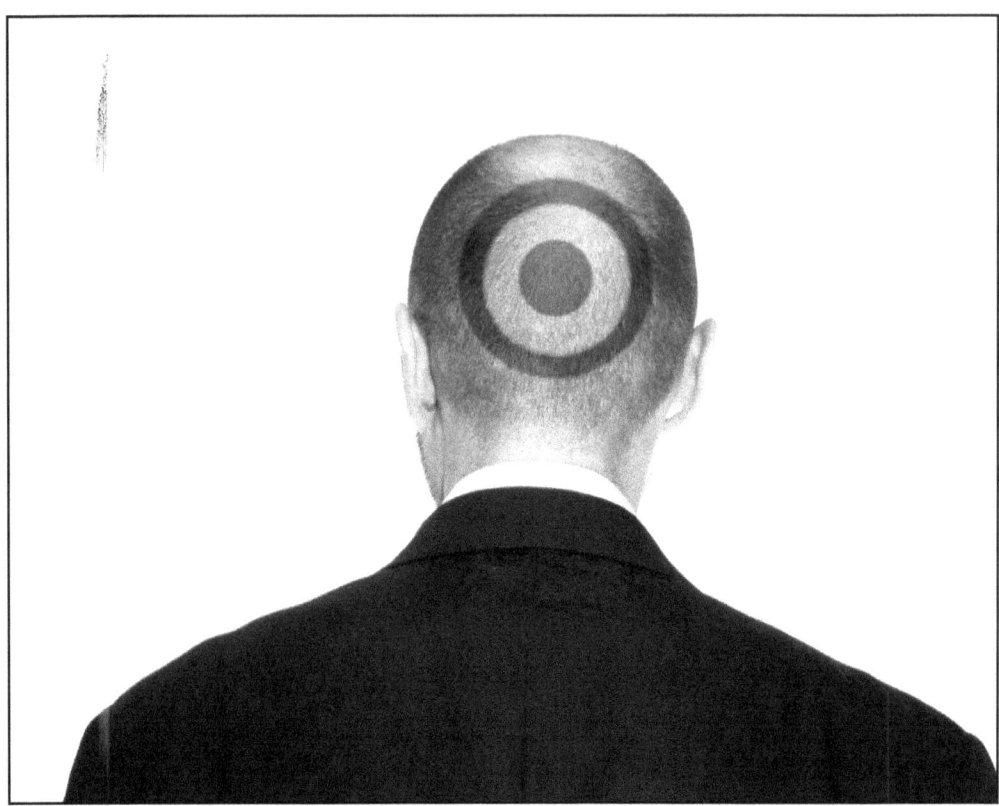

deterrence and action are the components of effective personal security. It is your responsibility, and yours alone, to make sure that you and your loved ones are protected. This job is not for cowards.

Three Principles of Personal Defense: Alertness, Decisiveness, and Aggressiveness

The law of self-defense is derived from English Common Law. It essentially states that you may use sufficient force and violence to prevent an assailant from inflicting death or serious bodily injury upon yourself or any other innocent party.

In the midst of a terrorist attack is not the time to worry about the law. Focus on surviving and getting out of the kill zone first, regardless of what measures you have to take to accomplish this. Worry about the law later.

Most people are not used to dealing with a violent or confrontational situation. As a rule, people live their lives peacefully and neither want nor expect to resort to violence in order to resolve a conflict. There are, however, some situations that can only be resolved by the use of force and violence on your part. In these circumstances you must transform yourself from the "prey" into the "predator".

Your life and the lives of your loved ones depend on your ability to be alert, decisive and aggressive. Pay attention to your "sixth sense" and be alert to what is going on around you. Once a situation begins to develop, take action immediately. Do not hesitate and do not over think what you must do. This is not the time to second guess yourself or rationalize your actions, falling prey to the "paralysis of analysis". Take immediate action and follow through by using speed, surprise and, if necessary, extreme violence to extricate yourself from the situation. Indecision leads to catastrophe! If you have given serious thought and planning to what you are going to do in an emergency, then you will be mentally prepared to deal with it. Correct tactical thinking leads to correct tactical solutions. This, in turn, leads to rehearsal of your plan, resulting in quicker reaction time. All of this leads to confidence in yourself and in your ability to handle any emergency.

It has been said that the best defense is a good offense, and I wholeheartedly agree. At the moment of a terrorist attack, your best bet is to launch an explosive counterattack and get off the "X" as quickly as possible. The plan is to catch the terrorists off guard, hindering their attack and buying yourself some time to make your getaway.

Don't worry about being "fair". This is not a fair fight. You did not start this fight, the terrorists did. Maintain your self-control and stay as calm as you can. Above all, do not panic. If you panic, you will go into "condition black" (frozen in indecision), which is the last thing you want to happen. That is why preparation is so important. If you expect something to happen, plan for it and rehearse your plan, you are much less likely to panic when the real thing happens. If you plan for an emergency and it does not happen, you are no worse off. If you fail to plan and it does happen, however, you have put yourself and your family at extreme risk. At the moment of truth, think of nothing else but staying alive and getting out of the "kill zone". Remember, the terrorist does not care about the law, courts, police or fairness. He only wants to succeed in his mission. Don't let him.

I am convinced that the best thing we can do in the civilized world to thwart terrorism is to educate our citizens. The terrorist is not concerned about the police or military launching a rescue operation to free you. To be sure, our record of successful hostage rescue operations is less than perfect. The terrorist does not fear the police, the law, judges or juries, so it is essential that he fear you.

You must have the skills necessary to detect, defeat and disrupt a terrorist attack on your own. You cannot depend on the police to protect you. A common fallacy is that the police are there to protect the citizenry. The fact is there are far too few police officers to do that. If you are depending on the police to protect you and your family, you are in serious denial. It's safe to say that a well-planned and rehearsed terrorist attack would stand very little chance of being stopped by the police. The primary responsibility for your safety and the safety of your family belongs to you. There are no guarantees of success, but when you make yourself a "hard target", your chances of survival are greatly increased.

Victimology

Victimology is the study of victims and the traits they possess that make them victims. In interviews with penitentiary inmates, the inmates were asked what criteria they used in selecting their victims and the results were quite revealing. The inmates almost universally cited one characteristic as an indicator that a person was an "easy mark". They advised that they selected potential victims predominantly on their demeanor. The victims chosen by these convicted rapists, robbers and murderers appeared to be absorbed in their own private world and were oblivious to their surroundings. These "easy marks" are known as "soft targets".

A person who is distracted and unfocused on his environment is setting himself up to be marked as a victim. As was revealed in the interviews with prison inmates, we know that criminals notice this; but what's even more alarming is that terrorists look for this trait as well. During the surveillance part of the terrorist cycle, terrorists pay particular attention to how you conduct yourself in public. They notice whether you are alert, aware of your surroundings, and paying attention to what is going on around you. They look at your demeanor and deportment in public. Terrorists want a "soft target", someone who goes about his or her daily routine in "condition white" (totally oblivious to anything around them, paying no attention to danger signals). They want someone who is time and place predictable and who goes about their business with little concern for their own security or that of their family.

If you want to avoid becoming a victim of terrorism (or crime, for that matter), "condition white" should not describe you. If it does, you are a "soft target" and you seriously need to consider making some changes in your life. You should give serious consideration to transforming yourself into a "hard target", a person who is observant and interested in his surroundings. Don't make it easy for the bad guys.

Being alert and aware of your environment, taking precautions to change your routes and times and having a viable plan are all things you can do toward making yourself into that "hard target". The terrorists who may be observing you are trying to determine what kind of target you are. Send a message to the terrorists that you are definitely a "hard" target and a bad choice for an attack. Avoid the "victim mentality".

The Victim Mentality

Just what is the victim mentality? Sadly, there are some people who just seem to attract trouble. They have a propensity to be victimized over and over again. These people have what I call a "victim mentality". Ironically, people who tend to be victimized the most are those who do not believe that anything bad will happen to them. "I can't believe this happened to me!" was a recurrent refrain I heard from crime victims when I was working as a street cop. Most of the time they didn't see the attack coming. They were taken totally by surprise, even though in retrospect there were clear indications of trouble prior to the event. The main problem was the victim just wasn't paying attention.

Whether you know it or not, the way you conduct yourself in public sends out messages to other people. Terrorists and criminals are predators. Like wild animals, they look for the weak prey first. Criminals usually pick on people who can't or won't defend themselves. On the African plain the lion always goes after the slowest or weakest wildebeest in the pack. They sense this weakness because their prey gives off subtle signals.

You also give off subtle signals that human predators quickly pick up on. Criminals and terrorists look for people who exhibit certain characteristics common to victims. When you walk with your head down while talking on your cell phone, totally oblivious to anything occurring around you, you are easy prey for the predator. If you look like a victim, walk like a victim, and act like a victim, chances are that sooner or later you will be a victim.

Many people today live their lives in denial, believing they have no enemy who would want to harm them. Webster's New World Dictionary states that denial is the "refusal to believe or accept". I believe that denial is the biggest obstacle people face in dealing with their personal security. Just getting people to believe that there is even a slight possibility they could be in danger is an accomplishment in itself.

Denial serves no useful purpose. Denial is your worst enemy and will convince you that the threat is not serious enough for you to bother taking precautions to protect yourself and your family. The first step you need to take is to be honest with yourself and admit it is a possibility you could become a target of a terrorist attack. Once you have admitted this possibility, the second step is to do something about it.

People who become victims are generally those living their lives in denial, which is precisely why they are victimized in the first place. I am not saying that if you follow the advice offered in this book you will never become a victim. It's entirely possible that if you do everything exactly right you will still be targeted. What I am saying is that by following my advice you will (a) become more alert and aware of your surroundings, lowering the risks of becoming a victim and (b) be better prepared to handle an emergency should one occur. Try not to get carried away to the point of becoming "obsessive" about your security. Nobody likes dwelling on the possibility of a terrorist attack 24 hours a day, seven days a week and nobody wants to be with someone who does. What I am advocating is facing the reality of the world in which you live. It's a dangerous place and preparation is a vital key. The first step in your preparation should be to banish denial from your life and determine to make your family and yourself into "hard targets".

It would be ludicrous to deny that the world is a far more dangerous place today than it was just a few years ago. Clearly, terrorism is on the rise worldwide and shows no signs of abating anytime soon. If you are an American citizen or a citizen of any of the Westernized nations, you are undoubtedly a "high value target" to terrorists. Government officials, businessmen and women and military personnel are particularly vulnerable. Al-Qaeda struck the World Trade center, a symbol of trade and commerce; and the Pentagon, a symbol of government and military power on September 11, 2001. No American or Westerner is safe from terrorism.

Like the common street criminal, terrorists also look for signs of weakness in their intended victims. They look for obvious signs, such as a lack of security precautions on the part of the prospective victim and for subtle signs, such as the victim's demeanor. If a terrorist is conducting surveillance to determine your suitability as a target, he is paying attention to how you carry yourself and to your public demeanor. A "hard target" walks with his head up and shoulders back. A "soft target" walks with his eyes affixed to the ground. A "hard target" appears confident and sure of himself. A "soft target" appears to be easily intimidated. A "hard target" looks people in the eye when they pass. A "soft target" averts his gaze and looks away. In addressing this last point, I m not suggesting you should stare at a stranger in a threatening manner. I'm simply saying to make it obvious you have observed him, are not intimidated and could likely identify him in a police lineup if necessary. Averting your gaze indicates submission and weakness, labeling you as a "victim".

Terrorists, when selecting their victim, want answers to the following questions:

- Are you aware of your surroundings?
- Do you walk with your head up, aware of what is happening around you, and alert to changes in your environment?
- Do you perform a cursory security check of your vehicle before getting in?
- Are you alert when driving? Do you constantly scan the area and the vehicles around you?
- Do you walk and drive while talking endlessly on your cell phone?
- Are you time and place predictable? Do you vary the times you leave home and work, and do you frequently change your routes?

- Do you have a habit of stopping at the same places every day?
- When stopped in traffic, do you leave enough room between you and the car in front of you so that you can make a quick exit if necessary?
- While sitting at stoplights, stop signs, and other traffic control devices do you constantly scan the area around your vehicle?
- While driving in your vehicle do you frequently look in the rear view mirror?
- Do you drive with your windows up and doors locked?
- Are you particularly observant when approaching chokepoints?
- Do you allow random strangers to approach you on the street and engage you in conversation?
- If you do allow strangers to approach you, do you allow them to distract you from your environment?

If your enemy is paying attention to these things, you should too. Make yourself a "hard target" by being alert, aware and observant at all times while in the public domain. Avoid becoming paranoid, but keep in mind that your security and that of your family does deserve your highest attention. Once you begin practicing being a "hard target", taking these precautions will become almost second nature. You will go through your daily routine with more confidence and the assurance that you are doing everything possible to enhance your security posture. Always stay in "condition yellow" when in public. Police officers know this and practice being in "condition yellow", both on and off duty. (Living to draw their retirement is important to them.)

What Police Officers Know

After graduating from the basic police academy in 1974 and beginning my rookie year on the streets, I quickly came to realize two important facts: (1) it is a dangerous world out there and (2) police officers know things about staying safe that the average citizen doesn't know. Police officers have certain "survival" habits they employ both on and off duty. After all, a police officer is never technically "off duty".

In the interest of self-preservation, I incorporated these "survival techniques" into my daily routine. At first, performing some of these steps to enhance my safety felt strange to me. They eventually became a habit and were so ingrained in my daily life that even now I do them almost unconsciously. This habit is known as "unconscious competence".

Before we discuss the things that police officers know and do and explain how you can apply them in your life, let's look at the four levels of competence. I believe it is important for you to know where you stand on the scale of competency, as this is the first step in developing your security awareness posture. How "competent" are you? The four levels of competence, according to the "Kirkpatrick model" (Donald L. Kirkpatrick is the author of *Evaluating Training Programs: The Four Levels*) are: Unconscious Incompetence, Conscious Incompetence, Conscious Competence and Unconscious Competence.

Unconscious incompetence

"Unconscious incompetence" means that you possess no knowledge about security awareness or survival whatsoever. What's worse, you don't even know that you are incompetent in this area. The bottom line is you are totally incompetent when it comes to handling emergency situations and you don't even know it (you don't know what you don't know!). This is not where you want to be on the scale of competence. This is a very bad place to be. If you are "unconsciously incompetent", you are simply prey waiting for a predator to attack. You might as well write "VICTIM" in big, bold letters on your forehead. Hopefully, after reading this book you will realize what you don't know and take the steps to increase your level of security awareness and competence.

Conscious incompetence

"Conscious incompetence" simply means that you are totally incompetent when it comes to your security and safety, but at least you know it. Knowing you are incompetent is a huge step toward preparing yourself to become competent with your personal security. Once you become aware that you are incompetent, you can then take steps to remedy the situation. The real crime is in knowing that you are incompetent and still refusing to do something about it. There are no excuses for being "consciously incompetent" and no one to blame but yourself.

Conscious competence

"Conscious competence" is when you fully understand there are gaps in your security and you know what to do to fix it. You have obtained some level of competency in the skills needed to protect yourself and your family and you are able to execute these skills. "Conscious competence" is clearly better than unconscious incompetence or conscious incompetence. The problem with "conscious competence" is that the person possessing it does not yet have the competency required to do things automatically. He or she must think about what they are doing before they do it. Don't get me wrong, they are competent and they know that they are competent. They have not practiced the necessary survival skills enough, however, to be able to react instinctively. They still have to think before they act, taking up precious time they cannot afford in an emergency.

Unconscious competence

"Unconscious competence" is the place you want to be. You possess the survival skills necessary to save your life in an emergency and you have practiced them enough to become extremely competent in their use. In fact, you are so competent that you can execute these survival techniques almost without thinking about what you are doing. In an emergency situation you react automatically, almost as if you are on autopilot. You do what you have been trained to do quickly, aggressively and with extreme competence. These "survival" techniques are hard wired into your central nervous system and your reactions are almost involuntary.

Professional athletes who have trained for hours, days, weeks, months and years to perfect their sport possess "unconscious competence". Professional fighters don't have to consciously think about blocking a punch that's coming toward their face -- they just do it automatically. They have cat-like reflexes that have been honed through constant, consistent and repetitive practice. Their reaction time is minimal and they execute their techniques flawlessly, aggressively, and without hesitation. This is where you want to be. You can become unconsciously competent through continual repetition of your survival techniques and by practicing these techniques perfectly. Contrary to popular belief, practice does not make perfect. Perfect practice makes perfect. So practice these survival techniques over and over, perfectly, until they are second nature. Repetition is the mother of competence. Practice and rehearse these techniques, both mentally and physically, as if your life depends on it. Guess what? It does. Mentally rehearse what you are going to do, physically practice your techniques over and over and develop a survival mindset. This is the pathway to becoming an "unconsciously competent warrior".

Survival Techniques for Your Daily Life

Once you have attained this level of "unconscious competence", you can now apply certain survival techniques to your daily routine. These techniques should become second nature to you, as natural as walking. Good police officers (the ones who live to collect their retirement) practice these techniques every day they are on the job. I strongly encourage you to adopt these routines into your life.

Following are some "survival techniques" that police officers know and practice. Doing these things every day will significantly increase your chance of survival in a dangerous world.

- **Look ahead – plan ahead.** I recently heard the story of a police officer who was killed when he unknowingly walked in on a robbery in progress at a convenience store. Going in for a cup of coffee, he did not see the masked man with a gun pointed at the clerk, and was killed when the gunman turned and fired on him as he walked through the door. Whenever I walk into a convenience store or similar type of business, I make it a habit to pay attention to what is going on inside. If I see something unusual I pause and take a closer look. Keep your eyes open when driving up to a building and when walking toward a door. Look and see what is going on inside. This goes for your office and home as well. As a police officer, I was always amazed at the people who came home to find that their front door had been jimmied open or a window broken, yet they went inside anyway. This is an excellent way to become a hostage or a rape or murder victim. Stop, look and listen. If something seems strange or out of place, back off and call the police. Good police officers always briefly scan the area around and inside any building they are preparing to enter. They don't want to walk into a crime in progress. You don't want to walk in on a situation where you can be abducted and end up becoming a hostage or worse. Pay attention. Stop, look, listen, and have a plan ready in case you observe suspicious activity.

- **Keep your eyes open.** On patrol, police officers continually scan the area around them looking for signs of unusual behavior or activity. Attacks don't usually come out of nowhere. The bad guys have to have an "eyeball" on you and make an approach before they are able to assault you. By constantly scanning the area around you, you are able to detect signs of people or vehicles that might be surveilling you. You will be able to detect them before they approach you.

While in a vehicle, you should scan right and left, using your side and rear view mirrors to see what's going on behind you. Avoid looking straight ahead using "tunnel vision". Focus your vision both far ahead and close in to you, using your eyes to scan from side to side. Maintain 360-degree security, checking your rear and side view mirrors every few seconds.

When on foot, use your eyes to focus your vision on people and objects both near and far, glancing behind you occasionally. You don't have to swivel your head like the little girl in The Exorcist, but you should look behind you from time to time. Some counter surveillance tricks you can employ are looking in store windows to reflect anyone behind you; doubling back briefly to determine if anyone is following you; and stopping to "window shop" taking a quick glance around. The important thing is to open up your vision, maintain 360-degree security and pay close attention to your surroundings.

- **Sit facing the front door in restaurants.** Whenever I am going out to dinner with another ex-cop, there is always the issue of who gets to sit facing the door. We want to make sure that one of us is positioned to be able to see the front door at all times. The reason for this is because the front door is most likely where the bad guys will enter to do their "dirty business" (robbery, kidnapping, etc.).

Restaurants, bars and cafes in foreign countries are favorite places from which terrorists abduct Westerners. Americans and other Westerners like to congregate in certain bars and restaurants and the bad guys know this. The last place I want to hang out when I'm overseas is in an establishment frequented by Americans and Europeans. You may as well hang a sign that says, "bomb this place", because that could very well happen.

In the United States, violence has been known to occur in restaurants and bars on a fairly routine basis. The 1984 massacre of 21 people in a McDonalds in San Diego, California by James Huberty, a 41-year-old former welder and security guard, is a grim reminder. Another dire example of a "restaurant attack" is The Luby's Cafeteria massacre in Texas, which claimed the lives of 23 people and wounded another 20. One trained individual with a gun could have stopped that shooter. If possible, sit with your back to the wall to avoid the risk of anyone attacking you from behind. If you are in a restaurant or bar and the shooting starts, get on the floor fast and stay there. Look for a secondary exit and head for that.

- **Avoid doorways, dark alleys and parked cars.** The bad guys like lurking around dark and hidden areas such as alleys and doorways. When walking and approaching these areas, move to the curb, giving it a wide berth. Swing wide around corners when approaching them, being especially alert to anyone hanging around in these areas. Bad guys are fond of standing next to the corner of a building, grabbing their victims as they turn the corner. Police officers know this and when chasing a suspect they are taught to approach corners carefully, swinging wide around them.

Be aware of people in vehicles, especially if they seem to have an unusual interest in you. One of the favorite kidnapping methods of terrorists worldwide is to jump out of a parked car, grab their victim and speed off. When walking to your vehicle in a parking lot, be particularly observant. Notice any suspicious people or vehicles in the vicinity of your car. If you even suspect something strange is going on, go back into the building and call the police or alert a security officer. Better to be safe than sorry. I know of a number of individuals, mostly women, who have been abducted in parking lots while walking to their cars. If you park in the same parking space or parking lot every day, you are easy prey for a terrorist. All they have to do is stake out your vehicle, wait until you leave work at the end of the day and grab you. As with your travel routes, don't be time and place predictable where you park either.

- **Be wary of strangers approaching you on the street.** No one likes being rude or unfriendly, but when it comes to your safety there are some precautions you should take if approached by strangers on the street.

When a police officer is conducting an interview of a suspect on the street, he assumes what is called the "field interview stance". In the field interview stance the officer avoids directly facing the person with both feet parallel to each other. Instead, he will position his body somewhat so that one foot is slightly in front of the other, and he presents his "weak" side to the suspect. Police officers do this to keep their gun side away from the subject and to respond with defensive measures should they be suddenly attacked. Their hands are up in a non-threatening and casual manner at about waist level. This is so they can (a) draw their weapon quickly if needed, and (b) have their hands up in a defensive position in order to fend off an attack. Most importantly, they never let the person get within an arm's length of them. If you are in a position where a person suddenly lunges at you, you will want time to be able to move out of the way and take defensive measures. Being outside of arm's reach buys you the time to react.

Never allow strangers to take your hand on the street. There is no good reason a total stranger should want to do that. It's highly possible this could be a diversionary technique. He could be trying to distract you while an accomplice approaches you from behind. When a stranger on the street stops you and attempts to engage you in conversation, your "threat" antennae should immediately go up. I have a friend who recently traveled to a major European city and became distracted by two guys engaged in a supposed "fist fight". While he was engrossed watching the fight, another person came up behind him, grabbing his bag containing his wallet and passport. All three of the men then ran off in different directions. It was a setup and he didn't see it coming. Terrorists have also been known to use similar distraction techniques prior to conducting attacks. Remember this when traveling abroad and don't be fooled by the "friendliness" of a stranger or allow yourself to be distracted by a "disturbance". The best thing to do in one of these situations is to leave the area quickly. It's okay to be reasonably friendly to strangers who approach you, but maintain caution at the same time. The bad guys want you to be at ease and, like a spider, draw you closer and closer into their web until you are trapped. Don't fall for it.

Use all of your senses, keeping your distance and maintaining a defensive posture and "360-degree security" while on the street. The encounter will most likely turn out to be innocent, but it could be a contrived incident to distract you, setting you up to be a victim.

- **When carrying a weapon, keep your "gun hand" free.** If you are fortunate enough to legally carry a firearm and have the training to use it safely and effectively, you should make it a point to keep your "gun hand" free whenever possible. Your gun hand is the hand (usually your dominant hand) that you use to draw and fire your weapon. Assuming you are right handed, carry all packages and other items in your left hand. If you have to quickly draw your gun, you will not be encumbered by anything in your "shooting" hand. Dropping a package that you are carrying takes time that you cannot afford to lose. Every second counts in a gunfight. In the "normal" world a second may not mean much. In the world of a shooter or gun fighter, a second is an eternity. It can mean the difference between winning and losing, life and death. Remember that you are reacting to someone else's action. Action is always quicker than reaction, so you are already behind the power curve. Don't make it worse by having packages in your hands that you have to drop before drawing your weapon. (This could be a good excuse to use for having your spouse carry most of the packages. "Gotta keep that gun hand free, honey!"). ❖

"Courage is resistance to fear, mastery of fear, not absence of fear".

~ Mark Twain

MANAGING FEAR AND STRESS

Police work is one of the most stressful jobs anywhere on the face of the planet. Police officers worldwide may go from absolute boredom one minute to unimaginable terror, stress and fear in the next. Good police officers know this and try to mentally prepare themselves for the day it will come. In this chapter we will discuss methods that will enable you, like the police officer, to better manage the fear and stress associated with a terrorist incident.

Research in the area of stress management indicates that when a person is subjected to a high level of unanticipated stress, such as that occurring in a terrorist attack, the body prepares for one of three options: fight, flight or freeze. We have already concluded in previous chapters that freezing (also known as "hyper vigilance") is not an option you have in an emergency situation. That leaves you with one of the remaining two options -- fight or flight. Depending on the situation, you may have to do both.

Flight or Fight

During an unexpected emergency, the body goes into a survival mode. There is a big dump of adrenalin rushing throughout your nervous system, resulting in certain physiological changes in your body. Several of these manifestations were discussed in an earlier chapter, but should be re-emphasized here. You can expect a significant rise in your heart rate, as well as in your rate of respiration. Research has shown that when a person's heart rate exceeds 145 beats per minute, his performance begins to deteriorate. There is a negative affect on mental and physical reaction time, as well as deterioration in muscle coordination. You may experience "tunnel vision" (perceptual narrowing) and auditory exclusion as well. These are normal responses to a sudden onset of stress and fear. Your body is trying to prepare you for action (flight or fight).

Knowing in advance that these physical changes will occur will help you deal with them. If you know that tunnel vision will most likely occur, you won't be surprised when it does. Once you recognize what is happening, you can make a conscious effort to "open up your vision", enabling you to see what is going on around you.

Auditory exclusion is another physiological phenomenon that may occur during a stressful event. Auditory exclusion limits your ability to hear. This may appear as either total hearing loss or selective hearing loss (the inability to hear certain sounds). I have observed people who, while participating in stressful training scenarios, fail to hear another person yelling in their ear. They later claimed they had never heard anything at all, or if they heard something, it was muffled or inaudible. That is why, during an emergency, you may have to repeat commands to a friend, family member or others with whom you are trying to communicate. In my experience, words and phrases generally have to be repeated at least three times before it begins to register with someone who is under stress.

Loss of manual dexterity is another physical manifestation of stress. Research indicates that fine motor skills are negatively affected during a stressful situation. Fine motor skills are anything requiring a high degree of manual dexterity, such as using tweezers or threading a needle. Gross motor skills are much more effective under stress. In a vehicle, smashing the accelerator down to the floor and driving straight ahead is an example of a gross motor skill. It takes no fine motor skills to perform this act. Be aware that your ability to execute any procedure requiring fine motor skills may be drastically diminished during a terrorist attack.

Not everyone manages the effects of stress in the same manner. The number and severity of mental and physiological stressors present in a critical incident vary from person to person. You may not react to stress the same as I would; however, almost everyone experiences some degree of reaction. You need to be aware of the probability of these physical manifestations occurring during a high-stress event. A surprise at such a critical time is a distraction you can't afford.

Reducing Your Stress in an Encounter

There are some other things you can do to help mitigate your stress during a violent encounter.

- Rehearse various scenarios in your mind. Mentally prepare yourself by playing the "When/Then" game. Use visualization techniques to help you plan a course of action. Should an emergency situation occur, instead of asking, "What is happening?" you will say, "I knew this could happen, I am prepared and I will survive."

- Get in shape. The better physical condition you are in, the better your body will handle the stress of an emergency.
- Have confidence in your abilities. If you have prepared mentally and physically, you are ahead of the game. Developing "unconscious competence" in your abilities will help you handle any stressful situation.
- Practice deep breathing techniques. Taking deep breaths when under stress helps get your heart rate and respiration under control. Once your heart rate and respiration are under control, the effect stress has on your body will begin to dissipate.
- Practice anticipation mindset. If you expect something to happen, you won't be surprised when it does. When in public, stay in "condition yellow".
- Have a backup plan. In the event the first plan doesn't work, be sure you have a secondary plan of action. Try to prepare yourself and your family for any eventuality. Have confidence that your plan will work, and mentally rehearse your plan often.
- Resolve in your mind that you will survive. If you understand that you have no option but to survive, regardless of how bad things may be, you will be more likely not to give up when faced with a stressful situation. Develop a "survival mindset".

The ability to control fear and stress is, in my opinion, clearly the most important factor in surviving a violent encounter. You can be a world-class shooter or an internationally known martial artist, yet your skills will do you no good if you allow fear and stress to overwhelm you. Stress-induced paralysis (Condition Black) is the single greatest threat you will face in an emergency situation. Faced with a violent encounter, the stress that you experience may seem overwhelming. You will freeze, fail to react, and become a victim. This is exactly what the terrorist expects you to do. The word "terror", as defined in the American Heritage Dictionary, is "intense, overpowering fear" and "the ability to instill fear". Deprive the terrorist of his ability to instill fear by refusing to be overpowered.

Making the decision to react quickly and violently is something you must decide beforehand. Resolve to do whatever it takes to survive the encounter. The easy way out is to do nothing and hope that the bad guys have mercy on you. They won't. At best, you will be taken hostage and later, after having used you for propaganda purposes, they may very well kill you. Decide to do something. Doing something, anything, is always better than nothing. Make your mind up now that you will fight, that you will get off the "X" alive, and you will survive whatever happens. Above all, never give up. To give up is to die.

Control the Fight

Most of us like to be in control, or at least we like to think we are. The reason many people don't like to fly is their sense of powerlessness as they cruise along at 32,000 feet. They feel much better driving their car than when they are flying, although statistics show they are much safer in the airplane than their car. Why is this? Because while driving they feel as if they have more control over the situation.

The problem you face during a violent encounter is that you are not in control—the aggressor is. He decides when and where to initiate the attack and by what means. In essence, he has your life in his hands. That's the way he wants it. Like everyone else, he wants to be in control too.

While it's true that the terrorist has initial control of the situation, it does not have to remain that way. You can and should take control of the fight as quickly as you can. Either you control the fight or the terrorist will. Taking control of the situation will give you a definite psychological advantage over your opponent, so take control as quickly as you can.

To attain this control, you must launch a swift, violent, aggressive and unrelenting counterattack. This could mean that you will have to use your vehicle to run over your assailants or to ram their vehicle. You might have to use whatever weapons you have at your disposal to commence a fierce counterassault against them. Whatever your tactics, fight back aggressively and keep fighting until you can get away from the attack site. Take the fight to the terrorists in an unrelenting onslaught of fury. Determine that you are not going to willingly give up your life or your freedom, at least not without a hell of a fight. Then do whatever it takes to facilitate your escape from the "kill zone".

Hesitating, reacting half-heartedly or being unsure of yourself will lose the fight every time. You have a very short window of opportunity to react swiftly and violently, catching your aggressors off guard. Remember, they don't expect this kind of reaction from you – they're expecting all out surrender. That is why an aggressive counterattack just might work for you. Your violent reaction to their assault could be just enough to stun and distract them, possibly breaking off the attack altogether or allowing you to make your getaway.

The great football coach Vince Lombardi once said that "winning is nothing compared to the will to win". When confronting a violent situation, you must have that determined will to win the fight and survive whatever is thrown at you. That "will" can be developed through confidence in your abilities, and that confidence is obtained through visualization and practice of your techniques.

Control your stress, stay in the fight and have the will to win. This is what it will take to get you through the fight and help you survive.

What to expect during a violent confrontation

Most people have never been involved in a violent confrontation and thus have no idea what to expect. Watching a shootout or bombing on television cannot come close to replicating what will happen in a real life encounter and there is no way to sufficiently describe it. You must experience it to know the abject terror and confusion that occurs during a violent emergency, and only if you manage to live through it will you be mentally prepared for the next encounter.

Every terrorist incident is different. While the basic elements in the attack may be the same, each incident has it's own unique characteristics. There is no possible way to define and describe every kind of terrorist incident you may face. Terrorists are a creative bunch. Just when you think you have them figured out, they come up with something even more deviously creative and unconventional. There is no way the military or law enforcement can possibly predict or prepare for every eventuality. No two terrorist attacks are the same. While they may share some similar characteristics, each terrorist incident is different.

Some commonalities are inherent in all terrorist incidents, however. During a terrorist attack some things are inevitable, and to be mentally prepared, you should be aware of what they are. Mental preparation is one of the keys to staying out of "condition black". Knowing what to expect in a violent confrontation goes a long way toward dissipating the stress and anxiety you will experience.

The first thing that you should expect in a terrorist attack is . . . Terror! Total, sheer, absolute terror! Fear, fright, alarm, horror, panic and trepidation are all emotions associated with terror. You should be prepared to experience any or all of the following:

- **Extreme confusion and uncertainty.** Your first response will be to wonder what the hell is going on. There will be disbelief and incredulity that a terrorist attack is actually underway and that you are the target of that attack. You will initially be confused about what is happening, where the attack is coming from and how many terrorists are involved. You will likely be confronted with a mass of people running around in shock, fear and confusion. In the early stages you will be uncertain how you should react. Should you "duck and cover", run, fight, or freeze? This is where playing the "when/then" game helps. If you expect it, you aren't as likely to be in denial and your mind will quickly accept the fact that you are, indeed, in extreme danger. Only then will you be able to recover from the initial shock, awe and confusion of the attack and transition into acting on your pre-determined plan.

- **Blood and gore.** Be prepared for the area to be littered with blood and body parts, particularly if the attack is initiated with a bomb or other improvised explosive device. Hopefully none of the blood or body parts will be yours, but if they are, don't just give up and lie down and die. Perform "self-aid" (stop the bleeding by applying direct pressure to the wound) and carry on with your plan to get off the "X" and out of the kill zone. That accomplished, immediately get to a safe place where you can seek medical attention. Even though they may look serious and produce a lot of blood, most wounds are not fatal. You can survive a fairly serious wound by using standard first aid techniques. (Note: I highly recommend that you sign up for a basic first aid/CPR course through your local Red Cross, YMCA, fire department or other agency, regardless of whether you travel overseas. It can't hurt and may just what you need to save your life or the life of another.) Many people freak out at the sight of blood (not to mention body parts). I have seen highly trained police officers and military personnel get faint at the sight of blood. If this describes you (and I must admit to having had that experience, myself), don't be surprised by it -- expect it. Expect it, fight through it and, above all, don't give up. You can faint later.

- **Noise.** For most of my career in the CIA, in law enforcement and the military I was exposed to gunfire and explosions on an almost daily basis. I am used to it. I do realize, however, that most people have no idea what five pounds of C-4 explosive sound like when it goes off, much less the destruction it causes. The sight and sound of an explosion can have a startling effect on you. The sound of an AK-47 assault rifle going off in your ear is going to be extremely loud. People are going to be yelling and screaming and confusion will reign. Do not let this distract you from your objective of getting off the "X". Try to filter out all extraneous noise, such as gunfire and people yelling and screaming. Pay attention to the noise that is important -- communicating with your friends or family. Stay focused, not allowing the noise to distract you. Whatever else you do, don't freeze – stay out of "condition black".

- **Fear.** Expect to be afraid. Courage is not the absence of fear – it's being afraid and acting anyway. If someone tells you that they aren't afraid during a violent confrontation, they are either (a) lying, (b) crazy, (c) stupid, (d) have never really been in a violent confrontation or (e) all of the above. In any case, you don't want someone with that attitude around you in an emergency situation. I have seen some of the biggest, seemingly toughest and self-glorifying police officers and "commandos" go into absolute "condition black" when faced with a crisis situation. On the other hand, some of the very people you would expect to panic in a violent situation come through like champs. Remember that it's perfectly okay to be afraid, but never let fear paralyze you, keeping you from doing whatever is necessary to survive.

Words cannot possibly do justice to what will happen in a real life terrorist incident. There is no way that we could possibly replicate the terror those passengers must have experienced on the 9/11 planes that crashed into the World Trade Center, The Pentagon, and in a field in Pennsylvania. However, knowing what to expect in a violent confrontation will help dissipate the fear, stress and confusion you will undoubtedly experience. Regardless of what happens, you can survive. Indeed, it is the "survival" attitude and mindset that you must take into the fight in order to survive. ❖

CHAPTER 21

"The best we can hope for concerning the people at large is that they be properly armed."

— Alexander Hamilton, The Federalist Papers

"I've got a firm policy on gun control. If there's a gun around, I want to be the one controlling it."

— Clint Eastwood

SHOULD YOU CARRY A FIREARM?

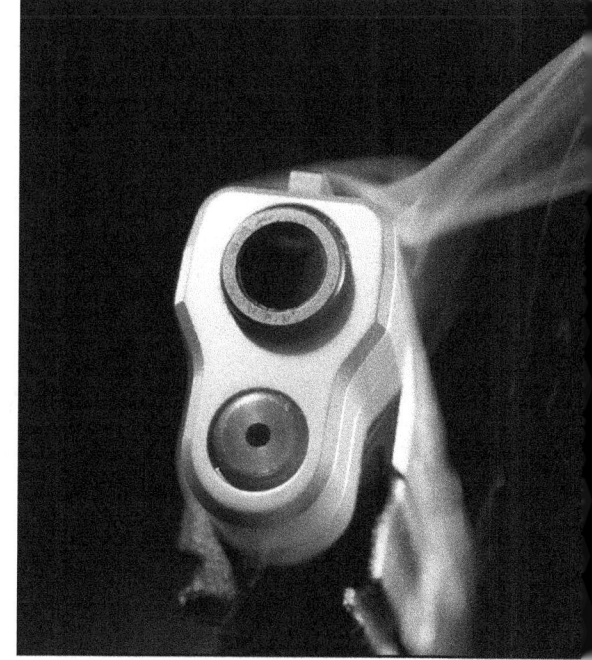

Although the main topic of this book is not gun fighting, the use of firearms deserves some consideration when we are discussing your safety. Some of you are authorized to carry firearms and do so on a daily basis. Others will carry a gun, authorized or not. Some of you may be authorized to carry a firearm, but have chosen not to for reasons of your own; and last are those who want nothing to do with firearms at all. This next section is specifically written for those of you giving consideration to carrying a firearm, and in it I address some questions you may have regarding carrying your weapon. It will also provide information on the different types of firearms available, with the goal of helping you make an informed decision when selecting and purchasing your weapon.

Now, About That Firearm..

Is it legal for you to carry, own or possess a gun? Legality, in my mind, takes second place to your safety and that of your family. In some jurisdictions it is against the law to even possess a firearm, the Second Amendment to the Constitution notwithstanding. Ironically, it is those cities that have the highest crime rate, including murder, rape and robbery. That said, it is almost always best if you operate within the law and I'm certainly not advocating that you do anything illegal. When overseas, you should become familiar with the weapons laws in that country. They may vary from state to state and province to province, so check with the U.S. Embassy if you need clarification. Again, it is best to follow all of the laws of the country in which you live, work and operate. You don't want to end up doing forty years in a South Asian jail because of a weapons violation.

- What type of firearm should you choose for self-defense? There are many schools of thought concerning the best weapon for self-protection. Almost everyone has a different opinion on this topic, and there is no single firearm that is suitable for everybody. Your choice should reflect the weapon that you are most comfortable with and that will suit your particular needs. Obviously, a belt-fed, fully automatic machine gun is an excellent defensive weapon. But how practical is it? What you choose should be small enough to conceal and comfortable enough to carry 24 hours a day, 7 days a week. For home defense, a shotgun is an outstanding weapon. However, if you want something that you can carry concealed on your person, a pistol is the obvious choice. (And I definitely recommend that you carry your gun concealed. You don't want it taken away from you and used against you). You also need a weapon in a large enough caliber to effectively stop a man-sized threat. Several gun manufacturers make small, lightweight and easily concealable handguns in calibers ranging from .22 to .45. For self-defense purposes, I recommend at least a 9mm semi-automatic pistol or a .38 revolver. My personal favorite is a .45 caliber model 1911 semi-automatic pistol. The weapon that you should choose, however, should be what you like and feel confident with. If you are not completely confident in your ability to carry and use your weapon, you might as well not even carry one.

- Are you well trained in the use of your chosen weapon? I can't stress enough the importance of obtaining sufficient training prior to carrying a firearm. By "sufficient training", I don't mean going to the local dump and plinking at tin cans in your spare time. Enroll in a good, well-known firearms training school. Yes, I know they are expensive, but you generally get what you pay for. You want to be instructed by someone who is an expert in defensive, combat shooting. Don't let the cost deter you. Get the best training possible. What you are buying is competence and confidence in your ability to handle a firearm, and peace of mind. The good schools are expensive, but the talent they have in terms of instructors is well worth it.

There are many firearms instruction schools in the United States, but make sure the one you choose stresses (a) safety and (b) defensive combat shooting. Obviously, safety is paramount in any firearms school. If you don't feel safe, you are not in the kind of environment that facilitates learning. You will also want a school that teaches defensive combat shooting, versus target shooting. The main difference between combat shooting and target shooting is that, while target shooting stresses good marksmanship, it does not address the tactical side of a gunfight. Combat shooting, however, stresses both marksmanship and tactics. In a good combat shooting course your training will replicate the stressful conditions you will encounter during in an actual gunfight. Schools that emphasize target shooting are generally geared toward people who want to participate in shooting competitions. Unless you plan on becoming a competitive pistol shooter, pick a school that emphasizes combat and survival type shooting. Many of the instructors are ex-cops or military combat veterans who have been in actual gunfights. They can teach you what to expect and how to react in an emergency situation, so pay attention and do what they tell you. What you will learn in these schools (at least in the good ones) could save your life someday. Consider the tuition a good insurance policy.

You must practice, practice, and then practice some more! Once you have obtained a certificate or two from a reputable firearms school, be sure to join a range and get in some quality practice time. Shooting skills are perishable. Aim for going to the range every month or so and perfecting the fundamentals that you learned in your training classes. Practice shooting from different positions and at different distances. Be sure to practice in low light and no light conditions, with and without your flashlight. Work on drawing your weapon from concealment. Whether you carry your gun in a hip type holster, ankle holster, a fanny pack, or simply keep the gun in your pocket, practice drawing and shooting the weapon from different positions. I recommend keeping your handgun in a good hip holster, since this is a safe and effective way to carry a firearm. If you keep a gun in your vehicle make sure it is readily accessible to you at all times. A gun will do you no good if, during a car jacking, you have to root around under your seat or in your glove box for your weapon. Also, don't keep your gun unsecured on the seat beside you. If you get in an accident, or if you have to ram your way through a terrorist attack, your gun may fall in the floor and slide under the front seat. The best way to secure your handgun in a vehicle is on your person, in a good quality hip holster. Practice drawing your weapon while seated in your car, with your seatbelt on. Make sure your weapon is unloaded when you practice this! You don't want any holes in either your car or your leg by practicing this technique with a loaded gun. Don't think that, just because you attended a one- or two-week firearms school, you are a "gunfighter". Only by constant and dedicated practice will you achieve the competence necessary to defend yourself with a firearm. Perfecting your self-defense skills should be a life-long pursuit.

- Where will you store your weapon at home? Generally speaking, your weapon should be readily accessible to you at all times when you are at home. However, where and how you secure your firearm largely depends on your personal situation.

Obviously, if you live alone you are going to secure your weapon differently from someone who has children in the house. The safety of your children takes precedence over the accessibility of your weapon, in my opinion. Having raised five children myself, I can tell you from first hand experience that they are going to snoop. You should make it crystal clear to them what to do if they discover a firearm in the house. They should be told to absolutely never touch or handle a firearm under any circumstances. Even if you, personally, don't own a firearm, you will never know when they will be in the home of someone else who does own a firearm. When my children were growing up, I instructed all of them on the dangers of handling firearms by an untrained person. I also took most of them out to the range to practice shooting on occasion. Although your children may be "gun savvy", you will never know when a child visiting in your home might accidentally stumble upon your firearm. If you have children, or if children have access to your home, I highly recommend that you secure all of your weapons. There are many good locking devices on the market that can ensure that your firearm is secure, yet readily available when you need it.

If you live alone and do not have children visiting in your home, store your weapon in a place that is secure, yet quickly accessible. Practice retrieving your weapon from storage, timing yourself to see how long it takes to get to your gun and ready it for firing. If it takes you longer than thirty seconds or so, consider making some changes in how and where you store your gun. As with anything related to firearms, safety is paramount. Safety should never be secondary to convenience when it comes to weapons.

I am a firm believer that having any kind of gun is better than having no gun at all. The type of gun you have can make a difference; however, it's your attitude and mindset that wins fights -- not your equipment. I have known people who have the absolute best equipment money can buy, but don't have the "combat mindset" attitude. If you don't possess that attitude, you should probably remain unarmed. I know of several instances where an unarmed criminal took a gun away from an armed citizen, turning the gun against its owner. How did this happen? It happened because the owner was unsure of himself, lacked confidence in his ability to use his weapon effectively and lacked the proper "combat mindset" to defend himself. If you carry a gun for personal defense, make sure that (a) you possess the skills necessary to use it safely and effectively and (b) you are willing to use it (having the "combat mindset"). If you don't think you have the mindset to use a firearm against another person in an emergency, then please don't carry one. The chances of someone taking it away and using it against you are too great.

Liability and Your Firearm

This brings us to the issue of liability. The last thing you need to worry about when you are trying to save your own life or the lives of your family members is liability. There is no doubt that we live in a litigious society today.

When teaching firearms courses I always get inundated with questions regarding liability. Most of them are legitimate questions and the topic of liability should be addressed in firearms training classes. Anyone who is authorized to carry a gun should be familiar with the laws concerning the use of deadly force in the jurisdictions in which they live and work. Generally, you are authorized to use deadly force only when you or someone under your protection is under threat of death or serious bodily injury. Laws may vary, however, from state to state, city to city, and country to country. Become intimately familiar with them if you carry or possess a firearm. Obey the law and make absolutely certain you have a clear understanding of when you can and cannot use deadly force. In the midst of a violent confrontation is not the time to begin questioning and second-guessing the legality of using your weapon. Many a police officer has been killed or seriously wounded in the line of duty when he stopped to consider the possible consequences, rather than taking the action that could have saved his life. Act first and worry about the consequences later.

If you don't have a weapon, chances are good the terrorist does. Therefore, one option you have is to take his gun away from him and use it against him and his associates. There are a couple of relatively simple techniques you can learn to take a firearm away from someone, but it takes diligent practice to master them. If you do decide to try and take a weapon away from a terrorist, you will probably get only one chance -- so make it count. Taking a pistol away from someone is easier than trying to take a long gun, such as a rifle, carbine or shotgun, but even that can be done with practice.

Upon getting the gun away from the terrorist, of course you must (a) know how to use it and (b) be willing to use it. Going to a range that has several different types of weapons and learning how to use them is good idea. If you are going into a high threat area you may want to concentrate on the gun most favored by terrorists, the AK-47 assault rifle or one of its variants.

Selecting Your Firearm

The AK-47 Assault Rifle

The AK-47 (Automat Kalashnikova 1947) is an assault rifle that is manufactured in several former Communist-bloc countries, notably the former Soviet Union and China, as well as some Eastern European nations. It is a relatively easy gun to learn to shoot. It is a weapon that was made for the "masses", those "peasant revolutionaries of the Third World", who neither had the time nor the ammunition necessary to learn how to operate a complicated weapons system. There are probably more AK-47s in the world than any other type of firearm, and more of them are produced each year than any other type of assault rifle. That and the ease of firing it are probably the reasons the AK-47 and its variants are generally regarded as the revolutionary's weapon of choice. Mir Amil Kansi used an AK-47 to murder two Agency employees in the 1991 terrorist attack at CIA Headquarters.

The Semi-Automatic Pistol

Some terrorists prefer to use semi-automatic pistols, since they are much easier to conceal than a rifle or other long gun. Most all pistols operate in basically the same manner, although you will want to become familiar with several different types. Some have external safety devices which have to be in the "off" position before you can fire the weapon, while others have internal safeties that require no external manipulation. Try to become familiar with and learn to safely manipulate both types of pistols.

The Revolver

Revolvers are another type of handgun, although they are increasingly becoming less popular than the semi-automatic pistol. Revolvers are easier to handle and manipulate than semi-automatic pistols, simply because there are no external safeties on contemporary revolvers. All that is required to make them fire is to pull the trigger. It is doubtful that most terrorists will be armed with revolvers, but you never know. Criminals, on the other hand, might very well be armed with a revolver, so it certainly wouldn't hurt you to become familiar with them as well.

Assuming you become proficient in taking a weapon away from a terrorist and know how to operate the weapon, will you actually be able to use it against him? Trust me, he is probably not going to throw up his hands and surrender to you, even if you now possess his weapon. Once you take his weapon from him, you will have to make sure you keep it from him. Chances are very good he will make a concerted effort to get it back from you. In that event, you will have no choice but to shoot him.

Shooting to 'Wound' or Shooting to Kill

Another question that I always get during a basic firearms class is, "Should I shoot to wound or shoot to kill?" There is a common misconception, largely obtained from television and the movies, which says you should shoot to wound an assailant. "Shooting to wound" is viewed as preferable to shooting to kill. In the first place, under stress you are not going to be able to effectively place a non-fatal shot to a person's arm, leg or other extremity. During a gunfight, which definitely qualifies as a stressful event, you will be lucky if you can get some shots off and hit the attacker anywhere on his body. Do not try to "shoot to wound" your assailant. Instead, you should shoot to stop your assailant. Your objective is to stop the attack as quickly and effectively as possible. If that means you have to shoot the terrorist multiple times to stop him, so be it. Shoot to the center mass of the body, where the vital organs are located. This is also the largest target on a man and the easiest to hit under stress. Keep shooting until the terrorist no longer presents a threat to you or your family.

I have worked with thousands of shooters during my career in the intelligence, law enforcement and military arenas, and have seen some excellent, world-class shooters. I am a pretty fair shooter myself and have been around firearms most of my life, both as a student and a firearms instructor. I can tell you most assuredly that, under the extreme stress of a gunfight, none of the shooters I have worked with, nor I, could accurately place a shot in the arm or leg of a moving target wounding him as to effectively eliminate the threat. If you did try, you would probably miss, since you are aiming at a small target (arm, leg, or other extremity) on a moving person. This would be wasting ammunition, as well as giving your opponent ample opportunity to take the weapon back from you and kill you with it. (Believe me, he will not be shooting to wound you!)

Secondly, a wounded animal is a dangerous animal. Do not assume that, just because someone has been shot in the arm or leg, he can't still be a threat. He can and will be a threat to you as a scared, wounded individual. There are numerous examples of wounded suspects assaulting and even killing police officers after the officer had shot them. Shooting to wound and then expecting the threat to give up works only in the movies.

If you are going to shoot someone, aim at his "center mass". This is the area of his body that comprises the upper chest. On most people, this is the largest area of their body and, therefore, the biggest target. Aim for the biggest target and keep shooting until the threat is eliminated. You are most likely going to have to shoot him more than once to stop him. Shoot to "center mass" and keep shooting until you are certain that the terrorist is no longer a threat.

"Wouldn't a shot to the head be more effective?" some have asked. That depends on several factors. First of all, how close is the threat? If he is right on top of you then, yes, you will probably need a head shot to stop him. However, if he is more than ten feet away, the chances of your hitting him in the head are not very good. I have seen outstanding shooters completely miss a shot to the head on a stationary paper target from that distance. Now, how do you suppose you will do against a moving target at ten feet or more? There is a high probability that you will miss and if he is closing on you fast, you may have blown your last chance to stop him. Again, if he is right on top of you and you know you can get an accurate head shot, then take it. This may be your last chance and you had better make it good. Shoot to the chest first and then, if he doesn't stop and gets within ten feet, shoot to the head. In most cases a shot to the head will immediately stop the threat -- but not always. I have seen people shot in the head and walk away with noting more serious than a headache. "How is this possible", you ask? The human skull is hard, and unless a bullet hits in just the right place, it can actually skim around the head on the surface between the skin and the skull bone. If you are going to shoot someone in the head, aim for the area around the eyes and the bridge of the nose. This area consists mainly of soft tissue and is apt to be more easily penetrated by a bullet. Of course hitting a small area such as this on a moving target takes considerable skill, luck or both. Aim for this area as a last resort and only after you have put several rounds into the chest area of the threat.

Another question I am often asked and is related to the last question is, "How many times should I shoot the terrorist?" Only in the movies and on television does the bad guy go down after one shot. It is probably going to take multiple shots to the chest in order to stop the threat and neutralize his ability to harm you. You must be ruthless and aggressive. Extreme, relentless violence is the only way to stop an aggressor of this nature. A terrorist who is high on adrenaline and determined to kill you will probably not be easy to stop, particularly if all you have is a handgun. If he doesn't stop after you shoot him several times in the chest, shoot to the head. Do whatever it takes to stop the threat. Keep shooting until he is down, and then get away from the area as quickly as possible. You don't want to hang around and give Mr. Terrorist's buddies a chance to succeed where he failed.

Even more important than your skill with a firearm is your willingness to use it against another person. The fact is that most people cannot bring themselves to take another person's life, even at the expense of their own. I have seen highly trained police officers fail to pull the trigger when they were not only justified in doing so, but should have done so to stop an advancing threat. Studies have indicated that even some soldiers in combat have failed to fire their weapons against the enemy.

Whether you will be able to pull the trigger on someone is a personal decision only you can make. I recently read two accounts of individuals who were kidnapped by terrorists and held hostage for an extended period of time before they escaped. In both accounts the hostages had several opportunities to grab one of the terrorist's weapons and use it against him. In one case, the terrorist actually gave the hostage his rifle to hold for him while he climbed over a fence. In the other instance, the terrorist had a habit of falling asleep and leaving his rifle within easy reach of the hostage (and did this on several occasions). In both instances the hostage could not bring himself to use the weapon against the terrorist. Maybe it was because they were not sure how to operate it, but most likely it was because they lacked the will to take another life. The decision to take a life is something you will have to resolve firmly in your mind before you have to do it. In the middle of a gunfight or when you are already captured and held hostage is not the time to wrestle with those types of personal and moral dilemmas.

Even if you carry a firearm, as I repeatedly said, I believe the most important factor in survival is your attitude and mindset. You can have an arsenal of high-powered weapons, be the best shooter in the world, and attend all of the top firearms schools. All of this will come to nothing if you don't have the "survival mindset". If you carry a firearm, you should be absolutely positive you could use it if you have to. You must resolve in your mind that you are ready and willing to take the life of another human (or sub-human, in the case of terrorists).

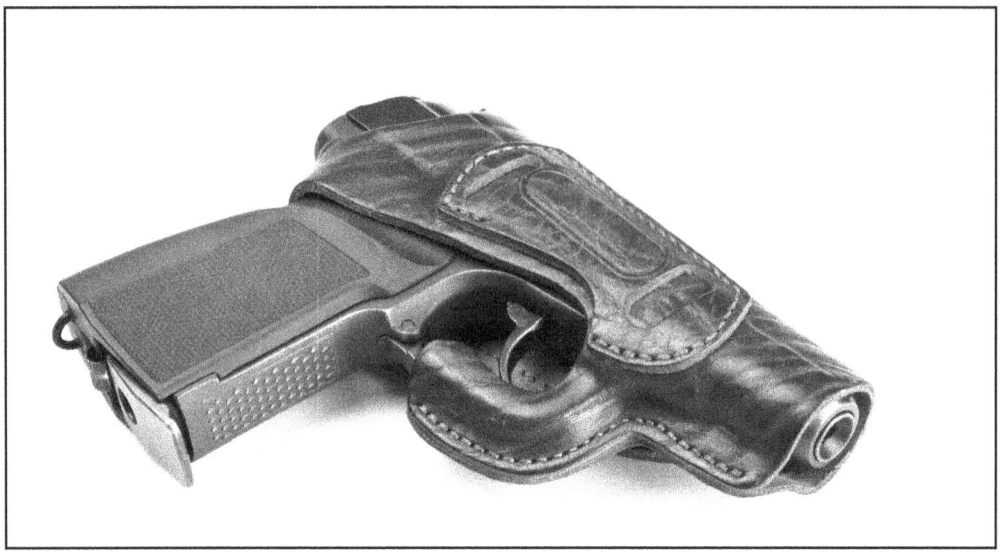

I clearly recall having a woman in one of my firearms training classes who was good student and a reasonably good shooter. In this course we typically did scenario-based training where we used simulated weapons (not live or real guns, but simulated guns that shoot a type of paint ball ammunition). In this particular scenario an "assailant" armed with a knife approached my student in a threatening manner. All she was to do was issue a command to stop; if the "assailant" refused and continued to advance toward her, she was authorized to shoot him. The "threat" (another instructor) presented himself and began advancing toward her with a rubber knife. In a trembling voice and with tears in her eyes, she kept commanding the perpetrator to stop. When he failed to stop, my student kept retreating backward toward a wall. Reaching the wall and unable to retreat any further, she immediately broke down in tears and refused to shoot her assailant. The "assailant" instructor simply walked up to her, took the gun from her hand and proceeded to shoot her with the "paintball" ammunition. It was a valuable lesson she learned that day. Although she failed the exercise, she now knows that she does not have the mindset to shoot an attacker. Obviously, if she can't "shoot" an instructor with paint rounds in a training exercise, how could she ever shoot a real threat with a live weapon?

If that scenario describes you, then you may be better off not carrying a firearm for personal protection. You don't want the bad guy to take the gun away and use it on you. You must be crystal clear in your mind that you can and will use a gun to prevent death or serious bodily injury to you or your loved ones. If you have not resolved this issue, do so before your purchase a gun.

Additionally, you might want to go to a gun range and rent or borrow a weapon to see if you can physically handle one. Shooting a handgun is not as easy as it looks on television. If you do go to a range, be sure that you have a certified firearms instructor with you. A good instructor can do a lot to help you alleviate your fears.

Owning a gun does not make you a gunfighter any more than standing in your garage makes you a Cadillac. Get good training, practice relentlessly and resolve in your mind to use your weapon safely, aggressively and efficiently to save your life and to protect your family.

Knife defense and take away

Ask most people on the street whether they would rather face an adversary armed with a gun or a knife and the vast majority will opt for the person armed with a knife. Ask a trained martial artist or a police officer the same question and many will say they would rather face an adversary armed with a gun, particularly if they are unarmed at the time of the incident. Why? Because it is much easier to take a gun away from someone than it is a knife. You might as well face it, if you attempt to take a knife away from an adversary, even one who is untrained in knife fighting or in the martial arts, you are probably going to get cut. On the other hand, if you know what you are doing, you stand a good chance of getting a gun away from a terrorist without getting shot. First of all, it takes some degree of skill to effectively use a gun, whereas it takes less skill to wield a knife. Secondly, the gun may not even be loaded or the shooter might have a malfunction with his weapon. I have taken guns from several bad guys, only to discover that the gun was either (a) not loaded, (b) was loaded with the wrong type of ammunition or (c) was broken and couldn't fire in the first place. A knife works all the time, and in the hands of a trained knife fighter, can be a deadly weapon.

Who would have ever thought that a simple box cutter would be used to perpetuate the worst terrorist attack in history? The terrorists on the ill-fated 9/11 flights were armed solely with box cutters. With minimal "weapons" they were able to take over four commercial airliners and cause the deaths of thousands of people.

Box cutters are knife-like tools that are primarily used, obviously, to open boxes. Most of them have plastic handles with maybe a one- or two-inch blade, at most. Prior to 9/11, a box cutter was never considered a serious weapon.

If you were on an aircraft with a hijacker armed with a knife, your best bet would be to recruit some people to help you. (See Chapter 16, Staying Safe While You Travel) Someone may get cut, but the terrorist won't be able to get everyone. Remember to use all of the "weapons" at your disposal. To help deflect the knife, wrap a towel, jacket, sweater, blanket, or whatever else you have around your forearm. Use overwhelming force and aggression to do this and once you get started – do not stop! Once his arm is pinned to the ground, wrench the knife from his hands. (Hint: A sharp object, such as a pen or fork, if jammed into the hijacker's eye socket with maximum force can do wonders here.)

Once the knife has been retrieved, restrain him (if he's still alive), using anything you can to tie him up. Again, think outside the box – a towel or blanket can be used for restraint; even shoestrings can be used to tie his hands behind his back. If his fellow bullies are in another part of plane, unaware of what's happening, remember to gag him to prevent him from warning them.

The thing to remember is that whatever the terrorist is armed with -- a gun, knife, bomb or box cutter, do something. And do it with everything you have. Don't hold back, be totally committed, and follow through with speed, surprise and maximum aggression.

The 21-foot rule

There is a very general rule in law enforcement circles that states that a person with a knife, standing within 21 feet of an intended victim, should be regarded as being a deadly threat. The assumption is that a person of average ability, armed with a knife, can cover 21 feet before his victim can effectively react, even if the intended victim has a firearm. I have seen this demonstrated on dozens of occasions and I agree that this rule is generally accurate. A lot, though, depends on the skill of

the attacker. A good, experienced knife fighter can cover 21 feet, cutting his victim several times before he even realizes what is happening. My advice to anyone facing an adversary with a knife is to either (a) run like hell or (b) have a gun and know how to use it.

Never take a knife to a gunfight

Usually, having a gun gives you a distinct advantage over someone armed with a knife. That doesn't mean you can totally dismiss a threat that is armed with a knife. On the contrary, you must take a person armed with a knife every bit as seriously as one armed with a gun. Even if you have a gun, don't take the "21-foot rule" too literally. Suppose you are armed with your favorite pistol and a knife-wielding attacker charges you. Do you wait until the person is within 21 feet before you fire? You could, but several things could happen, all of them bad. First of all, you could have a weapons malfunction in which your gun fails to fire. Perhaps you could have forgotten to load your gun at all (I have seen this happen way too many times during scenario-based training). Or, heaven forbid, you could fire at the attacker and miss. Let's say you do hit him and for some reason (high on drugs, adrenalin, bulky clothing or just one tough dude), he won't go down. The attacker can be on you before you know it. That is why running away might be a good option. An even better option would be steadily pumping rounds into your adversary as you run. The goal is to try and maintain as much distance as possible between you and the attacker. Whether he is armed with a knife, gun or a bomb, distance is always your friend. The further away from the threat you are, the better off you will be. ❖

CHAPTER 22

"Acquiring weapons for the defense of Muslims is a religious duty. If I have indeed acquired these weapons, then I thank God for enabling me to do so. And if I seek to acquire these weapons, I am carrying out a duty. It would be a sin for Muslims not to try to possess the weapons that would prevent the infidels from inflicting harm on Muslims."

~ Osama Bin Laden, in response to the question, "Are you trying to acquire chemical and nuclear weapons?"

THE CBRN ATTACK

Chemical, Biological, Radiological and Nuclear

There has been a lot of speculation recently regarding possible terrorist attacks using chemical, biological, radiological or nuclear devices (CBRN). The mere thought that a terrorist could set off a nuclear device or a "dirty bomb" is enough to terrorize an entire nation.

While the threat of a CBRN attack is very real and cannot be discounted as a legitimate threat, in my opinion we shouldn't be obsessing about it. The reality is that there are far more shootings, bombings and kidnappings going on in the world than CBRN incidents.

The fact that a CBRN attack is a relatively rare occurrence ensures that it will dominate the news for days or even weeks. Terrorists have used chemical and toxic substances in the past and will, in all likelihood, continue to do so, although not on the scale of "conventional terrorism". Some of the more recent CBRN incidents are:

- On March 20, 1995, Sarin gas attacks in the Tokyo subway system. The five coordinated attacks killed twelve people and injured approximately 1000 people.
- In 2001, several letters containing the bacterial agent, anthrax, were mailed to the offices of several news media and two U.S. Senators, killing five and causing seventeen people to become ill.
- The toxic chemical, Ricin, was mailed to several locations in the U.S. in 2003 and 2004, including the White House. (Note: Ricin is twice as deadly as cobra venom!).

Despite the tragic loss of life associated with these incidents, they pale in comparison to the loss of lives caused by gun and bomb attacks. It would be a mistake to totally discount the effect a CBRN attack would have on the security of the United States and following is a brief definition of chemical, biological, radiological and nuclear threats.

Chemical Threat

According to the Department of Homeland Security, "A chemical attack is the deliberate release of a toxic gas, liquid or solid that can poison people and the environment". Signs of a chemical attack can be nausea, choking, difficulty breathing and loss of coordination, among other symptoms. Just as in a biological attack, you must get away from the infected area as quickly as possible. If you are outside when the attack occurs, consider going into a building, attempting to seal the windows and doors. Use a water hose or shower to "decontaminate" yourself, and seek medical attention at once.

Biological Threat

The Department of Homeland Security website defines a biological threat as "the deliberate release of germs or other biological substances that can make one sick". Biological agents can be either inhaled or absorbed through the skin. During a biological attack you may not be immediately aware that you have been infected. If you suspect that you have been exposed to a biological agent, your best bet is cover your mouth and nose and get away from the area as quickly as possible. Get to a safe area and seek medical attention immediately.

Radiological Threat

A radiological threat, also known as a "dirty bomb", is composed of common explosives, intended to spread radioactive materials over a targeted area. Unlike a nuclear explosion, the blast is more centralized and the radioactive material is not as widespread. The initial explosion may seem like a "normal" bomb, and you will obviously not be able to observe the radioactive material around you. Once again, get away from the area and, if you suspect you have become contaminated, go to a hospital or decontamination facility as quickly as possible.

If there is a CBRN terrorist incident in your area, you may want to consider getting away from the area for a while. You should have a plan in place that includes a secondary location to which you and you family can evacuate and stay for a few days. Always keep at least half a tank of gas in your car and keep the windows up and doors tightly closed while making your escape. In your plan, you should have identified several alternate routes to your secondary location in case the primary route is blocked. It would be good to have a tertiary (third) location in case your secondary location is unavailable for some reason.

If getting out of town is not an option, you will have to "shelter-in-place". Make sure you seal your home as best you can to guard against outside contamination getting in. You will want to create a barrier between you and the contaminants outside. You may have to limit your activities to one room and that is where your "safe" room comes into play.

The Department of Homeland Security, on their website, recommends that you keep the following supplies available in the event it is necessary for you and your family to shelter-in-place:

- One gallon of water per day per person, for drinking and sanitation
- At least a three-day supply of non-perishable food
- A battery-powered radio and extra batteries
- Flashlight and extra batteries
- First aid kit
- Whistle to signal for help
- Dust mask or a cotton T-shirt to help filter the air
- Moist towelettes for sanitation
- Wrench or pliers to turn off the utilities
- Can opener (if your kit contains canned food)
- Plastic sheeting and duct tape for sealing windows, doors and vents
- Infant formula and diapers, if you have an infant
- Garbage bags and plastic ties for personal sanitation
- Miscellaneous needs, such as medications, pet food, paper and pens or books

Nuclear Threat

A nuclear attack by a terrorist organization would be difficult to accomplish, due to the technical aspects of developing and deploying a nuclear device -- but not impossible. It would be a grave mistake to discount the ability of a terrorist organization to conduct an attack utilizing a nuclear weapon. Believe me, if Al-Qaeda or another extremist terrorist group has the opportunity, they will not hesitate to use a nuclear device to achieve their objectives.

Growing up in the early 60's, I was well versed in what to do during a nuclear attack (which we expected any day from the Soviet Union). "Duck and cover" were the watchwords we frequently heard from our teachers, television and the educational films that attempted to educate us on surviving a nuclear attack. Believe it or not, during a nuclear attack we were supposed to "duck" under our desks, and "cover" our heads with our arms (as if this would save us!).

The Department of Homeland security uses better phraseology for what to do during a nuclear attack today. They use the terms, "shielding, distance and time".

Shielding

Shielding is the means whereby some sort of a thick shield or barrier is placed between a person and the blast. A shield, such as a wall, vehicle or large piece of furniture will not only shield you from the blast, but will also help protect you from the radioactive material produced by the blast (theoretically, at least).

Distance

Obviously, the farther away you are from the actual blast site, the more protected you will be. Get as far away from the blast site as possible and immediately seek medical attention.

Time

Limiting the time spent near the blast and radiation site will increase your chances of survival significantly. Do not linger in the affected area any longer than you have to. Leave the rescue work to the professionals.

Apart from a nuclear explosion, keep in mind that you could also be the victim of a conventional bomb that goes off in your building. The 1993 World Trade Center bombing and the 1995 bombing of the Alfred P. Murrah Federal Building in Oklahoma City are prime examples of conventional bombings

Regardless if you are the victim of a nuclear bomb or a conventional explosion, there are things you can do to increase your chances of survival. The U.S. Federal Emergency Management Agency recommends the following steps be taken during an explosion:

- Get under a sturdy desk or table to protect yourself from falling objects. Once you feel that you are relatively safe from falling debris, get out of the building as quickly as possible. Watch for weakened floors and stairways and continue to be aware of falling objects.
- Do not stop to retrieve personal items or make a phone call. Leave the building immediately.
- Use the stairs, not the elevators.
- Once you are out, get away from the building, avoiding standing in front of glass doors, windows or any other "potentially hazardous areas".
- Quickly move away from the building entrances to avoid blocking others trying to get out and emergency rescue personnel trying to get in. Do not crowd around the sidewalks or streets adjacent to the building. Emergency vehicles and rescue workers need unfettered access to the area.
- If you find yourself trapped in the building, use a cell phone, flashlight or whistle to signal your location to rescuers.
- Cover your mouth and nose, preferably with cotton fabric, such as a T-shirt or a similar item.
- Avoid unnecessary movement as much as possible, being careful not to disturb the dust and debris around you.

Should you purchase a gas mask?

Again, I believe the chance of terrorists using bombs, guns, and kidnappings as weapons are much greater than executing a chemical, biological, nuclear or radiological attack. I am certainly not saying that a CBRN attack will never occur and, yes, we should be prepared as much as possible for any eventuality.

Gas masks, however, are not the solution to every CBRN problem; in fact, I find them to be highly impractical for that purpose. Israel is the only country to have issued gas masks to all of its citizens, which occurred during the 1991 Gulf War. Ironically, more people died attempting to put on their gas masks than from Scud missiles. To be effective, the masks must be personally fitted to you and you must have them with you 24 hours a day, seven days a week. Obviously, they would be of little use in a nuclear attack, particularly if you were at "ground zero", as would be the case in a direct hit. To adequately protect yourself in the event of a biological attack (which you wouldn't be able to hear or see coming), you would have to wear one constantly. How many people are willing to do that? ❖

"Every American man is an enemy to us. We call on every Muslim who believes in God and wishes to be rewarded to comply with God's order to kill the Americans and plunder their money wherever and whenever they find it."

~ Osama bin Laden

CONCLUSION

We are at war. Unlike conventional wars, the War on Terror knows no boundaries. There is no such thing as a non-combatant in the War on Terror. Every country on the face of the earth is subject to becoming a target of terrorism, making every citizen in those countries terrorism's victims. In the War on Terror we are all on the front lines, whether we like it are not.

By definition, the very act of terrorism evokes crimes perpetrated against innocent civilians. This is the way it has been for centuries upon centuries. The difference with terrorism in the 21st century is that the world has gotten a lot smaller and terrorists have become more technologically advanced. In the past, to avoid becoming a victim of a terrorist incident, all you had to do was stay out of those areas of the world in which terrorist groups operated. No longer is that true. As we so graphically saw on September 11, 2001, the long tentacles of terrorism now reach around the world. No place is safe anymore.

Corporations are duty bound to provide their employees who live, work, and travel abroad with an education in self-protection. Civilian government agencies and the military must also bear the responsibility of educating their employees and troops. Tourists should be aware of the terrorist threat in the areas in which they travel and should be trained in basic survival skills. The bottom line is that we are ultimately the ones responsible for our own safety and security and that of our loved ones. We must be proactive in preparing ourselves to confront terrorism.

To date, the War on Terrorism has been going on for several years, with no sight in end. The reality is that we have been in a war on terrorism for decades, long before September 11, 2001. I believe that if we are to win this war, we must equip our citizens to do a better job of detecting, defeating and disrupting terrorist acts themselves, lessening our total dependency on the local police, FBI, and other law enforcement agencies. These organizations are doing an outstanding job of protecting us from terrorism. It is a testament to the dedication and professionalism of America's law enforcement and intelligence organizations that we haven't been hit on U.S. soil by a major terrorist attack since 9/11, in spite of concerted efforts by terrorists. Having said that, even enforcement and intelligence organizations face major obstacles in fighting the war on issues, liberal courts, lack of cooperation from foreign governments, bureaucratic in- the list goes on and on. Our law enforcement and intelligence agencies have an difficult job and it's not getting any easier.

When I began my career in law enforcement in the early 1970s, attention was being focused on "crime prevention". This was a relatively new concept in criminal justice at that time and the idea behind "crime prevention" was novel, in that more of the responsibility for safety was placed on the average citizen. Because of an overwhelming crime rate, the police looked to its citizens for help in their "war on crime". From this concept sprang programs such as Neighborhood Watch, school resource officers, business crime prevention, and other such programs. No longer was the public expected to look to the police solely for their protection. The citizens began to realize that they bore some of the responsibility for their own safety and protection.

As a result, today we have thankfully seen a dramatic resurgence of concealed carry laws whereby law-abiding citizens are authorized to carry a gun for self protection. Why? Because the police cannot possibly be everywhere all the time. Today we make sure our children are exposed at a very young age to the realities of "stranger danger" and similar programs designed to teach them to avoid stranger abductions and other child-targeted crimes. Such programs were unheard of in my community when I was growing up in the 1950s – it just wasn't necessary then. The changes in our world since that time are truly mind boggling.

We have seen vast improvements in security in the business world today. Employees of retail businesses are now briefed on handling a robbery attempt, dealing with shoplifters and other crimes. Corporate America employees are trained in spotting and reducing internal theft. Civil Service workers are encouraged to identify and report waste, fraud and abuse in the government. All of this is important, but the ability of the average citizen to detect, deter and prevent terrorist attacks is a critical skill in the 21st century.

Just as people in the twentieth century prepared for a nuclear holocaust between the world's superpowers, people in the twenty-first century must face the realities of terrorism. The key difference is that in the twentieth century the nuclear war that everyone expected thankfully never materialized. Terrorism, on the other hand, has become a reality and by all indications it is here to stay. Terrorism is the new "conventional warfare" of the twenty-first century. Just like soldiers preparing to face the enemy in battle, we must prepare to confront and defeat terrorism in all its many forms. This will take a concerted effort by our intelligence agencies, law enforcement community, military, and perhaps most importantly, the civilian population.

Pray for the best, but be prepared for the worst. Become knowledgeable of your enemy, learning how he operates and how you can defeat him. Practice anticipation mindset. Don't be time and place predictable. And above all, never give up.

"Never give in! Never give in! Never, never, never…. We shall go on to the end. We shall never surrender".

~ Sir Winston Churchill